# THE SOVIET UNION
# AND THE ARMS RACE

# THE SOVIET UNION
# AND THE ARMS RACE

Second Edition

## David Holloway

YALE UNIVERSITY PRESS
NEW HAVEN AND LONDON

TO THE MEMORY OF MY FATHER,
ERNEST HOLLOWAY

Second edition 1984.
Third printing 1986.

Designed by Caroline Williamson and set in Compugraphic Times by Red Lion Setters, Holborn, London.
Printed in Great Britain by Butler & Tanner Ltd, Frome, Somerset.

**Library of Congress Cataloging in Publication Data**
Holloway, David, 1943 –
  The Soviet Union and the arms race.

  Includes index.
  1. Soviet Union – Military policy. 2. Soviet Union – Defenses. 3. Soviet Union – Armed Forces. 4. World politics – 1945 – . 1. Title.
UA770.H63 1983   355′.033047   84-40205
ISBN 0-300-03280-3 (cloth)
ISBN 0-300-03281-1 (paper)

# Contents

# Acknowledgements

This book draws on work done in recent years for a number of different projects and for that reason my intellectual debts are numerous. I would particularly like to acknowledge the help I have received from colleagues at several different institutions: in the Department of Politics, University of Edinburgh; in the Centre for Russian and East European Studies at the University of Birmingham, from whom I learned much while collaborating on a study of Soviet technological performance; in the International Security Studies Program at the Woodrow Wilson International Center for Scholars in Washington, D.C., where I spent a year working on a study of early Soviet nuclear policy; and at the Peace Studies Program of Cornell University, where this book was completed. My thanks are due also to the Institute of World Economy and International Relations of the Soviet Academy of Sciences for inviting me for a visit during which some of the topics in this book were discussed. I have learned so much from so many people that it would be invidious to try to name them all. I would like to express my particular thanks, however, to Ron Amann, Julian Cooper, Bob Davies, Mary Kaldor, Judith Reppy and Jane Sharp. None of these people or institutions should be held responsible for the views, arguments and deficiencies of this book.

In writing this book I have drawn in some chapters on earlier published work. I am grateful to the copyright holders for permission to reuse material that has appeared elsewhere. The Macmillan Press has given me permission to draw at various points on a chapter on 'Foreign and Defense Policy' in Archie Brown and Michael Kaser (eds.), *Soviet Policy for the 1980s*, published in 1982 by the Macmillan Press in London and the Indiana University Press in the United States. I am grateful to the Peace Studies Program at Cornell University for permission to draw in chapter seven on a paper on 'The Soviet Style of Military R & D' in F.A. Long and Judith Reppy (eds.), *The Genesis of*

*New Weapons: Decision-Making for Military R & D*, published in 1980 by the Pergamon Press, New York and Oxford.

I would like to acknowledge also the financial support I received from the Woodrow Wilson International Center for Scholars, from the Nuffield and Ford Foundations, and from the Institute for the Study of World Politics, for my study of early Soviet atomic energy policy, on which I have drawn for the second chapter of this book.

My thanks are due to the Yale University Press for suggesting this book to me, and for being so patient while I wrote it.

Finally, my greatest indebtedness is to my wife Arlene, for her support and encouragement.

NOTE TO THE SECOND EDITION

I have not changed the text of the first edition, but I have added a new introduction to bring the analysis up to date.

David Holloway, February 1984

# Introduction to the Second Edition

In this book I tried to examine, as clearly and carefully as possible, a number of specific questions about the Soviet Union's role in the nuclear arms race. I did not attempt a comprehensive analysis of the Soviet Armed Forces, for their organization and equipment are described in other works. I decided to focus on the influence of international military rivalry, and of the Soviet efforts to build up the Red Army, on the formation of the Soviet state; on Soviet thinking about nuclear war and the uses of military force in the nuclear age; and on the economic and political institutions that sustain the military effort.

I did not set out to write a detailed history of Soviet military policy in the nuclear age, but I did adopt a historical perspective in the belief that this would help to throw light on current issues. I hoped that such an approach would prevent the book from being rendered too quickly out of date by the course of events. But since it was completed in the spring of 1982 a great deal has happened both in the Soviet Union and in the nuclear arms race, and it is appropriate therefore to take the opportunity presented by this edition to comment on recent developments.

## Brezhnev, Andropov and Chernenko

Since this book was written the General Secretaryship of the Party has changed hands twice. Leonid Brezhnev died in November 1982, and was rapidly succeeded by Yuri Andropov. In May 1983 the Minister of Defence, Marshal D.F. Ustinov, revealed that Andropov was Chairman of the Defence Council. In June Andropov became Chairman of the Presidium of the Supreme Soviet, or President of the Soviet Union.[1] But his health was poor, and after August 1983 he made no public appearance. He died on 9 February 1984 and was succeeded by

Konstantin Chernenko, who had been a protege of Brezhnev's, and Andropov's rival for the General Secretaryship in 1982. Chernenko is 72 years old and suffers from ill health. It is not clear what kind of mark he will leave on Soviet policy.

Brezhnev's legacy was a mixed one. He left his country more power-ful in military terms than ever before. Under his leadership the Soviet Union attained strategic parity with the United States, increased and modernized its nuclear and conventional forces in Europe and built up its military strength along the frontier with China. The Navy now shows the Soviet flag on the oceans of the world. This growing military power has supported Soviet claims to a global role in world politics. At home the Soviet Union enjoyed political stability and rising living standards.

But the Soviet Union's international position was far less favourable than one might suppose merely from counting missiles, tanks and ships. By the time of Brezhnev's death, the United States, alarmed by the growth of Soviet military power, and by the use of that power in Angola, Ethiopia and Afghanistan, had embarked on a major build-up of its Armed Forces. The Soviet Union's chief adversaries – the United States, China, Japan and Western Europe – had drawn closer together to oppose the expansion of Soviet power and influence. The Soviet Union was still embroiled in a war in Afghanistan, while the Soviet-backed governments in Angola and Ethiopia continued to face internal opposition. The crisis in Poland pointed to a fundamental weakness in the Soviet position in Eastern Europe. At home the slowing rate of economic growth in the last years of Brezhnev's rule was making policy choices more difficult.

At the 26th Party Congress early in 1981 Brezhnev acknowledged that the previous five years had been a 'complex and stormy' period in international affairs, but he did not chart a new course for Soviet foreign policy. In the last months of his life, however, there were signs that a new assessment of the international situation had been made. The initial Soviet complacency that the Reagan Administration would prove to be more accommodating than its rhetoric had by now been dispelled. In July 1982, Defence Minister Ustinov accused the United States of striving for military superiority, of trying to set up military blocs to encircle the Soviet Union, and of orchestrating an economic and technological war against the socialist countries, with the aim of destroying socialism as a socio-economic system.[2] In October, less than three weeks before his death, Brezhnev told a gathering of five hundred senior officers that the United States and its allies had unleashed an unprecedented arms race in order to achieve military superiority, and were trying to isolate the socialist camp politically and weaken it economically.[3]

These assessments indicated that the Soviet leaders had concluded in 1982 that there was little prospect of better relations with the Reagan Administration. They now tried to improve their international position by continuing to play on West European opposition to the deployment of Ground Launched Cruise Missiles (GLCMs) and Pershing 2 missiles in Western Europe, and by exploiting differences between Western Europe and the United States over trade policy towards the Soviet Union. They may have hoped to influence American policy through the European members of NATO, or to salvage detente with Western Europe, even though that with the United States had collapsed; failing that, they may just have wanted to sow dissension in the West.

The Soviet Union also tried to prevent the growing cohesion among its adversaries by seeking a *rapprochement* with China, whose relations with the Reagan Administration had worsened over the issue of Taiwan. Three times in 1982 Brezhnev expressed interest in improving relations with China, and a very limited relaxation of tension began before his death.

But these measures did not succeed in solving the Soviet Union's problems. During the fifteen months of Andropov's rule, Soviet foreign policy suffered further setbacks. In spite of some signs of improvement in the summer of 1983, relations with the United States deteriorated to the point where Andropov could state in September 1983 that 'if anyone had illusions about the possibility that the policy of the present American administration would evolve for the better, then the events of the recent period have finally dispelled them'.[4] This statement came only weeks after a Soviet air defence interceptor had shot down a South Korean airliner near the island of Sakhalin. Much remains unclear about that incident, but it had the immediate effect of embittering Soviet–American relations still further. President Reagan portrayed it as evidence of the brutal and callous nature of the Soviet leaders. Andropov presented the Reagan Administration's treatment of the incident as confirmation that it had no interest in good relations with the Soviet Union and was eager to undermine Soviet prestige and influence.

In November 1983 NATO began to deploy the new American missiles in Europe. This was a serious setback for Soviet policy, which had tried strenuously to prevent the deployment. The Soviet leaders may have thought in 1979 and 1980 that Western Europe was the weakest link in the chain of encirclement around the Soviet Union, and believed that political opposition would prevent NATO from carrying out its decision. But the deployment demonstrated that the most important West European governments were united with the Reagan Administration on this issue. The Soviet Union withdrew from the INF (Intermediate-Range Nuclear Forces) talks and refused to set a date for the resumption of START (Strategic Arms Reduction Talks). Soviet–American relations now seemed to have reached their lowest point since the Cuban Missile Crisis of 1962.

Andropov continued the policy of seeking better relations with China, but this has not yet yielded significant results. There are still serious obstacles in the way of a full *rapprochement*. China has laid down three conditions for a normalization of relations: a reduction of Soviet forces on the Chinese frontier, removal of Soviet troops from Afghanistan, and withdrawal of Soviet support for the Vietnamese-backed government in Kampuchea. These are tough conditions, though it is not impossible that some progress will be made on them. But a limited accommodation is much more likely than a full *rapprochement*, for suspicion and mistrust remain strong on either side and will not be dispelled easily.[5]

It would be wrong to exaggerate the problems the Soviet Union faces. It remains a very powerful state, and there are tensions and disagreements among its adversaries which it will try to exploit. But its present problems show that the Soviet Union was not able to translate its military power into commensurate political gains in the 1970s. Brezhnev had hoped that Soviet military power would help to make detente irreversible. But it did not do so. Indeed, the growth of that power and its exercise in support of foreign policy contributed to the collapse of detente by inspiring widespread anxiety abroad. If the Soviet Union now finds itself in a difficult international position, that is at least partly the consequence of its own policies in the 1970s.

Andropov's legacy to Chernenko was if anything less cheering than that which he had inherited fifteen months before. In 1982 tactical adjustments were made in Soviet foreign policy, but these have not met the challenges the Soviet Union faces. The Soviet leaders have so far failed to devise a long-term, or even a medium-term, strategy to deal with these challenges. They have seemed bewildered by the complexity and intensity of the problems that confront them.

Andropov's death will hardly lead to a major reassessment of policy. Although it might now be easier for the Soviet Union to move away from some of its policy positions, there is in fact likely to be little change. Defence Minister Ustinov and Foreign Minister A.A. Gromyko are still powerful figures in the Politburo and can be expected to press on with the policies they have been pursuing. Continuity was the keynote of the early days of Chernenko's rule as General Secretary.

## Military Doctrine and Military Strategy

In the last years of his life, Brezhnev formulated a defensive and deterrent rationale for Soviet strategic policy (see Chapter Three). This rationale, which has not changed since his death, can be summarized as follows. Soviet strategic forces are intended to prevent an attack on the Soviet Union and its allies; if such an attack is launched, the attacker will receive a 'crushing rebuff'; the present strategic relationship with the United States is one of parity, and neither side can outstrip the other in the arms race; the Soviet Union is not striving for superiority, but neither will it allow the United States to attain superiority; nuclear war would be immensely destructive, and it would be suicidal to start one; it is dangerous madness to expect to win a nuclear war.

This new formulation of doctrine has been greeted with scepticism in the West. Some scepticism may well be in order, for it is not entirely clear what practical consequences follow for military strategy or weapons procurement. What this new statement of doctrine does express clearly, however, is a keen appreciation of the terrible consequences of nuclear war, and an awareness that, for the time being at least, the Soviet Union and the United States are destined to live in a relationship of mutual vulnerability to devastating retaliatory strikes.

Marshal Ogarkov, the Chief of the General Staff, wrote in September 1983 that with the present balance of forces, 'the defending side will always retain such a quantity of nuclear means as will be capable of inflicting "unacceptable damage", as the former Defence Secretary of the USA R. McNamara characterized it in his time, on the aggressor in a retaliatory strike'.[6] And, in words that echo the opening Soviet statement at SALT, he added that 'in contemporary circumstances only suicides can wager on a first nuclear strike.' (See pp. 46, 49.)

But the recognition that this is now the nature of the Soviet–American relationship does not mean that the Soviet Union has adopted a strategy of assured destruction, in the sense of seeking only to destroy American cities in the event of a nuclear war. In the words of the *Military Encyclopedic Dictionary*, published in 1983 and edited by

Marshal Ogarkov, 'in accordance with Soviet military doctrine, which has a profoundly defensive character, the main task of Soviet military strategy is the development of means of repulsing the aggressor's attack and of utterly defeating him by means of decisive military operations'.[7] Soviet military strategy continues to stress the importance of preparing to defeat the enemy in nuclear war, while military doctrine emphasizes the need to prevent such a war from taking place (see pp. 31–5).

In Brezhnev's reformulation of military doctrine the problem of managing the strategic relationship with the United States occupies a central place. The key concept here is parity, the basis on which Soviet nuclear programs are justified, and on which arms control agreements are supposed to be concluded. In accordance with this principle the Soviet Union has declared that it is not pursuing superiority. But it has also stressed that it will not reduce its forces unilaterally and that it will match new weapons programs on the Western side. In December 1982, for example, Andropov warned that the Soviet Union would counter the United States' MX ICBM by deploying an analogous missile of its own, and that it would deploy its own long-range cruise missile, which it was already testing, to counter the American cruise missile.[8]

In line with its conception of parity the Soviet Union has pressed ahead with the development of new strategic weapons. In 1983 the first Typhoon class submarine, armed with twenty SS-N-20 SLBMs, each of which carries from six to nine warheads, was due to become operational. In late 1982 and early 1983 two new solid-fuel ICBMs were tested: the SS-X-24, which is akin to the American MX, and a smaller, potentially mobile missile, the SS-X-25. Under the SALT II Treaty (which both sides have committed themselves not to violate, even though it has not been ratified by the U.S. Senate), each side may test only one new type of ICBM before 1985. The Soviet Union has informed the United States that the SS-X-24 is its new ICBM, and argues that the SS-X-25 is merely a modification of the SS-13, which is already deployed. The Reagan Administration, however, claims that the SS-X-25 may infringe the Treaty by exceeding the limits set for defining a new type of missile, but it does not have conclusive evidence of this.

These programs show that the Soviet Union is trying to alter the structure of its strategic forces by placing more warheads on SLBMs, and by developing mobile ICBMs. These steps are evidently designed to counter the threat that new American systems – the MX ICBM and the Trident 2 SLBM – will pose to Soviet ICBM silos. Soviet programs show a determination to ensure that, even if the United States should strike first, the Soviet Union will retain a large retaliatory missile force. At the same time, the testing of the SS-X-24 suggests that the Soviet Union, for its part, will continue to deploy warheads that can strike hardened targets in the United States.

The development of such systems as the SS-X-24 has raised doubts about the meaning of the Soviet commitment not to be the first to use nuclear weapons. Brezhnev announced this commitment in a message to the United Nations in the summer of 1982. Ustinov later stressed that this would entail practical measures, since it established an 'even stricter framework in the training of troops and staffs, in the determination of the composition of armament, in the organization of still firmer control which will exclude the unsanctioned launch of nuclear weapons, from tactical to strategic'.[10]

The Soviet commitment not to be the first to use nuclear weapons was widely regarded in the West as no more than propaganda. It undoubtedly has an important element of propaganda in it, and is clearly designed to embarrass NATO, which refuses to make such a commitment. But there is more to the Soviet position than that, for the renunciation of the first use of nuclear weapons fits into the pattern of recent organizational changes in the Armed Forces. The Ground and Air Forces have gone through a period of reorganization that points to a determination to achieve the goals of war in Europe as quickly as possible by conventional arms.[11]

If the Soviet leaders believe, as they say they do, that general nuclear war would be catastrophic for all concerned, and that nuclear war in Europe would be difficult if not impossible to limit, then it follows that they should try to keep the nuclear threshold as high as possible. In this context the Soviet commitment not to be the first to use nuclear weapons makes a great deal of sense. Soviet military planners may believe that their theatre nuclear forces would be able to deter NATO from resorting to nuclear weapons in Europe.

The position is less clear at the strategic level. In the late 1950s and early 1960s Soviet military strategy assumed that a war with the West would be nuclear from the outset, and stressed the importance of preempting an enemy attack. In the 1960s Soviet strategic thought recognized that war might grow out of a regional conflict and start with a conventional phase, but it still stressed the importance of preempting an enemy nuclear strike before it got off the ground. The Soviet Union has continued to deploy strategic missiles that seem to be designed to strike hard targets such as ICBM silos, and would thus be suitable for a preemptive attack (though it certainly does not have the capacity for a disarming first strike).

There is some evidence that in the 1960s the Soviet Union decided that, if war seemed imminent but not certain, it would adopt a launch-on-warning posture for its missile force. Dangerous though such a posture might be, it would be less so than a strategy of preemption alone. It would not preclude a decision to preempt, but it would lessen the urgency of such a decision, and hence the risk of miscalculation.

It is hard to know what the commitment not to be the first to use nuclear weapons means in practice. It does not mean that the Soviet Union will eschew counterforce systems in favour of those that are to be used only in retaliation against cities. It does not seem to rule out a preemptive strike against an enemy who is preparing a nuclear attack on the Soviet Union. But the Soviet commitment does reflect an awareness that nuclear war would have catastrophic consequences; it is rooted in the belief that nuclear war, once started, would be extremely difficult to limit; and it is consistent with the trend of Soviet strategic thought, which stresses that even in the event of war it would make sense to try to prevent the use of nuclear weapons.

Since the late 1960s the Soviet leaders seem to have been reconciled, for the time being at least, to living with the United States in a relationship of mutual vulnerability. But that relationship was called into question by President Reagan in his 'Star Wars' speech of 23 March 1983 when he held out the hope that new defensive systems could be developed that would render nuclear weapons 'impotent and obsolete'.[12]

In his reply to Reagan Andropov made it clear that he thought the President had a more sinister aim in view. The United States, he said, was aiming to disarm the Soviet Union in the face of the United States' nuclear threat, by rendering it incapable of dealing a retaliatory blow. Defences against ballistic missiles might appear attractive to the layman, Andropov said, but 'those who are conversant with such matters' could not view them in the same way. The SALT I Agreements had been based on the realization that an 'inseverable relationship' existed between offensive and defensive strategic systems, and the implementation of Reagan's plan would 'open the floodgates to a runaway race involving all types of strategic weapons, both offensive and defensive'.[13]

Ironically, the arguments that Andropov used were akin to those that the United States had advanced in the late 1960s when the Soviet Union was deploying an ABM (anti-ballistic missile) system of its own. In 1967 Kosygin spoke in much the same terms as Reagan used in 1983:

defensive systems, he said, were not a 'cause of the arms race but designed to prevent the death of people' (see p. 45). But in spite of Kosygin's assurances, the United States was alarmed by the Soviet ABM deployment, and feared that if the Soviet Union could made itself invulnerable to an American retaliatory strike, it might well be tempted to launch a nuclear attack. In the late 1960s the Soviet leaders took the point that defensive systems could play an offensive role, and Andropov repeated it in his reply to Reagan in 1983.

The development of highly (say 95 per cent) effective ABM systems looks extremely problematical, even with the use of exotic laser technologies. Even if it does prove possible to develop such systems, it will be a long time before they are deployed. At least until the end of the century the Soviet Union and the United States will be locked into a relationship in which each is vulnerable to a devastating retaliatory strike by the other. The race to develop defensive systems will complicate an already complex strategic relationship, but will not change its basic character in the next fifteen to twenty years, and may not do so after that. On the ability of the Soviet Union and the United States to manage this relationship, even while they are in conflict on so many issues, hangs the fate of us all.

## *Arms Control*

The precise definition of parity may be a matter of serious dispute, as START and the INF talks show. At START, which began in June 1982, the Soviet Union proposed a reduction in the number of strategic nuclear delivery vehicles on either side to 1800 by 1990. Unspecified but equal limits would also be set for warheads.

The initial American proposal was very different, and aimed to reduce the Soviet ICBM force, which poses a threat to the United States' land-based missiles. The United States called for reductions in two stages. In the first, each side would cut to 850 the number of its ICBMs and SLBMs, and to 5,000 the number of its warheads, with no more than half of these to be deployed on ICBMs. The Soviet Union was quick to reject this proposal, on the grounds that the United States was trying to gain a unilateral advantage by compelling the Soviet Union to restructure its forces. It also objected to the fact that the American proposal deferred to a vague second stage the heavy bombers and cruise missiles in which the United States enjoys a lead.[14]

There have been some changes in the American and (to a lesser extent) the Soviet positions. In spite of these, however, there has been little progress at START, and the negotiations have now been made more difficult by the collapse of the INF talks. The original Soviet proposal at START would have prohibited the deployment of new American forward-based systems that could strike Soviet territory, on the grounds that such systems would enable the United States to circumvent an agreement. The Soviet Union withdrew from START when it left the INF talks, and if START resumes, the Soviet position will be modified to take account of INF.

The INF talks are a striking example of how arms control negotiations can go wrong. From the very beginning there existed, as Chapter Four explains, a basic disagreement about the nature of the military balance in Europe. In May 1982 the Soviet Union tabled a draft treaty which proposed that each side reduce its INF to 600 systems within five years, and to 300 by 1990. (The draft also included a provision that no new type of system – e.g. GLCM or Pershing 2 – be deployed.) This proposal was based on the Soviet assessment of the nuclear balance in Europe, an assessment that was disputed by the West (see p. 74).[15]

In line with its own view of the balance the Soviet Union argued that British and French missiles should be counted on the NATO side. In December 1982 Andropov offered to reduce the number of SS-20s in the European part of the Soviet Union to 162, to match the number of British and French missiles; this would have meant a reduction of about 80 in the number then deployed.[16] Andropov later explained that the Soviet Union would destroy the missiles that were withdrawn, and would not redeploy them to the Far East. In May 1983 Andropov offered to balance Soviet INF warheads against those on British and French missiles. This would have meant a reduction to about 140 SS-20s, but it would also have constrained the British and French programs to modernize their forces. Britain and France, with the support of the United States, refused to have their missiles weighed in the balance, claiming that these were strategic, not theatre systems.

The Soviet Union's rejection of Reagan's 'zero option' proposal of November 1981 (in which he offered to abandon deployment of the new American systems if the Soviet Union dismantled its intermediate-range missiles) followed naturally from its conception of the nuclear balance. In March 1983 Reagan made another proposal, but this too was rejected by the Soviet Union because it was still based on the idea that parity should be created, on a global basis, between Soviet and American land-based intermediate-range missiles. Foreign Minister Gromyko spelled out the Soviet objections to the new proposal: it took no account of aircraft; it omitted the British and French systems; and it made no allowance for the Soviet requirement for medium-range systems in the Far East.[17]

In the summer of 1982 the Soviet and American positions seemed for a moment to draw closer together. In July, during a walk in the woods near Geneva, the chief Soviet and American negotiators, Yuli Kvitsinskii and Paul Nitze, agreed to take back to their governments an exploratory document containing the outlines of a treaty. According to this, the Soviet Union and the United States would be allowed 75 intermediate-range missile launchers apiece in Europe; Pershing 2 would not be deployed; there would be a freeze on SS-20 deployment in the Far East; restrictions would be placed on the deployment of medium-range bombers and on missiles with a range of less than 1,000 kilometres. British and French forces were not covered.[18]

This proposal was rejected in Washington. It was also turned down in Moscow, apparently on the grounds that British and French forces were not included. Yet it retains considerable interest, for it shows the kind of compromise the chief negotiators thought could be struck. In particular, it shows the terms that Kvitsinskii thought might just be acceptable in Moscow: in return for a major cut in the SS-20 force the Soviet Union would gain a limit on GLCMs, and prevent the deployment of Pershing 2.

The 'walk in the woods' episode suggests that there may have been disagreement among the Soviet leaders about the concessions they should be willing to make in order to stop or to limit the NATO deployment. A curious incident in November 1983, just before the Soviet Union broke off the talks, seems to support this view. Kvitsinskii suggested to Nitze that if the United States proposed equal reductions, leaving the Soviet Union with 120 SS-20s and NATO with none of its new systems, the Soviet Union might respond favourably. Kvitsinskii later denied that this had been a Soviet proposal.[19]

Some progress towards an agreement was made during 1983, but this was not sufficient to prevent the Soviet Union from withdrawing from the negotiations in November, when NATO began to deploy the new missiles. The Soviet Union contended that there was now no basis for an agreement. There is very little chance that these talks will be resumed in their original form, although it is possible that INF will be incorporated into START.

The analysis given in Chapter Four suggested that the Soviet Union – and certainly the military – intended to have a substantial medium-range missile force irrespective of whether or not the NATO deployment went ahead. Soviet proposals indicate that 120 SS-20s (about half the present number) would meet the military requirement. But Soviet policy was guided by broader considerations, for the INF negotiations were the focus of a political struggle over the deployment of the American missiles in Western Europe. For Washington the talks were part of an effort to secure the deployment of the missiles. Moscow saw them as a means of preventing deployment and thus disrupting what it interpreted as Reagan's grand strategy for weakening the Soviet Union. It is this political element that accounts for the Soviet refusal to countenance any new American missiles in Western Europe. When deployment started, the Soviet Union withdrew from the talks.

In line with its argument that parity existed before the NATO deployment began, the Soviet Union has announced countermeasures to redress the balance in Europe, and has said that it will pose a threat to the United States analogous to that which the GLCMs and Pershing 2s pose to the Soviet Union. The Soviet Union is reported to have started deploying SS-22 missiles (which have a range of about 900 kilometres) in East Germany and Czechoslovakia, and may station new missile-carrying submarines off the east coast of the United States.[20]

The INF talks show how ambiguous a concept parity is. It requires that any attempt to attain superiority be countered, and this creates pressure to match the other side in all respects. At first sight parity appears to provide an equitable basis for arms control agreements, but it is difficult to translate into practice in such a way as to halt the competition in armaments.

Since early 1982, when this book was written, no new arms control agreements have been concluded, and the current talks do not look like providing significant results in the near future. The Reagan Administration has accused the Soviet Union of seven violations or possible violations of existing agreements. In the interests of parity the Soviet Union responded with a similar list of charges.[21] It is often said — and rightly — that arms control agreements do not depend on trust between the states involved, but a minimum level of serious diplomatic dialogue is needed to resolve the difficult issues of treaty compliance. This has been lacking since the Reagan Administration took office, and the prospects for cooperative efforts to halt the arms race will remain bleak until it is reestablished.

## The Politics of Defence Policy

Early in 1983 the CIA (Central Intelligence Agency) concluded that its estimate of the rate of growth of Soviet military expenditure in the late 1970s and early 1980s had been too high. Instead of its previous estimate of a growth rate of 4–5 per cent, the CIA now thinks that Soviet military expenditure grew at no more than 2 per cent a year from 1977 to 1981 (the latest year for which estimates are available). It concluded after looking at the figures for arms production that procurement outlays had not grown at all during this period (see Table 1).[22] The new estimate is of course subject to all the same uncertainties and qualifications as the earlier one (see Chapter Six), but the evidence does point towards a slackening of the Soviet military build-up.

The slowdown in the rate of growth of defence expenditure has lasted too long to be plausibly explained as a lull caused by the phasing out of old programs and the introduction of new ones. It seems more reasonable to interpret it as resulting from a policy decision on the part of the Soviet leaders. It coincides with the decline in the rate of growth of the economy as a whole. From 1966 to 1976 the Soviet GNP grew at 2.2 per cent a year, and defence outlays at 2.0 per cent.[23] The slowdown in the rate of growth of defence expenditure can be interpreted, therefore, as a response to the more general slowdown in economic growth, and to the pressures on resource allocation that have followed from this.

The slowdown in the growth of defence expenditure also coincided with Ustinov's appointment as Minister of Defence. When the previous Minister, Marshal Grechko, died in April 1976, the Politburo moved quickly to replace him with Ustinov, an old associate of Brezhnev's who had spent most of his career in managing weapons development and production. Although hardly the archetypal civilian, Ustinov is not a professional soldier, and his appointment marked the first time in twenty-one years that a non-military man had held the post of Minister.

Ustinov's appointment thwarted the ambitions of the then Chief of the General Staff, Army General Kulikov, a protege of Grechko's who had hoped to succeed his patron. Within nine months Ustinov removed Kulikov from the General Staff and gave him the less important post of Commander-in-Chief of the Warsaw Pact. Ustinov replaced him with his own protege, and Kulikov's rival, Ogarkov, who still heads the General Staff.[24]

Within a month of Ustinov's appointment, Brezhnev was made

Table 1: *Production of major items of equipment for Soviet forces, 1977–1981 (Military production less exports)*

| | 1977 | 1978 | 1979 | 1980 | 1981 |
|---|---|---|---|---|---|
| Tanks | 2,200 | 2,000 | 2,000 | 2,500 | 1,400 |
| Armoured Vehicles[1] | 3,700 | 4,400 | 4,500 | 4,800 | 4,000 |
| SP Field Artillery | 900 | 400 | 100 | 50 | 150 |
| Towed Field Artillery | 1,000 | 1,100 | 1,200 | 1,000 | 1,400 |
| Tactical Aircraft | 750 | 950 | 700 | 750 | 750 |
| Helicopters | 850 | 600 | 600 | 650 | 650 |
| Naval ships: major combatants | 10 | 10 | 9 | 9 | 7 |
| Naval ships: minor combatants | 27 | 26 | 27 | 33 | 25 |

SP: self-propelled.

1 This figure includes between 600 and 800 vehicles imported yearly from Eastern Europe.

*Source:*

U.S. Defense Intelligence Agency figures quoted in Richard F. Kaufmann, *Soviet Defense Trends*, A Staff Study prepared for the use of the Subcommittee on International Trade, Finance, and Security Economics of the Joint Economic Committee U.S. Congress, September 1983, p. 8.

Marshal of the Soviet Union, and his chairmanship of the Defence Council was revealed. In the following year it was made known that he was Supreme Commander-in-Chief of the Armed Forces. These moves symbolized the assertion of his – and of the Party's – authority in military affairs. This assertion was soon followed by Brezhnev's reformulation of military doctrine. In January 1977 he gave a speech at Tula in which he declared that superiority was not the goal of Soviet policy (see pp. 48, 115).

These circumstances – the slowdown of economic growth, Ustinov's appointment as Minister of Defence, the assertion of Party authority, and the reformulation of doctrine – all coincided with the reduction in the rate of growth of defence expenditure. This suggests that the reduction was the result of a conscious policy decision. If this interpretation is correct it helps to set the context for the choices the Soviet leaders now face.

In speeches and articles in 1980–2 Marshal Ogarkov issued sharp warnings about the dangers facing the Soviet Union. These could be read as an argument that military preparations should not be neglected, and that military outlays should grow more rapidly in order to match the United States' military build-up (see pp. 71, 94). But the Party leaders did not respond eagerly to Ogarkov's warnings. Ogarkov stressed the dangerous and aggressive nature of American policy, and its search for global military superiority.[25] But the assessment of American policy given by Ustinov in July 1982 was different in emphasis. He portrayed the American threat not merely in military terms, but as an all-round political, ideological and economic challenge. The implication of this analysis was that the Soviet response must have a similarly all-embracing character: more military spending by itself would not solve the Soviet Union's problems.

Brezhnev delivered the same message to the extraordinary meeting of senior officers in October 1982.[26] He tried to assuage military disquiet about the policies being pursued in the face of the worsening international situation. But he gave little comfort to the military. He painted a rather bleak picture of the state of world politics, but he seemed to suggest that the Soviet Union had room for diplomatic manoeuvre, for he noted that the Reagan Administration's policies were causing alarm even among America's allies, and he pointed to the possibility of an improvement in relations with China.

Brezhnev also stressed the importance of industrial development at home, and spoke of the 'exceptional significance' of the Food Program, which had been adopted in May, thus suggesting that only very limited additional resources for the military would be forth-coming. He spoke of the support that the Armed Forces were already receiving, and said that it was up to the military leadership to ensure that they were capable of discharging their responsibilities effectively. His speech seemed to rule out a major increase in military expenditure, though it is possible that some additional growth was approved in the policy review of the summer of 1982.

Brezhnev died within three weeks of giving this speech. Ustinov appears to have played a key role in Andropov's emergence as Brezhnev's successor, and this presumably meant that Andropov had the support of the military too. But Ustinov's role under Brezhnev suggests that he should be regarded not merely as a mouthpiece or creature of the military, but as a powerful Party figure in his own right. Ustinov's support for Andropov did not mean that Andropov was beholden to the military. Nor does the support that he seems to have given Andropov's successor imply that Chernenko is the creature of the military. On the contrary, the choice of Chernenko as General Secretary shows the key role of the Party's central apparatus in the political system.

While he was General Secretary, Andropov gave no clear sign that he was willing to make a major increase in military expenditure. He made it his most urgent priority to restore some vigour to the economy. He tried to improve labour discipline and productivity by cracking down on absenteeism and corruption, and launched some limited experiments in economic reform. His policies had some success in raising labour productivity in 1983.[27]

The emphasis on economic problems did not mean that international politics had lost its significance for the Soviet Union. On the contrary, a major reason for the effort to revitalize the economy has been the fear that economic and technological weakness would undermine the international position and future military power of the Soviet Union. The Soviet leaders seem to feel beleaguered abroad and to have turned inwards to deal with their problems at home. They will not withdraw from world politics of course, as their decision to build up Syria's air defences after the Lebanese war of 1982 shows. But they may concentrate for the time being on consolidating their power rather than on trying to expand it. They are under considerable pressure, however, to increase once again the rate of growth of defence expenditure, in order to maintain their position vis-à-vis the United States. In the five years from Fiscal 1979 to 1983 United States defence outlays increased at 4.1, 3.0, 4.6, 7.6 and 9.5 per cent (in real terms), and even larger increases are planned.[28] If the CIA's estimates are to be believed, Soviet military expenditure has been rising at a much slower rate than this since 1977.

## Conclusion

Soviet foreign and defence policy has been marked by a great deal of continuity during the two successions. This is partly because some adjustment had already been made to the pressures for change during Brezhnev's last years. It now appears that in the late 1970s defence expenditure was brought into line with the declining rate of economic growth. Moreover, in the summer of 1982 there seems to have been a reassessment that laid down the guidelines for the policy pursued by Andropov. The Reagan Administration was seen as implacably hostile, and the prospect of accommodation was judged to be remote. Soviet policy was decided with this in mind, and any move that would look like capitulation to American pressure was of course ruled out.

But the Soviet leaders have failed to find an effective strategy to cope with their problems in foreign and defence policy. In spite of the continuity of policy over the last two years, the question of change is still on the Soviet agenda for the longer term. For this reason it is more important than ever for the West to work out a policy that would provide the basis for cooperative efforts to manage the immensely dangerous rivalry with the Soviet Union. In recent years Western policy has not come close to doing this.

David Holloway
Stanford
February 1984

## NOTES

1. Andropov's position as Chairman of the Defence Council was made known by Ustinov in *Pravda*, 9 May 1983.
2. *Pravda*, 12 July 1982.
3. *Pravda*, 28 October 1982.
4. *Pravda*, 29 September 1983.
5. See William E. Griffith, 'Sino-Soviet Rapprochement?', *Problems of Communism*, March–April 1983, pp. 20–9, and Edmund Lee (pseud.), 'Beijing's Balancing Act', *Foreign Policy*, No. 51, Summer 1983, pp. 27–46.
6. *Krasnaya Zvezda*, 23 September 1983.

7.   *Voennyi Entsiklopedicheskii Slovar'*, Moscow: Voenizdat, 1983, p. 712.
8.   *Pravda*, 22 December 1982.
9.   Hedrick Smith, 'U.S. Sees New Soviet Arms Violation', *New York Times*, 12 May 1983, p. B9.
10.  *Pravda*, 12 July 1982.
11.  See Phillip A. Petersen and John G. Hines, 'The Conventional Offensive in Soviet Theater Strategy', *Orbis*, Fall 1983, pp. 695–739.
12.  *New York Times*, 24 March 1983, p. 20.
13.  *Pravda*, 27 March 1983.
14.  'Dva podkhoda k peregovoram po OSSV', *Pravda*, 2 January 1983.
15.  The terms were already set out in *Pravda*, 10 February 1982.
16.  *Pravda*, 22 December 1982.
17.  *Pravda*, 4 April 1983.
18.  For accounts of this episode see John Newhouse, 'Arms and Allies', *The New Yorker*, 28 February 1983, pp. 64–81; John Barry, 'Geneva Behind Closed Doors', *The Times*, 3 May, 1 and 2 June, 1983; Strobe Talbott, 'Behind Closed Doors', *Time*, 5 December 1983, pp. 22–32.
19.  *Time*, 5 December 1983, pp. 13–15; Yuli Kvitsinsky, 'Soviet View of Geneva', *New York Times*, 12 January 1984, p. 31.
20.  See Andropov's statement in *Pravda*, 25 November 1983; John F. Burns, 'Soviet is Manning New Missile Units', *New York Times*, 18 January 1984, p. 5, and Gerald F. Seib, 'New Soviet Submarine Moves Close to U.S. in a Move Seen as Politically Motivated', *Wall Street Journal*, 27 January 1984, p. 6.
21.  *The President's Report to the Congress on Soviet Noncompliance with Arms Control Agreements*, Washington D.C.: The White House, Office of the Press Secretary, 23 January 1984; 'SShA narushayut svoi mezhdunarodnye obyazatel'stva', *Pravda*, 30 January 1984.
22.  Richard F. Kaufman, *Soviet Defense Trends*. A Staff Study prepared for the use of the Subcommittee on International Trade, Finance, and Security Economics of the Joint Economic Committee, U.S. Congress, September 1983, p. 6. According to the U.S. Department of Defense's *Soviet Military Power*, 2nd ed., Washington D.C., March 1983, pp. 78–80, the production of basic types of equipment did not increase in 1982. Compare the figures for 1982 with those given for 1980 on p. 122 below: tactical aircraft – 1,100; helicopters – 700; tanks – 2,500; armoured vehicles – 4,500; artillery – 1,700. These figures are for total production, including production for export.
23.  *Ibid.* p. 19.
24.  On the relationship between Grechko and Kulikov, and between Kulikov and Ogarkov, see Andrew Cockburn, *The Threat: Inside the Soviet Military Machine*, New York: Random House, 1983, pp. 65–9.
25.  See p. 94 below; also N.V. Ogarkov, 'Na strazhe mirnogo truda', *Komunist*, 1981, no. 10; and N.V. Ogarkov, *Vsegda v gotovnosti k zashchite otechestva*, Moscow: Voenizdat, 1982, pp. 15–17.
26.  *Pravda*, 28 October 1982.
27.  *Pravda*, 29 January 1984.
28.  *National Defense Budget Estimates for FY 1984*, Office of the Assistant Secretary of Defense Comptroller, Department of Defense Washington D.C., March 1983, Table 6–10.

# Introduction

In the early 1980s anxiety about the prospect of nuclear war has risen to a higher pitch in Western Europe and the United States than at any time since the nuclear age began. Political relations between East and West have deteriorated sharply: the hopes of detente have given way to pessimism and disillusionment. Against the background of a worsening international situation, major decisions about nuclear weapons and nuclear strategy have been taken that seem to presage, at the very least, a new and more intense phase in East–West, and in particular in Soviet–American, military rivalry.

The growing anxiety about the possibility of nuclear war is directed in large measure against the policies of the NATO governments, and in particular of the United States. But the policy of the Soviet Union is also the focus of concern. Three main elements of Soviet military policy have alarmed and worried people in the West in recent years. The first is what is commonly referred to as the 'Soviet military build-up': the steady accumulation of military power over the last twenty years or so. The second is the nature of Soviet thinking about nuclear war, and in particular its stress on the need to prepare to fight and win such a war. The third is often called Soviet 'expansionism': the increasing use of military power to expand Soviet influence throughout the world.

Not everyone in the West, of course, shows the same degree of concern about these aspects of Soviet military power and policy; nor is everyone concerned in just the same way. The Reagan Administration has presented its decision to increase American military power as a necessary counterweight to Soviet power. Its critics, on the other hand, argue that its policy will make things worse, not better. Yet the concern about Soviet power and policy is very widely shared, even if the conclusions drawn are not always the same. People have come to ask more and more often: what is it that drives Soviet military policy?

This book tries to help answer this question by examining three aspects of Soviet military power: the role of the military factor in the formation of the Soviet state; Soviet views about the uses of military power in the nuclear age; and the economic and political institutions that sustain the Soviet military effort. The first two chapters look at the Stalin period: at military power as an objective of Stalin's industrialization policy, at the trial of a terrible war with Germany, and at the Soviet entry into the nuclear arms race. The next three chapters examine Soviet thinking about nuclear weapons and nuclear war, Soviet arms and arms control policy, and Soviet use of military power as an instrument of foreign policy. In the last three chapters the domestic bases of Soviet military power are discussed: the defence economy, military technology, and the politics of defence.

This book does not attempt to provide a comprehensive analysis of Soviet military power and policy. It does not, for example, look in detail at Soviet forces or operational doctrine; nor does it try to analyze in detail the military balance between East and West. These topics have been extensively examined in other works. My chief concern has been to look at the historical experience, the policy objectives, and the institutions that have sustained the Soviet military effort – to look, in other words, at the bases of military power in the Soviet state. I have written on this topic because I believe that Soviet military power can be understood only in the context of the Soviet state and its history. Although this book is very selective in the issues it examines, I hope that it will help to throw some light on Soviet military power and policy and thus contribute to the current Western debates about war and peace in the nuclear age.

# CHAPTER ONE

# Military Power and the Soviet State

In the months before the October Revolution of 1917, the Bolsheviks did what they could to further the disintegration of the Russian Army and to enlist the support of disaffected soldiers and sailors. But, as Lenin later admitted, they made no preparation for raising an army to defend the revolution.[1] As Marxists, they regarded the standing armies of the capitalist states as instruments of aggression abroad and repression at home. Like most socialists of the time they thought that the proper form of military organization for a proletarian state was a people's militia in which workers and peasants would serve on a part-time basis. This, they believed, would not degenerate into a military caste or lead to the creation of a military realm separate from other areas of social life.[2]

These ideas about military organization did not survive the early trials of the Soviet state. The Bolsheviks seized power quickly in October 1917, but they had to wage a bitter civil war to consolidate that power throughout the country. They were soon forced by the war, and by the intervention of the leading capitalist powers, to raise an army. In the spring of 1918 Lenin called for an army of one million men, and soon for three million, to defend the young Soviet state.[3]

In organizing the Red Army, Trotsky imposed strict discipline and centralized control, and recruited between 50,000 and 100,000 former Imperial officers. He claimed that these steps were necessary to make the Red Army an effective fighting force, but they evoked widespread criticism within the Party. The 8th Party Congress in March 1919 pronounced the existing organization of the Red Army transitional, and declared that it would be transformed into a territorial militia after the Civil War. In *The ABC of Communism*, written in 1919, Bukharin and Preobrazhensky, two of the Party's leading theoreticians, argued that the Party must convince all the proletarian and peasant troops 'that the workers have only become soldiers for a brief space and owing to a temporary need, that the field of *production* is the natural field of their activities, that work in the Red Army must on no account lead to the formation of any caste permanently withdrawn from industry and agriculture.'[4]

As the Civil War ended, an intensive debate took place about the transition to a territorial-militia system. Commissions were set up and reports prepared. But the circumstances did not favour reorganization. In 1920 the Bolsheviks tried to take the revolution into Poland on the bayonets of the Red Army, but met defeat outside Warsaw. In 1921 they used the Red Army to suppress the peasant insurrection in Tambov and the sailors' mutiny in Kronstadt. It was clear that, although victorious in the Civil War, the Bolsheviks still faced enemies abroad and opposition at home. A disciplined standing army under tight central control appeared to be a more reliable instrument for protecting Bolshevik power than a militia that might be ineffective as a military force and open to hostile political influences. The promised transition was not made.[5]

The organization issue was finally settled by the military reform of 1924–5, which created a mixed system, with the emphasis on standing forces; the territorial-militia element was retained for economic reasons rather than on grounds of principle. The Bolsheviks still claimed that the Red Army was an army of a new type, because its mission was to defend the proletarian revolution of October 1917. It differed in important respects from capitalist armies of the mid-1920s. Its commanders were not drawn predominantly from upper and upper-middle class backgrounds, and it had a system of military commissars – political officers through whom the Party sought to exercise control and instil loyalty. But the Red Army was far from embodying pre-revolutionary socialist ideas of military organization. It had been shaped primarily by the Bolsheviks' determination to defend their power against enemies at home and abroad.

## Industrialization and Military Power

In 1905 Lenin wrote that two conditions were necessary for successful revolution in Russia: a socialist revolution in one or more of the advanced countries, and an alliance between workers and peasants in Russia. By the end of the Civil War both of these conditions were threatened. Europe had not been swept by proletarian revolution, and the failure of the Polish workers to greet the Red Army as liberators in

1920 dealt a further blow to the hope of revolution in the immediate future. Moreover, War Communism, with its forced requisitioning of food in the countryside, had the effect of turning the Russian peasants against the Bolsheviks. Lenin repeated the two conditions for the success of socialism in Russia when he introduced the New Economic Policy at the 10th Party Congress in March 1921.[6] The new policy was designed to secure peasant support by ending state requisitions of food and allowing the market a greater role in the economy. The change in domestic policy was accompanied by a foreign policy designed to secure a breathing space for the Soviet state.

It became increasingly clear in the early 1920s that revolution in Europe, by which so much store had been set, was not about to happen. The Soviet Union would have to survive as the only proletarian state in a capitalist world. The idea of building 'socialism in one country' began to gain ground in the Party in the mid-1920s. Trotsky attacked this notion as a betrayal of the revolution, and as a surrender to the peasantry. At first it did seem that 'socialism in one country' implied a continuation of the New Economic Policy. But its ultimate significance was very different.

The New Economic Policy proved successful in bringing disused plant back into production, but it did not provide the basis for further industrialization. A bitter and wide-ranging argument broke out in the Party about the correct strategy for industrial development. Military considerations were not decisive in this debate, but they were important.[7] The Bolshevik leaders realized that the economic basis of Soviet military power was even weaker than that of Russia in 1914. As the idea of 'socialism in one country' gained acceptance, the lack of modern armaments grew more worrying. The Soviet state might have to fight alone against the capitalist powers; and although it might have the support of revolutionary elements in those countries, it would face a formidable enemy.

In January 1925 Frunze, Trotsky's successor as Commissar of War, warned that a future war would not be like the Civil War:

> Of course it will have the character of a class civil war in the sense that the White Guards will be on the enemy's side, while we, on the other hand, shall have allies in the camp of our enemies. But in equipment, in the methods of waging it, it will not be a war like our civil war. We shall have to deal with a splendid army, armed with all the latest technological advances, and if we do not have these advances then the prospects for us may prove very very unfavourable. This

should be taken into account when we decide the question of the
general preparation of the country for defence.[8]

The issue of industrialization was linked in the late 1920s with the task
of re-equipping the Red Army. In December 1927 Voroshilov, the
Commissar for Army and Navy Affairs, told the 15th Party Congress
that the chief military purpose of the First Five Year Plan was to raise
'the technical strength of the Red Army to the level of first class
contemporary armies'.[9] The economic Five Year Plan was accompanied by a Five Year Plan for the development of the Red Army, which
was drawn up by the military authorities and approved by the Party
and government in 1928.[10]

In 1929 Stalin, who had now defeated his political opponents on
both left and right of the Party, set his own brutal stamp on Soviet
industrialization. He launched the forced collectivization of agriculture, and pushed for an increase in the targets for industrial production. 1929 was also a key year for military policy. In July the Politburo
issued a decree on 'The State of Defence of the USSR', calling for an
even faster drive to reequip the Red Army.[11] The targets in the military
plan were revised upwards: the Red Army was to have no fewer troops
than its probable enemies in the main theatre of war, and was to attain
superiority in the decisive types of armament – aircraft, artillery and
tanks.[12] In the same year the Red Army adopted new Field Service
Regulations. The Regulations Commission noted that 'we have every
reason to expect that [our] technological might will increase from year
to year. We must not only refuse to accept a technological lag, but on
the contrary, we must surpass our bourgeois neighbors in arms and
equipment.'[13] In 1931 the guidelines for military planning were altered
once again: the Soviet Union was to have more troops than the enemy
in the main theatre of war.

Industrialization was launched under the slogan of 'catching up
and overtaking' the advanced capitalist powers economically and
technologically. In 1931 Stalin spoke of Russia's traditional backwardness and its suffering at the hands of its enemies: the only way
to avoid being beaten again was to catch up with the capitalist
world.

Do you want our Socialist fatherland to be beaten and to lose its
independence? If you do not want this you must put an end to its
backwardness in the shortest possible time and develop genuine Bolshevik tempo in building up its Socialist system of economy. There is
no other way. That is why Lenin said during the October Revolution:

'Either perish, or overtake and outstrip the advanced capitalist countries'.

We are fifty or a hundred years behind the advanced countries. We must make good this distance in ten years. Either we do it, or they crush us.[14]

The true significance of 'socialism in one country' was that, far from leading to a policy of gradual change, it helped to inspire the Bolsheviks to transform Russia by their own efforts. The drive to build socialism in one country brought a fusion of socialist and nationalist loyalties. Russian destiny and Marxism joined hands in the effort to industrialize the Soviet Union and make it a great and independent power.[15]

The Bolsheviks believed that they needed a strong army, because they were likely to face a coalition of powerful capitalist states in a future war. They believed too that military power rested upon industrial power, and consequently gave high priority to the creation of a modern armaments industry. Tsarist Russia had had an extensive arms industry, to which the First World War had given new impetus. But this was neglected under the New Economic Policy, and by the late 1920s the Soviet Union had virtually no tank industry, little or no warship production, and low artillery and ammunition production; the aircraft industry was the brightest spot in an otherwise gloomy picture. Besides, most of the Red Army's weapons were of pre-revolutionary or foreign design. During the years of the First Five Year Plan (1928–32) the production of arms and equipment rose rapidly. It remained more stable during the Second Five Year Plan (1933–7), but rose again after that as the threat of war loomed larger (see Table 1). In the early 1930s foreign weapons were acquired and used as the basis for Soviet designs. By 1940 the Soviet Union had a strong defence industry and military-technological base,[16] and had gone a long way towards attaining the goal of strategic self-sufficiency.[17]

In re-equipping the Red Army the Soviet leaders rejected the concept, which was popular with Western military theorists at the time, of small highly-mechanized forces. They sought instead to marry the mass army to modern military technology. During the 1930s the Red Army's leaders devoted a great deal of attention to determining how the new weapons would be employed in war. Tukhachevskii, the Red Army's Chief of Armament, and a group of officers close to him developed the concept of the 'operation in depth' as a way of using modern arms in mobile offensive warfare. The main idea was that modern armaments made it possible to strike the enemy not only in his front line, but

Table 1.1: *Annual average production of basic types of armament (units), 1930–1940*

| | 1930–1 | 1932–4 | 1935–7 | 1938–40 |
|---|---|---|---|---|
| Aircraft: | | | | |
| total* | 860[1] | 2,595[1] | 3,758[1] | 8,805[2] |
| bombers | 100[1] | 252[1] | 568[1] | 3,571[3] (1940 only) |
| fighters | 120[1] | 326[1] | 1,278[1] | 4,574[3] (1940 only) |
| Tanks** | 740[1] | 3,371[1] | 3,139[1] | 2,672[2] |
| Artillery pieces*** | 1,911[1] | 3,778[1] | 5,020[1] | 14,996[2] |
| Rifles ('000) | 174[1] | 256[1] | 397[1] | 1,379[2] |
| | *1928–32* | *1933–6* | *1939* | |
| Naval Shipbuilding (tonnes displacement) | 2,400[2] | 14,000[2] | 30,460[2] | |

*Sources*
1. M.V. Zakharov, 'Kommunisticheskaya partiya i tekhnickeskoe perevooruzhenie armii i flota v gody predvoennykh pyatiletok', *Voenno-istoricheskii zhurnal*, 1971, no. 2, p. 7.
2. Julian Cooper, *Defence Production and the Soviet Economy 1929–1941*, CREES Discussion Paper, University of Birmingham, 1976, pp. 46–50.
3. G.S. Kravchenko, *Ekonomika SSSR v gody Velikoi Otechestvennoi voiny*, Moscow: Ekonomika, 1970, p. 297, and Cooper, *op. cit.*, p. 46.

*Notes*
\* This figure includes civil aircraft.
\*\* Tank production fell in the late 1930s. This may be explained partly by a switch to new models, but may also reflect the loss of faith in tank forces that followed the purge.
\*\*\* This does not include naval artillery. Nor does it include mortars, which began to be produced in 1937. In 1940 38,500 mortars were produced (see Cooper, *op. cit.*, p. 49).

simultaneously in the whole depth of his order of battle. The enemy could be prevented from bringing up his reserves and stopping the breakthrough.[17] This new operational concept tried to embody the qualities of manoeuvre and offensive that were said to spring from the class character of the Red Army. (The influence of the secret ties that the Red Army had with the Reichswehr from 1922 may have been considerable too.) This concept, which was based on the massed use of tanks, artillery and aircraft, reflected – and in turn reinforced – the belief that military power rested on industrial might.

The Soviet leaders built up heavy industry in order to provide the basis for economic growth and for military power. Through an exceptionally high rate of investment they brought about a major and rapid change in the structure of the economy. A large network of planning and management bodies directed resources to the goals set by the Party leaders, without reference to the market. High priority sectors, including the defence industry, had first call on scarce resources, and tight central control was imposed to ensure that targets in these sectors were met. In 1956 the Polish economist Oskar Lange described the Soviet economy as a 'war economy' because the instruments of economic management were the same as those used in capitalist economies in wartime.[18]

Lange was not referring to the level of military expenditure: his point was that there was nothing inherently socialist about the instruments of management and hence that to abandon them was not tantamount to abandoning socialism. But the requirements of defence did have an important influence on the whole pattern of industrialization. Besides specialized plants for turning out weapons, military production needed the support of a strong industrial base, and in particular of the metallurgical, fuel, machine-tool, electrical supply and chemical industries. The Party tried to ensure that civilian industry could produce arms if the need arose. New civilian plant was designed with this in view, and towards the end of the 1930s special workshops were set up in many factories to smooth the way for military production. In this way the Party tried to make sure that the drive for economic growth and the preparation for war complemented each other.[19]

In 1930 Stalin rejected a proposal from Tukhachevskii for expansion of weapons production, on the grounds that it would lead to an end of 'socialist construction' and its replacement with a system of 'red militarism'. Less than two years later he said that he had been wrong to turn down the proposal.[20] 'Red militarism' is an apt term for many aspects of Soviet life in the 1930s. The creation of military power was one of the main objectives of the industrialization drive, and military requirements had an important effect on the pattern of industrial development. The Party saw itself as a disciplined army, combating hostile forces in Russian society. The style of political and economic leadership was military: the economic system is often called a 'command economy'. Official language was suffused with military images: problems were 'attacked'; everyone belonged to one 'camp' or another; enemies were 'crushed'; the Party conducted struggles on various 'fronts': industrial, agricultural, ideological, scientific.[21] 'There is no fortress', it was said, 'that the Bolsheviks cannot storm.'

Finally, the need for security was offered as one of the chief justifications for the ruthlessness of Soviet rule. In 1936 Stalin declared that socialism had been built in Russia and that antagonistic classes no longer existed there; this should, in Marxist theory, have helped the state to 'wither away'.[22] But in 1939 Stalin justified the strength of the Soviet state by reference to capitalist encirclement and the efforts of the capitalist states to undermine Soviet power.[23]

## The Test of War

Stalin manipulated the threat from abroad in order to strengthen his own power. The great purge he carried out between 1936 and 1938 did incalculable damage to the ability of the Soviet Union to defend itself in 1941. Soviet rule had already seen repression on a large scale, as in the forcible collectivization of agriculture. But the arrests of 1936–8 remain difficult to fathom, for they were made on the basis of fabricated charges, and lacked any obvious rationale. Perhaps Stalin was seeking to eliminate potential sources of opposition, and certainly the process developed, like a witch-hunt, its own dynamic of denunciation and forced confession. In 1937, at the height of the purge, Stalin struck at the Red Army. The great majority of the Red Army's commanders at brigade level and above were arrested. The Naval Command and the military commissars were similarly hit. The ranks of field-grade and junior officers also suffered enormous losses. Some were shot, others were sent to the camps. The Red Army lost more officers in these peacetime years than any army ever did in war.[24]

The purge destroyed the High Command that had been trying to mould the Red Army, with its new arms and its new doctrine, into an effective fighting force. Most of the military innovators, including Tukhachevskii, were arrested, to be replaced by men with less experience and ability. Military doctrine remained unchanged in its general outlines, but many operational concepts, including that of the operation in depth, came under suspicion because they were associated with those who had now been branded enemies of the people.[25] The resulting loss of direction was reflected in the general disarray of the Red Army in 1938–41, and contributed to its poor showing in the war with Finland in the winter of 1939–40.

On 22 June 1941 Germany attacked the Soviet Union. The war that the Soviet Union had anticipated for so long took Stalin by surprise and caught the Red Army unprepared. By the end of November several million Soviet troops had been killed or taken prisoner, and the German armies had reached the outskirts of Moscow. The Soviet authorities had lost control of 40 per cent of the population, 40 per cent of the grain production, and 60 per cent of the coal, iron, steel and aluminium output of the country.[26] On the eve of the German attack Soviet military doctrine rested on three basic principles: constant readiness for a crushing repulse of any aggressor; defeat of the enemy on his own territory; and attainment of victory with little bloodshed.[27] But the Red Army was not ready to meet the German attack, and Germany quickly occupied large areas of Soviet territory. By the end of 1941 much blood had already been spilt and victory was by no means certain.

The disaster of 1941 has been one of the most important and most controversial issues in Soviet historiography. How could Stalin have been taken by surprise when his whole policy had been based on the need to prepare for war? Stalin had used the respite afforded by the Ribbentrop–Molotov pact of August 1939 to try to strengthen the Soviet position. He extended the Soviet frontier westwards by occupying Eastern Poland, the Baltic States and Bessarabia. He made an effort to repair those of the Red Army's deficiencies that had been exposed in the Winter War with Finland in 1939–40. But in spite of many warnings of an impending German attack, he failed to take the precaution of bringing the Red Army to a high state of readiness or to prepare the country psychologically for war. He misread Hitler's intentions, hoping to forestall an attack by adopting a conciliatory and unprovocative policy, even to the point of helping the German war effort with Soviet exports. Germany had the advantage of surprise, and as a result inflicted great losses on the Red Army in the initial attack.[28]

While Stalin lived, Soviet historians were not able to attempt a serious analysis of why and how Germany had achieved surprise. The Red Army's retreat was presented as part of a preplanned strategy of active defence.[29] In the 'secret speech' of February 1956, however, Khrushchev placed the blame for the success of the German surprise attack on Stalin. He listed some of the warnings Stalin had received and ignored, and he condemned him for his failure to make the country ready for war.[30] This speech opened the way to franker discussion of the initial setbacks of the war. Writers of memoirs and historians followed Khrushchev in stressing Stalin's responsibility, and the 'mistakes' he had made; his purge of the Red Army, his trust in Hitler, and his failure to heed the warnings were all condemned.

In 1967, however, the situation changed. A.M. Nekrich's book *June 22, 1941*, which had been published two years earlier, was savagely attacked in the Party's historical journal.[31] This book examines in telling detail the contribution of Stalin's policies to the disaster of 1941. The attack on it was intended, apparently, to show that criticism of Stalin and his rule should now be muted, and was part of a general policy of changing the picture that Khrushchev had presented of Stalin in the secret speech. Certainly since 1967 the treatment of Stalin's role in the war has changed in tone.[32] The failure to anticipate the German attack is still seen to have had dreadful consequences, but Stalin is no longer held solely responsible for this. Less emphasis is laid on his mistakes, and more on the complexity of the situation in which he found himself. The focus of attention has moved away from one man's failings to the performance of the system as a whole in preparing for war and in withstanding the shock of the German attack. This change of emphasis can be seen as an attempt to present a more balanced picture of Stalin. But the restrictions on writing about Stalin are a serious hindrance; how can the performance of the system be examined properly when its chief architect and central figure cannot be studied critically?

The intensity of the arguments about 1941 reflects the intensity of the experience itself. The German attack left a deep mark on the Soviet consciousness, and particularly on the minds of political and military leaders. The memory of 22 June 1941 has had a profound effect on post-war military policy. Much of the writing about that day can be read as an exploration of the problem of surprise attack and the initiation of war. The connection with the nuclear age is not always made explicit. But historical analysis is one way of reflecting on current problems, and the shifts in historical interpretation are linked with changes in thinking about nuclear war.[33]

In December 1941 the Red Army launched a counter-offensive outside Moscow and halted the German advance. But the Soviet Union could take the offensive in an effective manner only when industry began to turn out armaments in large numbers. Losses of equipment were enormous in the opening stage of the war, and military production was disrupted by the German advance. By the end of 1941, however, more than 1,300 major plants and ten million people had been evacuated to the east of the country, and in the following year arms production started to rise sharply. Once it was supplied with weapons, the Red Army could search for the right combination of arms, men and doctrine to put into practice the principles of manoeuvre and offensive that had been espoused in pre-war military thought. A High Command of great ability emerged from the early setbacks to prove itself at the battles of Stalingrad and Kursk. The Red Army went over to the attack, pushed the German armies back and liberated Eastern Europe from Nazi rule. In May 1945 the Red Army took Berlin and raised the Red Flag over the city.

The war with Germany is known in the Soviet Union as the Great Patriotic (or Fatherland) War. When Molotov broadcast the news of the German attack on 22 June 1941 he recalled the patriotic war of 1812 when the Russian people had risen to crush Napoleon's invasion; Hitler, he said, would meet the same fate. On 3 July Stalin spoke on radio for the first time since the invasion and produced a profound effect by addressing his listeners as 'Comrades, citizens, brothers and sisters, fighters of our Army and Navy!' He went on 'I am speaking to you, my friends!' Throughout the war he appealed to the patriotism of the Russian people. They were urged to fight, not for socialism, but for Mother Russia. During the war the union between Russian nationalism and the Soviet state became closer than ever. Stalin made concessions to national sentiment that seemed to hold out the promise that after the war the Soviet Union would be a happier place than before.

The Soviet Union bore the brunt of the war against Germany. Soviet losses were immense. More than twenty million people were killed. Hundreds of towns and thousands of villages were destroyed. The people endured terrible hardships, as in the 900-day siege of Leningrad, where the suffering of the inhabitants was matched only by their heroism. There was opposition to Bolshevik rule during the war, particularly in the occupied areas. But the savage and inhuman nature of the German occupation soon showed that the familiar, though repressive, Soviet rule was preferable to that of the Nazis.[35] In spite of (or perhaps because of) the upheavals caused by Stalin's repressive rule, the German invasion drew regime and people closer together than at any time since the revolution. Domestic divisions were submerged in the struggle against a common enemy.

## Conclusion

Neither of the two conditions that Lenin pointed to in 1905 as necessary for successful revolution in Russia had been met. With the failure of revolution in Europe, the Bolsheviks had decided to build socialism in one country. In order to pursue the goal of rapid industrialization, Stalin had collectivized agriculture by force and thus destroyed the 'alliance of worker and peasant' that the New Economic Policy had been designed to cement. He proceeded to build a powerful state that could repress any opposition at home and meet any threat from abroad.

Stalin's industrialization drive followed a familiar Russian pattern in which rivalry with other, economically more powerful states has provided the stimulus to domestic change. This was true of Peter the Great's reforms, and of the reforms that followed the Crimean War. As a result of this pattern, the state has been the main agency of change in Russian society. The state has altered economic and social relationships with the aim of mobilizing resources to increase its own power. In Tsarist Russia a powerful state ruled over a weak and inchoate civil society. Only in the last century did civil society begin to emerge as a coherent entity. In 1911 the Russian historian Kliuchevsky characterized the growth of the Russian state thus: 'the state swelled up; the people grew lean'.[36] Stalin destroyed those elements of civil society that still existed. The state swelled up further, and the people grew leaner.

In July 1940 Hitler told his High Command that the attack on the Soviet Union would 'make sense only if we can smash the state with one blow'.[37] The initial disasters of the war did indeed call into question the survival of the state. In 1917 the Tsarist state had collapsed under the combined pressure of an unsuccessful war and domestic unrest, and the Bolsheviks won considerable support after the February revolution with their call for peace. Stalin may have had this in mind when he referred, in his victory toast to the Russian people, to the desperate situation in 1941–2: 'A different people would have said to our Government: "You have failed to justify our expectations. Go away. We shall install another government, which will conclude peace with Germany and assure us a quiet life."' [38] But the Soviet state proved more resilient than Russia in the First World War, thanks in large measure to the courage and sacrifices of the 'lean people'.

In February 1946 Stalin declared that the Soviet social order had successfully passed the test of war and proved its 'unquestionable vitality'. He claimed that 'the Soviet social order has shown itself more stable and capable of enduring than a non-Soviet social order, that the Soviet social order is a form of organization, a society superior to any non-Soviet social order . . . ' [39] He said in the same speech that the policies of collectivization and industrialization had made victory possible, and he announced that the Soviet Union would return to the task of building up heavy industry. It would take at least three more Five Year Plans before the Soviet Union would be ready for 'all contingencies'.[40] That meant a return to the prewar policy of building up the power of the state.

# CHAPTER TWO

# Entering the Nuclear Arms Race

Victory over Germany brought the Soviet Union political gains that must have been inconceivable in the early months of the war. Stalin now had a say in the political arrangements of Eastern Europe, and Soviet security was thereby enhanced. Stalin's policy in Eastern Europe, however, soon brought him into conflict with his allies. Strains were evident at the Potsdam Conference in July and August 1945. This was the last meeting of the allied leaders to try to resolve their differences about the post-war settlement. It was also the first occasion on which the atomic bomb cast its shadow over relations between the Soviet Union and the Western powers.

The Americans and the British had pondered for some time what to tell Stalin about the atomic bomb. Neither Roosevelt nor Churchill had been impressed by the advice of the great Danish physicist Niels Bohr that they should inform Stalin before the bomb was tested and try to get agreement on international control.[1] The first atomic bomb test took place on 16 July while the Potsdam Conference was in progress. On 24 July President Truman approached Stalin after the formal session had broken up and 'casually mentioned' to him that 'we had a new weapon of unusual destructive force.' Truman wrote later that Stalin replied that 'he was glad to hear of it and hoped we would make "good use of it against the Japanese".' Truman and Churchill (who was watching intently from nearby) were convinced that Stalin had not grasped what the President was referring to.[2] They were mistaken, however, for Stalin knew of the Manhattan Project and had initiated Soviet work on the bomb early in 1943.

## Deciding to Build the Bomb

When nuclear fission was discovered in Berlin in December 1938, Soviet physicists were as quick as their counterparts in other countries to see that one of its potential applications was the creation of a bomb with unprecedented destructive force. In 1939 Igor Tamm, a leading theoretical physicist, remarked to a group of students, 'Do you know what this new discovery means? It means a bomb can be built that will destroy a city out to a radius of maybe ten kilometers.'[3]

The discovery of nuclear fission at once stimulated new directions of research in the Soviet Union. Leningrad was the leading centre for this work. Here the prime mover was Igor Kurchatov, who headed the nuclear laboratory at the Leningrad Physicotechnical Institute and was later to be scientific director of the atomic project. He coordinated the research not only of his own laboratory, but also of scientists working at the Radium Institute and at the Institute of Physical Chemistry. The Radium Institute was directed by V.G. Khlopin, a radiochemist who later developed the industrial processes for producing plutonium. The director of the Institute of Physical Chemistry was N.N. Semenov, who had done important work on chain reactions for which he later received a Nobel Prize.

Nuclear physics in the 1930s was the very model of an international scientific community. The dramatic progress of research was built on discoveries by scientists in several different countries. Although they had no centre of nuclear research to compare with Paris, Cambridge or Copenhagen, Soviet physicists followed international progress avidly and made some significant contributions to it. Now their work on nuclear fission parallelled that done elsewhere. In April 1939 two of Kurchatov's junior colleagues established that each fissioned nucleus emitted between two and four neutrons, thus indicating that a chain reaction might be possible. Two physicists at Semenov's institute investigated the conditions under which a chain reaction would take place in uranium, and concluded early in 1940 that an experimental attempt to achieve a chain reaction could now be undertaken. In the same year two other physicists, working under Kurchatov's close direction, discovered the spontaneous fission of uranium (i.e., fission without bombardment by neutrons). Inspired by these results, Kurchatov and his colleagues wrote to the Presidium of the Academy of Sciences, urging an expansion of work on nuclear fission.

In June 1940 the Academy set up a Uranium Commission, with Khlopin as chairman, to direct research on the 'uranium problem'. This commission was a clear sign of the Academy's interest in nuclear fission. Work was now to proceed on a broad front: exploration for uranium deposits (lack of uranium was an important constraint on early Soviet work); the production of heavy water; rapid construction of cyclotrons; studies of isotope separation; measurement of the nuclear constants. But Kurchatov was disappointed with the scale of this effort. In August he and a colleague sent the Academy Presidium a plan of research, proposing that an experimental reactor be built. They drew attention to the military and economic importance of nuclear energy and urged the Academy to approach the government for additional funds in view of the exceptional significance the uranium problem had for the defence of the country.

In November, at a conference on nuclear physics in Moscow, Kurchatov received a reply to his proposal. Speaking after a paper by Kurchatov, Khlopin, the head of the Uranium Commission, declared that some young physicists, in particular Kurchatov's students, were so captivated by the uranium problem that they forgot about current needs. Nuclear energy, he said, was still a distant prospect, still a beautiful dream; it would be wrong to draw creative minds and national resources into unreal schemes. Khlopin thus made it clear that the Uranium Commission would not act on Kurchatov's proposal.

Work on nuclear fission continued, though not at the pace or on the scale that Kurchatov desired. He made a further attempt to put his case before the authorities. Semenov wrote on his behalf to the government about the possibility of creating a bomb, the destructive power of which would be incomparably greater than that of any existing explosive. This letter, written at the end of 1940 or early in 1941, elicited no response before the German invasion brought nuclear research in the Soviet Union to a halt.

Early in 1942 the possibility of an atomic bomb became a serious issue for the Soviet leadership, as a result of information obtained about British, American and German work on the bomb. In April M.G. Pervukhin, Deputy Premier and People's Commissar (i.e. Minister) of the Chemical Industry, was sent for by Molotov, who gave him a thick file containing secret reports about the foreign work. Soviet sources do not say what was in the file, but it may have contained Klaus Fuchs's earliest reports on British work; it appears also that the Soviet Union had by this time received information about German interest in the bomb. Molotov told Pervukhin that he was giving him the papers on Stalin's instruction, and that he was to read them and advise what should be done. Pervukhin recommended that the papers be shown to physicists who would be able to make a precise evaluation of their significance. He himself was given responsibility for the uranium problem.[4]

Information came also from an unexpected source. In May 1942 G.N. Flyorov, one of Kurchatov's former students, wrote to Stalin that 'it is essential not to lose any time in building the uranium bomb'. Flyorov, now a lieutenant in the Air Force, was serving at the front in Voronezh, where he had visited the University library to look at the physics journals. He was anxious to see if there had been any response to the discovery, which he had helped to make, of spontaneous fission. A note about this had been published in the American journal *Physical Review*. On looking through the journals, however, he found no reaction to this discovery; moreover, he saw that little of importance was being published about nuclear fission, and that the big names in the field had vanished from the journals. He concluded, rightly, that research was now secret and that the Americans must be working on an atomic bomb. Hence the letter to Stalin.

In the course of 1942 Soviet leaders held consultations with prominent scientists about the development of an atomic bomb. In one meeting Stalin made clear his anger that it was a young lieutenant at the front, and not the members of the Academy, who had drawn the possibility of such a bomb to his attention. He was worried about the cost of developing a bomb, for he was advised by two of the scientists that it would cost as much as the whole war effort. He decided, nevertheless, to initiate a small-scale project. Kurchatov, who had abandoned nuclear research on the outbreak of war, was chosen as scientific director. He finally began work in February or March 1943.

The decision to build an atomic bomb was taken when the war with Germany still hung in the balance. (The counteroffensive at Stalingrad, planned in September and October 1942, had the codename *Uran*, which though normally translated as Uranus, is also the Russian for uranium. This may indicate that the atomic bomb was preying on Stalin's mind at the time.)[5] There were many who thought the effort a pointless waste of resources which could be used to meet more pressing needs. Stalin can hardly have thought that a Soviet bomb could be built in time to affect the outcome of the war. Soviet physicists had estimated in 1942 that the development of a uranium bomb would take between ten and twenty years. Perhaps Stalin had it in mind that after the war the Soviet Union would have to face a nuclear-armed Germany, for at this early period he may have had only minimum war aims, which did not necessarily include the destruction of the Nazi state. Perhaps he foresaw that even with the defeat of Germany the Soviet Union would come into conflict with Britain and the United States; after all, they were conducting their atomic projects in great secrecy, without informing the Soviet Union. More probably, the decision should be seen as a hedge against uncertainty. Given that Germany, Britain and the United States were interested in the atomic bomb, was it not as well to initiate a Soviet project, even though the circumstances in which the new weapon might be used could not be foreseen?

Kurchatov drew up a plan of research with three main goals: to achieve a chain reaction in an experimental reactor using natural uranium; to develop methods of isotope separation; to study the design of both the U-235 and the plutonium bombs. He built up his team slowly, drawing largely on those with whom he had worked before. By the end of 1943 he had fifty people working in his new laboratory; by the end of 1944 he had one hundred scientists. This was a tiny effort compared with the Manhattan Project. As the country was liberated, other institutes were drawn into the project, and in 1945 some German scientists and technicians were brought to the Soviet Union to take part. In the spring of 1945 Kurchatov ordered work to begin on the design of an industrial reactor for producing plutonium.[6] By the time of the Potsdam Conference the Soviet Union had a serious atomic bomb project under way.

In spite of this, however, the American success in building the bomb came as a blow for the Soviet Union. Alexander Werth, who was in Moscow at the time, wrote that the news of Hiroshima had 'an acutely depressing effect on everybody'. The atomic bomb was seen as a threat to Russia, and 'some Russian pessimists ... dismally remarked that Russia's desperately hard victory over Germany was now "as good as wasted".'[7] In December 1945 the British Ambassador wrote to the Foreign Secretary:

> the German invasion caught them still unready and swept them to what looked like the brink of defeat. Then came the turn of the tide and with it first the hope and then a growing belief that the immense benison of national security was at last within their reach. As the Red Army moved westwards belief became confidence and the final defeat of Germany made confidence conviction ... Then plump came the Atomic Bomb. At a blow the balance which had now seemed set and steady was rudely shaken. Russia was balked by the west when everything seemed to be within her grasp. The three hundred divisions were shorn of much of their value.[8]

Ambassador Harriman reported to Washington in much the same terms.[9]

The small Soviet project laid the basis for the all-out effort that was now launched. Stalin's immediate reaction to Truman's casual remark was to tell Kurchatov to speed up his work. In the middle of August, shortly after his return from Potsdam, Stalin summoned B.L. Vannikov, the People's Commissar of Munitions, and his deputies to the Kremlin. There they were joined by Kurchatov. 'A single demand of you, comrades,' said Stalin. 'Provide us with atomic weapons in the shortest possible time. You know that Hiroshima has shaken the whole world. The balance has been destroyed. Provide the bomb – it will remove a great danger from us.'[10] Kurchatov and his colleagues were asked how long it would take to build the atomic bomb if they received all-round support. Five years, they replied. In the event, the first Soviet test took place four years to the month after that August meeting with Stalin.

Compared with his failure to heed the warnings of a German attack in 1941, Stalin's decision about the atomic bomb in 1942 showed considerable foresight. The last thing he can have wanted to hear then was that Germany, Britain and the United States were working in great secrecy to develop a weapon of unprecedented destructive force. In spite of the critical war situation, he took the precautionary step of setting up a small-scale project. The Soviet leaders were nevertheless shaken by the American success in building a bomb. When Molotov heard what Truman had said at Potsdam, he saw it as an attempt to gain concessions from the Soviet Union. The Soviet leaders regarded the use of the bomb in Japan as part of an effort to put pressure on them, as a demonstration that the United States was willing to use nuclear weapons. Soviet security now seemed to be at risk from a new threat.

If Niels Bohr's advice had been heeded, and Stalin had been told officially about the bomb, his post-war policy might have been just the same. But Western secrecy contributed to Soviet suspicion and spurred the Soviet Union to develop its own bomb. As Margaret Gowing has written, 'If Russia had been formally consulted about the bomb during the war . . . it might have made no difference. The fact that she was not, guaranteed that the attempts made just after the war to establish international control, which might have failed anyway, were doomed.'[11]

## Post-war Weapons Programs

In the late 1920s the Soviet leaders adopted the goal of 'catching up and overtaking' the advanced capitalist powers. They made it clear that they would not accept economic or technological backwardness, least of all in military affairs. Now, at the end of a terrible war with Germany, the Soviet Union once again faced the prospect of rivalry with states that were economically and technologically more advanced. The war in the West had provided a greater stimulus to the development of new military technologies than the slogging-match in the East. Atomic energy was the most important of these, but long-range rocketry, radar and jet propulsion were other fields where the Soviet Union lagged behind. Once again the imperative of 'catch up and overtake' had to be obeyed if the Soviet Union was not to find itself inferior to the leading capitalist powers in military strength.

The post-war programs were not started from scratch. The atomic bomb project had already begun, and in the 1930s the Soviet Union had done pioneering work in rocket engineering and radar. But in both of these fields research was hit by the great purge, and it was only towards the closing stages of the war that their significance was clearly realized. In 1933, for example, the Reaction Research Institute (*RNII: Reaktivnyi nauchno-issledovatel'skii institut*) was set up at Tukhachevskii's instigation to develop rockets of various types. Because of its association with Tukhachevskii, however, the institute suffered badly in the purge, and many of the leading rocket engineers were arrested. After 1938 work was confined mainly to rocket artillery (the famous *Katyusha* system) and to rocket boosters for aircraft. The appearance of the German V-1 and V-2 rockets in 1944 revived Soviet interest in long-range rockets. Those engineers who had survived the purge and the war were now set to work to examine German achievements and to build on them.[12]

On 8 August 1945, two days after Hiroshima, the Politburo initiated work on a new Five Year Plan, which was formally adopted in March 1946. The Soviet leaders had to make decisions about the plan in the context of the new weapons programs. The then Minister of Finance has written in his memoirs that finding the financial resources for the plan proved more difficult than anticipated because the drop in defence spending was not as great as expected, and because 'significant resources' were required for the development of military technology.[13]

By the summer of 1946 the basic institutional framework had been created for developing nuclear weapons, long-range rockets, radar and jet propulsion. Special bodies were set up in the Party, the government, the secret police and the Armed Forces to direct these programs. In 1945 Scientific-Technical Councils were created for atomic bomb and rocket development. These consisted of scientists, engineers and industrial managers, and discussed the major technical and industrial problems connected with the programs. B.L. Vannikov headed the atomic council, with Pervukhin and Kurchatov as his deputies. The rocket council was chaired by D.F. Ustinov, the present Minister of Defence, who was then the People's Commissar of Armament. A special department of government, also headed by Vannikov, was set up to manage the nuclear program. The secret police had a department for atomic energy; half of all research for nuclear weapons development was done in prison institutes, while most of the construction and mining was done by prison labour. Overall control of the nuclear program lay in the hands of Beria, the chief of the secret police.[14]

The object of these arrangements was to exercise tight central control over the new weapons programs, and to ensure that they had first claim on resources. Soon after the Potsdam Conference Kurchatov became a regular visitor to the Kremlin. One of the industrial managers remarked to him that 'It's easy for you to solve problems: you meet Stalin every day.' Kurchatov replied that problems were indeed solved quickly in meetings with Stalin.[15] (The Soviet authors who recount this exchange comment that Kurchatov kept to himself the thought that dealing with Stalin almost every day was more difficult than walking a tightrope across an abyss; and it can have been no easier to deal with Beria, who is never mentioned now in Soviet accounts of their early nuclear program, but with whom Kurchatov must have had frequent contact.) Policy was developed in meetings between the Party leaders and those directly in charge of the programs. In April 1947, for example, Stalin summoned scientists, industrial managers and military men to the Kremlin for a series of meetings to decide on an overall plan for rocket development.[16] Stalin's personal interest ensured that these programs had the highest priority; the best scientists, engineers, workers and managers were assigned to them. Each decision was backed by Stalin's authority, and this helped to overcome obstacles in the way of executing policy.

The war provided the Soviet Union with a major infusion of foreign technology, mainly in the form of captured German scientists, technicians, equipment and production plant. Foreign technology also came through Lend-Lease, and by more fortuitous routes. The Tu-4 bomber, for example, was a copy of the American B-29, three of which made a forced landing on Soviet territory in 1944. Foreign technology was important for the post-war programs, but its contribution varied from field to field.[17] In 1945 the Soviet atomic bomb project was better organized than the German, and while the Soviet Union acquired some scientists, technicians and equipment, most of the leading German nuclear scientists fell into Western hands. The information passed by Klaus Fuchs and other atomic spies was more important for the Soviet effort, perhaps speeding up the development of the atomic bomb by as much as a year or two. But it is certainly wrong to say that this is how the Soviet Union acquired the 'secret' of the atomic bomb, for, as Niels Bohr remarked, the only secret of the atomic bomb is that it can be built.

The Soviet Union gained more from German rocket technology. In 1945 a team of Soviet rocket scientists was sent to Germany to study the German effort, and the first Soviet long-range rocket, the R-1, which was test fired in October 1947, was a modification of the German V-2. The United States too gained from the German rocket program, for as the Red Army approached Peenemunde, the main centre of German rocketry, Wernher von Braun took his team and their most important papers to meet the American forces. Unlike the United States, however, the Soviet Union gave high priority to rocket development.[18] In October 1946 thousands of German engineers and technicians were taken to the Soviet Union, where they worked under Soviet supervision. In spite of the purge, there was still a cadre of experienced and gifted rocket scientists who were able to build on the German technology. In 1947 a Council of Chief Designers was set up to coordinate the Soviet program. It was chaired by S.P. Korolev, who was later to design the first Soviet intercontinental ballistic missile. The other leading designers of the time, who were probably on the Council, were V.P. Glushko (whose design bureau was to develop the liquid-propellant rocket motors for most of the Soviet strategic missiles), A.M. Isaev (Chief Designer of a bureau for rocket motors since 1944), and A.N. Pilyugin (Chief Designer of Control Systems).[19] In 1950 the Soviet Union test fired the R-2, a development of the R-1, but with a range of 600 km, about twice that of the earlier rocket. By this time work had begun on the SS-3, which was deployed in the mid-1950s.[20]

## The Development of Thermonuclear Weapons

On 29 August 1949 the Soviet Union tested its first atomic bomb. (This was a plutonium bomb; the first test of a U-235 bomb took place in 1951.)[21] The United States detected the first Soviet test and made it public, to the apparent consternation of the Soviet government, which had made no announcement. News of the test caused a shock in Washington where, despite some accurate forecasts, it was generally believed that the Soviet Union would not have an atomic bomb until the early 1950s. This shock contributed to the decision announced by President Truman on 31 January 1950 to speed up work on thermonuclear weapons.[22] Such bombs have a yield many times greater than the atomic bombs used in Japan, and the decision to develop them marked a major new stage in nuclear arms competition. The decision was a particularly controversial one in the American scientific community, and the General Advisory Committee of the Atomic Energy Commission, under Oppenheimer's chairmanship, had recommended in October 1949 against an all-out effort, arguing that 'the extreme dangers to mankind inherent in the proposal wholly outweigh any military advantage that could come from this development'.[23]

It is sometimes argued that Truman's decision was correct because the Soviet Union was the first to test a thermonuclear bomb, in August 1953. Soviet writers indeed consistently claim that the Soviet Union developed the thermonuclear bomb before the United States, and portray this as a great triumph of Soviet science and technology. But this argument is misleading for, as Herbert York has shown, the bomb tested by the Soviet Union, while thermonuclear – or, in the curious Soviet phrase, 'one of the types of a thermonuclear bomb' – was not a 'superbomb'.[24] It was not based on the principle that makes it possible to obtain an almost infinite explosive yield from a combination of fission and fusion reactions. The Soviet test of August 1953, dubbed in the West 'Joe-4', had a yield in the order of 200–400 kilotons, while the American thermonuclear device (not a deliverable bomb) tested in October 1952 had a yield of 10 megatons, and the American bomb tested in February 1954 had a yield of 15 megatons. It was not until November 1955 that the Soviet Union tested a superbomb, with a yield of 1.6 megatons.[25]

The Soviet atomic bomb test of August 1949 helped to speed up American work on thermonuclear weapons, and American policy in turn stimulated Soviet weapons research and development. Soviet work on the thermonuclear bomb began in 1948 when Kurchatov set up a theoretical group (which included Andrei Sakharov) under Igor Tamm, after reports of a superbomb had been received from the West. Soviet interest in thermonuclear weapons may have been aroused by Klaus Fuchs, who told his Soviet contact about studies of these weapons at Los Alamos. He could have told the Soviet Union that in the spring of 1946 discussion had taken place about two possible types of thermonuclear bombs: one in which a relatively small amount of thermonuclear fuel is ignited by a relatively large fission explosion (later known as a boosted fission weapon) and the other in which a relatively small fission explosion ignites a very large mass of thermonuclear fuel (the superbomb). Fuchs's account of these early discussions of the superbomb would have been misleading rather than helpful to Soviet scientists in a scientific sense, because the early ideas were later shown not to work. But it is possible that Fuchs's reports stimulated Soviet work on these weapons.[26]

By the time of the first atomic bomb test, Tamm's group had concluded that thermonuclear weapons were possible, and two months after the test – that is, about 1 November 1949 – Kurchatov began to work on the development of a thermonuclear bomb as a matter of priority. The first thermonuclear bomb test took place almost four years later, on 12 August 1953. Soviet writers tend to stress the role of American actions in stimulating Soviet nuclear weapons development. It is therefore interesting that they do not mention as providing any impetus to Soviet efforts Truman's announcement on 31 January 1950 of his decision to accelerate development of the superbomb. But one of Kurchatov's biographers does stress that the American test of October 1952 led to an intensification of Soviet work; after the test 'Kurchatov and those taking part in the creation of the terrible new weapon increase the tempo of work. Alongside the design work, experiments are conducted to investigate different variants.'[27] This implies that besides working on the 'Joe-4' bomb, Soviet scientists now worked to develop a superbomb. The American test stimulated Soviet research, and analysis of the fallout from the American test would have helped Soviet scientsts to discover the mechanism behind the very high yield of the explosion. The first Soviet superbomb was tested in November 1955 (see Table 2.1).

This episode in the nuclear arms race is of interest for several reasons. First, it helps to give a clearer picture of the relative stages of development of American and Soviet nuclear weapons. In the mid-1950s the Soviet Union lagged at least three years behind the United States in the development of high yield weapons. Second, it shows how American and Soviet actions helped to stimulate each other's nuclear weapons development. Yet the actions that were salient on one side were not necessarily so on the other. American accounts of the period highlight the Soviet atomic bomb test of August 1949 and Truman's announcement of 31 January 1950. But Soviet accounts (such as they are) suggest that the Truman announcement was not as important to their own decisions as the early reports of American work on thermonuclear

Table 2.1: *Important dates in the early nuclear weapons program*

| | |
|---|---|
| 25 December 1946[1] | First chain reaction in an experimental pile. |
| 10 June 1948[2] | Plutonium production reactor goes critical. |
| 29 August 1949[3] | First test of a plutonium fission bomb. |
| October 1951[4] | First test of a U-235 fission bomb. |
| 12 August 1953[5] | First test of a thermonuclear bomb, with a yield of 200– 400 kilotons ('Joe-4'). |
| 22 November 1955[6] | First superbomb test, with a yield of 1,600 kilotons. |

*Notes*
1. I.F. Zhezherun, *Stroitel'stvo i pusk pervogo v Sovetskom Soyuze atomnogo reaktora*, Moscow: Atomizdat, 1978, p. 114.
2. *Ibid.*, p. 133.
3. W.J. Schultis *et al.*, *Analyses of Research and Development Trends in the U.S. and the U.S.S.R.*, vol. 2, Institute for Defense Analyses: Arlington, Virginia, 1971, Appendix B, p. B–47.
4. *Ibid.*, and *Announced Foreign Nuclear Detonations – Through December 31, 1978*, U.S. Department of Energy, Office of Public Affairs, Nevada Operations Office: Las Vegas, Nevada, p. 1. The Soviet Union held only two nuclear tests in 1951; the actual test dates are not known, but the U.S. government made the announcements in October, on the 3rd and the 22nd.
5. Herbert York, *The Advisors: Oppenheimer, Teller and the Superbomb*, San Francisco: W.H. Freeman and Co., 1976, pp. 89–91; see also David Holloway, 'Soviet Thermonuclear Development', in *International Security*, Winter 1979/80, vol. 4, no. 3, pp. 192–7.
6. York, *op. cit.*, pp. 92–3; Holloway, *op. cit.*, p. 195. The yield is taken from a declassified intelligence document quoted in full in the latter source.

weapons and the American thermonuclear test of October 1952. Third, Soviet decisions show elements both of reaction to American actions and of an internal dynamic. The early thermonuclear studies were initiated in response to reports of American work. The development of a thermonuclear bomb began after the first atomic bomb test and was not, as far as one can tell, directly triggered by American actions. The development of the superbomb was stimulated by the American test of October 1952.

York is surely right to argue that American national security would not have been harmed if the advice of Oppenheimer and the General Advisory Committee had been followed, and development of the superbomb delayed. The Soviet Union would not have been able to gain a lead in nuclear weapons technology, for the United States would have had time to respond to a continuing Soviet program. Had restraint been practised, the opportunity might conceivably have emerged after Stalin's death for political moves to restrain Soviet–American nuclear arms competition. In the event, the competition in nuclear arms continued unabated.

## Nuclear Weapons and Military Policy

Stalin was determined to hold on to the gains that the Red Army's liberation of Eastern Europe had brought for the Soviet Union, even though this was bound to lead to political conflict with Britain and the United States. The Soviet leaders differed among themselves in their assessment of how the capitalist world would develop, but they all seem to have shared the belief that the conflict between capitalism and socialism would sooner or later lead to a new world war. With disagreements between the allies coming to the fore, it was not clear how long a breathing space there might be before another war. The postwar years, in other words, were viewed by the Soviet leaders as a prewar period, and this reinforced the conclusion that the Soviet Union should once again give priority to increasing its military power. In November 1945 Molotov said that the Soviet Union 'must equal the achievements of contemporary world technology... We will have atomic energy and much else.'[28]

From August 1945 Stalin faced a dual problem: to build a Soviet bomb as quickly as possible, and to deprive the United States of any military or political advantage from its atomic monopoly. The first part of this problem was solved by launching the new research and development programs. The second was tackled by providing a counterweight to American air power. Soviet forces in Eastern Europe were the main element in this policy. American bombers could threaten Soviet cities and industrial centres, but Soviet forces could not strike the United States. Consequently the Soviet Army was deployed in Eastern Europe not only to safeguard Soviet interests there, but also to strike Western Europe in the event of war. (Soviet forces were certainly not strong enough for Stalin to contemplate an invasion out of the blue.) Conventional weapons were modernized and air defences strengthened.[29]

Stalin took pains to play down the significance of nuclear weapons. In September 1946, for example, he said that 'I do not consider the atomic bomb as serious a force as some politicians are inclined to do. Atomic bombs are meant to frighten those with weak nerves, but they cannot decide the fate of wars since atomic bombs are quite insufficient for that.'[30] The effort the Soviet Union was making to develop the atomic bomb makes it clear that Stalin did in fact attribute great importance to nuclear weapons. Such statements were designed to weaken any American attempt to use its atomic monopoly to put pressure on the Soviet Union, and also to prevent Soviet troops, who would have to fight without nuclear weapons, from being intimidated by the threat of nuclear war.

Stalin may well have thought that, important though the atomic bomb was, it would not change the character of warfare. He launched major programs to develop the atomic bomb and other modern weapons, but he did not permit any thought to be given to their effect on the conduct of war. Weapons development and military doctrine existed in separate worlds: the former was pushed at a rapid pace, the latter was stifled. Major-General Kozlov wrote later that 'Stalin's scornful statements about atomic weapons were the reason why our military thought was not directed in time to an objective and far-reaching evaluation of the new instruments of warfare, to the discovery and analysis of new phenomena of armed conflict and of the revolution in military affairs which had developed.'[31] Strategic thought was regarded as 'the prerogative of the "leader of genius" and not subject to elaboration on a lower level'.[32] By 1952 there were some signs that the implications of nuclear weapons were being reconsidered, but it was not until after Stalin's death in March 1953 that a full reassessment of military thought began.

# Thinking about Nuclear War

The October Revolution brought about, in Bolshevik eyes, a fundamental change in the class character of the Russian state and its military forces. In the early years after the revolution intense arguments
erupted about the practical implications of this political transformation. Among the issues involved was military doctrine. In 1921 Frunze
stressed the importance of doctrine, arguing that it was essential to
have a set of agreed views on the nature of a future war, since this alone
could give direction to the development and training of the Red Army.[1]
Trotsky opposed this argument on the grounds that military doctrine
had been appropriate for the states of the old regime when a stable
international system had existed; in a revolutionary period, he warned,
doctrine, with its implications of set and fixed views, was inappropriate
and might degenerate into doctrinairism. The tasks facing the Red
Army were more prosaic ('to teach how to oil rifles and grease boots')
than the abstractions of doctrine.[2]

Frunze won the argument (on political rather than intellectual
grounds) and the definition he gave to military doctrine is now the
accepted one in the Soviet Union. According to the *Soviet Military
Encyclopedia*, military doctrine is the system of views that a state holds
at a given time on 'the purposes and character of a possible war, on the
preparation of the country and the armed forces for it, and also on the
methods of waging it'.[3] In the Soviet definition, military doctrine has
two closely connected aspects: the political (which is supposed to be
dominant) and the military-technical. The former sets out the political
purposes and character of war and the way in which these affect the
development of the armed forces and the preparation of the country
for war. The military-technical aspect deals with the methods of
waging war, the organization of the armed forces, their technical
equipment and combat readiness. In practice these two aspects are not
only connected, but overlapping, and in the formulation of policy the

relationship between political and military responsibilities has often been contentious. Yet the analytical distinction should be borne in mind, because it is important for an understanding of Soviet thinking about nuclear war.

The Soviet concept of military doctrine cannot be properly understood without reference to the concepts of military science and military art. Military science is defined as the system of knowledge about the character and laws of war, the preparation of the armed forces and the country for war, and the methods of waging it; the significance of military science is clearer if we call it the science of war, *Kriegswissenschaft*.[4] Military art is the theory and practice of preparing and conducting military operations, and thus embraces strategy, operational art and tactics. But the *theory* of military art – and hence strategic and tactical *theory* – form part of military science.[5]

These definitions may seem scholastic, and thus irrelevant to an understanding of Soviet thinking, and it is indeed true that their apparent precision becomes blurred when one tries to distinguish the substance of doctrine from that of military science. It is impossible, for example, to find a statement of Soviet military doctrine that goes beyond the most general points. Nevertheless, these definitions are relevant to an understanding of Soviet policy-making, for they express a definite conception of the proper relationship between political authority and professional military expertise. In the Soviet view, military doctrine embodies the agreed views of the state on questions of war and military policy. It is defined by the Party leadership, who have to take account of economic and political circumstances in formulating doctrine. Military science, on the other hand, studies war and the methods of waging it, and is largely the prerogative of the General Staff and the military academies. It is not constrained in the same way by economic and political considerations, and develops more quickly than doctrine, which can remain stable for some time, being revised only in response to major political or military developments. Military doctrine expresses the political character and purposes of the state, but draws on military science in the formulation of its military-technical aspect.[6]

The distinction between military doctrine and military science has been strongly emphasized in Soviet writings in the post-Stalin period. Two points about it should be noted. The first is the stress laid on the primacy of Party authority in formulating doctrine. The Party leaders have to take account not only of professional military advice, but also of wider economic and political considerations. The second is that military writers have argued that military science should influence doctrine.

Although it is accepted that military doctrine sets the general goals towards which military science should orient itself, it is also argued that a military doctrine that is divorced from military science – that is, from professional military advice – will be marked by 'subjectivism' and 'voluntarism' and thus prone to serious error.[7] In other words, these abstract definitions reflect a certain tension between Party and military prerogatives in Soviet military thought.

## The Political and Military Aspects of Doctrine

1953 marked a major turning-point in Soviet military thought, for in that year Stalin died, thus making it possible to move away from the rigid orthodoxies of 'Stalinist military science'; in the same year the Soviet Armed Forces first received nuclear weapons, thus making it imperative to reassess Soviet thinking about war.[8] There are some indications that the reassessment began in Stalin's lifetime, for in *Economic Problems of Socialism in the USSR*, published in September 1952, Stalin wrote that 'It is said that Lenin's thesis that imperialism inevitably generates war must now be regarded as obsolete, since powerful popular forces have come forward today in defense of peace and against another world war. That is not true . . . To eliminate the inevitability of war, it is necessary to abolish imperialism.'[9] It appears that even before Stalin's death some members of the Soviet leadership believed that the fundamental aggressiveness of imperialism could be contained, and hence that war between the Soviet Union and the leading capitalist powers was not inevitable. This belief was apparently based in part on the growth of the peace movement in Western Europe; it may also have been associated with Soviet progress in developing nuclear weapons, though there is no direct evidence that this was so.[10]

In any event, it did not take long for the issue to come into the open after Stalin's death. In 1953 and 1954 several articles were published implying that the 'law of the inevitability of war' could be rendered inoperative. In March 1954 one of the Party leaders, Mikoyan, argued that the danger of war had receded now that the Soviet Union possessed both the atomic and the hydrogen bomb. On the same day Malenkov, Chairman of the Council of Ministers, declared that world war in the nuclear age would mean the 'destruction of world civilization'.[11] In saying this he was echoing a statement made by President Eisenhower the previous December. He was not being un-Marxist, for both Engels and Lenin had pointed to the possibility that weapons might be developed that would make war senseless.[12] But he was being less than astute in terms of the leadership politics of his day, and was criticized for his outspokenness. In February 1955 he was forced to resign as head of government, after a number of policy disagreements with Khrushchev.

At the 20th Party Congress in February 1956 Khrushchev announced that war was no longer to be considered 'fatalistically inevitable'. He noted the Marxist-Leninist thesis that 'wars are inevitable as long as imperialism exists', but claimed that the situation had changed. There now existed a world socialist camp, and in this camp the forces of peace found the moral and the material means to prevent aggression. The labour movement in the capitalist countries was also a major force for peace. 'In these circumstances', he said,

> certainly the Leninist precept that so long as imperialism exists, the economic basis giving rise to wars will also be preserved, remains in force. That is why we must display the greatest vigilance. As long as capitalism survives in the world, the reactionary forces representing the interests of the capitalist monopolies will continue their drive towards military gambles and aggression, and may try to unleash war. But war is not fatalistically inevitable. Today there are mighty social and political forces possessing formidable means to prevent the imperialists from unleashing war, and if they actually try to start it, to give a smashing rebuff to the aggressors and frustrate their adventurist plans.[13]

This was an important new position, and it has remained central to Soviet thinking ever since. War was less likely because the Soviet Union was increasingly able to prevent an attack on itself and its allies. This ability did not rest, in Soviet eyes, on Soviet military power alone, but Khrushchev's reference to the 'formidable means to prevent the imperialists from unleashing war and . . . to give a smashing rebuff to the aggressors' suggests that, besides new political relationships, he had military power, including nuclear weapons, in mind when he stated that war was no longer 'fatalistically inevitable'.

This thesis has remained a key element of Soviet military doctrine. The political aspect of doctrine stresses the possibility, and the importance, of preventing a world war between capitalism and socialism. The military-technical aspect of doctrine attends to the question of fighting such a war 'if the imperialists should unleash it' (to use the standard Soviet qualification). In Soviet thinking, deterrence is a political rather than a military concept and has received relatively little attention in military writings, which are concerned primarily with the preparation for war and the conduct of war; there is no Soviet equivalent to the theory of deterrence developed in the United States in the late 1950s and early 1960s. Soviet leaders have seen the prevention of war as something to be achieved by means of a 'peace policy' – a foreign policy that seeks to reduce the risk of war – backed by military might. According to Marshal Ustinov, the present Minister of Defence, the basis of Soviet military doctrine lies in the 'unity of the peaceful foreign policy of the Soviet state and its readiness to give the necessary rebuff to an aggressor'.[14] No contradiction is seen between the prevention of war and the preparation for war; war can be prevented only if the Soviet Union prepares to wage it.

The Soviet conception of deterrence is thus different from the American, and is embedded in the wider notion of war prevention. There is in fact no precise Russian equivalent for the term 'deterrence'. One Soviet commentator has written that

> the Russian language comes up with two corresponding terms – keeping out (*sderzhivanie*) and intimidation (*ustrashenie*), though the latter term was more often used in the '50s and '60s. When used in Soviet military vocabulary proper, and not as a Russian equivalent for the American term, the word is invariably *sderzhivanie*, i.e., keeping out, dissuasion. For the American reader of Soviet literature on the subject, matters are made worse because two widely different English words – containment and deterrence – are usually translated into Russian by the same word *sderzhivanie*, i.e., keeping out, not letting go, restraining – evidently due to some unfortunate initial slip. Even some Soviet theorists who do not read English are confused, as they study translations of U.S. writing on post-World War II strategy, because one Russian word is used to denote two diverse concepts – containment and deterrence.[15]

Of these two terms it is *sderzhivanie*, restraining or holding back, that is used to describe Soviet policy; when *ustrashenie*, intimidation, is used it is applied to Western policy. The fact that the same Russian word can denote both 'containment' and 'deterrence' underlines the point that deterrence is conceived of more broadly in the Soviet Union than in the West, where it is often seen solely in terms of the balance of armaments between the two sides.

This emerges more clearly in a discussion of deterrence by Fyodor Burlatskii, one of the Soviet Union's leading social scientists. In Burlatskii's view the strongest argument the advocates of nuclear deterrence have is that, in spite of international crises and tension, a third world war has been avoided. He claims, however, that three different hypotheses can be advanced to explain this. The first is that war has been made senseless by the threat of mutual destruction or irreparable damage. The second is that the creation of a bipolar international system after the Second World War led to a balance of power which made victory by one side over the other doubtful (or impossible). The third is that the forces of peace have been stronger than the forces interested in unleashing thermonuclear war.[16]

Each of these factors, writes Burlatskii, has played its part in preventing world war, but the third has been most important. While war may have become senseless in a technical sense, he argues, the crucial question is whether the 'imperialist conquerors' take this into account; nuclear war may be senseless, but someone might start it nonetheless. War must be prevented not merely through the threat of destruction, but by tackling the political conflict that might give rise to it. That is why the third factor is decisive for Burlatskii. By the relationship between the forces of war and the forces of peace, he means not only the balance of power within the bipolar system (with the Warsaw Pact naturally identified with the forces of peace). He has in mind also those political elements in the West which oppose a strengthening of NATO, as well as the non-aligned and anti-Western policies of the new states of the Third World.

Burlatskii's identification of the forces of peace may be crude, but his overall argument is interesting. It reflects a widely-held Soviet view that the threat of assured destruction is not the only, or the best way of preventing nuclear war, and *a fortiori* that the relationship of mutual assured destruction is not a sound basis for peace. Burlatskii echoes the argument put forward by Khrushchev at the 20th Party Congress, that it is not only the balance of armaments that prevents nuclear war, but the strength of the forces of peace. In Soviet eyes, the prevention of war is not only a matter of the balance of military power, important though that is, but the object of a wider policy that embraces political elements as well.

Since 1956 Soviet military doctrine has adopted the position that war is no longer 'fatalistically inevitable'; nor has world war been held necessary for the triumph of socialism. At the same time, however, Soviet doctrine has not ruled out the possibility of a general nuclear war, for such a catastrophe is seen as possible, in spite of the Soviet Union's best efforts. Most Soviet military theorists adhere to Clausewitz's thesis that war is a continuation of policy by other means. One of the implications of this is that the possibility of war has to be assessed not merely in terms of the balance of armaments, but – at a more fundamental level – in terms of the political conflicts that might give rise to it. Two consequences follow from this view. The first, which Burlatskii advocates, is the pursuit of radical moves to change the character of international relations. The second is to prepare for the wars that might take place.

## Rethinking Military Doctrine

Soviet military theorists divide the history of their military doctrine into several periods. They identify 1929 as the first major turning-point after the Revolution, and date the transformation of the Red Army into a mechanized force from that year. The war with Germany had a profound influence on Soviet strategic and tactical thought, but it did not bring major changes in military doctrine, in the Soviet sense of that term. 1953 saw the opening of the next major period, in which military thought began to confront the problems raised by nuclear weapons. In January 1960 Khrushchev announced the outlines of a new doctrine for the nuclear age.[17]

Between 1953 and 1960 the Soviet Union began to acquire a stockpile of nuclear weapons, along with the intercontinental, medium-range and battlefield systems to deliver them. Conventional forces were reduced as the nuclear arsenal grew: naval shipbuilding programs were cut in the mid-1950s, and the number of men under arms fell from 5,763,000 in 1955 to 3,623,000 in 1958.[18] This shift of emphasis made it necessary to rethink military doctrine. Colonel-General Povaly, Chief of the Operations Directorate of the General Staff in the 1960s, wrote that the new weapons 'persistently demanded a fundamental reexamination of all fundamental principles of military doctrine and all military art, primarily strategy.'[19] In 1953 the central focus of Soviet military thought was a conventional war in Europe. In December 1959 the Strategic Rocket Forces were established as a separate service, and in January 1960 Khrushchev declared that a future world war would inevitably be a nuclear rocket war.

This change of emphasis was not determined solely by the Soviet acquisition of nuclear weapons. Soviet policy had to take account of the heavy American reliance on nuclear forces. American defence policy during the period rested on the doctrine of 'massive retaliation', which envisaged massive and immediate use of nuclear weapons in response to Soviet aggression. The American nuclear stockpile was larger than the Soviet, and the American ability to launch nuclear strikes against the Soviet Union remained far greater than the Soviet ability to strike the United States. Moreover, in 1952 the United States introduced tactical nuclear weapons into Europe, thus changing the character of ground operations on the continent.[20]

At the end of 1953 the Ministry of Defence ordered that 'nuclear weapons and the particular features of preparing, conducting and securing an operation and combat in conditions of the use of such weapons' should be studied. This caused the General Staff Academy, the most senior of the Soviet military academies, to revise its research and teaching program radically. At the beginning of 1954 *Red Star*, the newspaper of the Ministry of Defence, published a series of articles on nuclear weapons, thus breaking a seven-year silence on the subject. In September of the same year the first large-scale troop exercise was held in which an atomic bomb was exploded; the results were studied carefully to gain information for anti-nuclear defence. In February 1955, in the post-Malenkov reshuffle, Marshal Zhukov became Minister of Defence, and on the eve of his appointment made a speech to senior officers in which he called for a more thorough study of the impact of nuclear weapons on the conduct of war.[21]

The effect was seen first in discussion of the role of surprise in war. Stalin had described surprise as a 'fortuitous' and 'transitory' factor in deciding the outcome of war, which would depend, he said, on the 'permanently operating factors': stability of the home front, morale of the army, quantity and quality of divisions, equipment of the army, the organizing ability of the commanding personnel of the army. Stalin had first used this formula in November 1941, when he claimed that the advantages the Germans had gained from surprise had evaporated. At the time it was sensible to assert that the gains of surprise were transitory, and it helped to sustain Soviet morale. But after the war the formula of the 'permanently operating factors' became enshrined as part of the orthodoxy of Stalinist military science. Discussion of strategic surprise was inhibited by Stalin's view that it was not a decisive factor, and this judgment was closely linked with post-war historiography, which played down the disasters of 1941 and portrayed the Soviet retreat as part of preplanned strategy.[22]

The issue of surprise attack was raised in 1953 and 1954, but the most outspoken statement came in February 1955, when *Military Thought* published an article by Marshal of Tank Forces Rotmistrov, who was teaching at the General Staff Academy. Rotmistrov wrote that

It must be plainly said that when atomic and hydrogen weapons are employed, surprise is one of the decisive conditions of the attainment of success not only in battles and operations, but also in war as a whole . . . Surprise attack with the massive employment of new weapons can cause the rapid collapse of a government whose capacity to resist is low as a consequence of radical faults in its social and economic structure and also as a consequence of an unfavorable geographical position.[23]

Since the advantages to be gained by surprise attack had become so much greater with the advent of nuclear weapons, it had become more important than ever to prevent it:

the duty of the Soviet Armed Forces is not to permit an enemy surprise attack on our country and, in the event of an attempt to accomplish one, not only to repel the attack successfully but also to deal the enemy counterblows, or even pre-emptive [*uprezhdayushchie*] surprise blows, of terrible destructive force.[24]

In spite of the importance now given to surprise, Soviet military theorists did not believe that a surprise attack would lead to victory. Rotmistrov wrote that 'surprise cannot yield a conclusive result, cannot bring victory, in a war with a serious and strong enemy'.[25]

The problem of surprise attack once again became bound up with the historiography of the war. In March 1955 *Military Thought* launched a campaign against the orthodox Stalinist interpretation of the events of 1941, and criticized those who represented the failure of 1941 as a victory, as a classic example of 'active defence'. A parallel was seen between a surprise nuclear attack and the German invasion. Although there were major differences, the parallel was close enough to allow lessons to be drawn from history. Hence, in the view of *Military Thought*, it was important not to misrepresent what happened in 1941. In his secret speech to the Twentieth Party Congress in February 1956 Khrushchev attacked Stalin's leadership in the war, and in particular his failure to anticipate the German attack. This opened the way to a much franker discussion of 22 June 1941.

Khrushchev's attack on Stalin finally destroyed the authority of 'Stalinist military science', while the growing stockpile of nuclear weapons now made it imperative to conduct a systematic review of military thought. In May 1957 the Ministry of Defence organized a conference to discuss the state of Soviet military science. In the following year the General Staff held a series of seminars, in which senior officers took part, to study the problems of a future war. In 1958–9 the General Staff Academy held conferences at which the character of a future war and of modern operations was discussed. By 1959 it had been agreed that the development of nuclear weapons and rockets made it necessary to revise Soviet military doctrine. This conclusion was accepted by the Party leaders, who had been following the military discussions. Senior officers were instructed to prepare studies of the impact of nuclear-armed rockets on the conduct of war, and in January 1960 *Military Thought* began to publish papers prepared by this group. The first was written by Lieutenant-General A.I. Gastilovich, Deputy Chief of the General Staff Academy for military-scientific work. In December 1959 the Strategic Rocket Forces were established as a separate service, and in the following month Khrushchev unveiled the main outlines of the new doctrine in a speech to the Supreme Soviet.[26]

Khrushchev stated that the Soviet Armed Forces had already gone over, to a considerable degree, to rocket-nuclear weapons, and that these weapons were being improved and would continue to be improved until they were banned. The Soviet Union did not regard war as inevitable, but if a world war were to take place it would begin with missile strikes deep into the enemy's interior. It was possible that a surprise attack would be launched against the Soviet Union, but the Soviet Union would be able to retaliate:

> Let us assume . . . that some state or group of states manages to prepare and carry out a surprise attack on a power which possesses nuclear and rocket weapons. But could the attacking side, even if we suppose for a moment that it succeeded in striking the blow by surprise, immediately put out of action all the nuclear weapons stocks, all the rocket installations in the territory of the power which is attacked? Of course not. The state which suffers the attack, if, of course, we are speaking of a sufficiently large state, will always have the possibility to give the proper rebuff to the aggressor.[27]

In saying this Khrushchev implied that both the United States and the Soviet Union could retaliate against the attacker and inflict massive damage on him; in other words, that a relationship of mutual assured destruction existed.

At the same time, however, Khrushchev argued that in a nuclear war the West would suffer incomparably more than the Soviet Union, because the Soviet state was so large and its population less concentrated. The Soviet Union would survive, but if the aggressors unleashed a new war it would be not only their last war, but also the end of capitalism, because people would understand that 'capitalism is the source that breeds wars and would no longer tolerate that system, which brings sufferings and disasters to mankind'.

## Military Strategy in the Nuclear Age

Khrushchev's speech was the first public statement of the new doctrine, and the characterization he gave of a future world war has remained central to Soviet thinking ever since. In a world war between socialist and capitalist states the chief means of destruction would be the nuclear-armed rocket. Because of the profound social nature of the conflict (it would be a war between social systems) and the power of thermonuclear weapons, such a war would be bitter and destructive to an unprecedented degree. But the new doctrine was outlined only in the most general terms. Soviet military thought was still trying to determine what a nuclear war would be like and what forces would be required to wage it.

Khrushchev was expressing a view held by Party and military leaders alike when he declared that a future war would be a rocket-nuclear war. The Soviet Union had tested the world's first ICBM in 1957, and had begun to deploy the SS-4 MRBM in 1959. A decision had already been taken to adopt the rocket rather than the bomber as the main delivery vehicle for nuclear weapons. The Strategic Rocket Forces had been set up the month before, and all land-based missiles with a range of over 1,000 km had been assigned to it. In his speech Khrushchev said that bomber production might be discontinued, but that the Soviet Union would try to maintain its leading position in rocket development.

Although military doctrine had been reoriented to focus on thermonuclear war, no consensus existed on what forces were needed to fight such a war.[28] Differences existed on questions of strategy and force structure: would a rocket-nuclear war be long or short? Were the Ground Forces essentially occupation forces, which would move into enemy territory after a nuclear strike, or would they take a major part in combat? Khrushchev went beyond what was generally accepted when he said in his January 1960 speech that

In our time the defense capability of the country is defined not by how many soldiers we have under arms, how many people are wearing soldiers' greatcoats. If one abstracts from the political and economic factors . . . the defense capability of a country depends to a decisive degree on what firepower and what means of delivery that country has at its disposal.

He proposed that the armed forces be cut by one third, to 2,423,000. He also declared that 'military aviation and the navy have lost their former significance with the present development of military techno-logy'. He apparently had it in mind to cut back conventional forces, while emphasizing the firepower of nuclear weapons. In this he was proposing to carry further the policy that Marshal Zhukov had pursued as Minister of Defence from 1955 to 1957. But Khrushchev's ideas about military power were resisted by the High Command, and his proposed manpower reductions were not made in full.

Whatever their disagreements about force structure, the different schools of thought in the Armed Forces agreed that the problem they had to solve was how to wage and win a nuclear war. This was made clear in 1962, when a volume entitled *Military Strategy* was published. This was written by a military group under the direction of Marshal Sokolovskii, who had been Chief of the General Staff from 1952 to 1960. Sokolovskii characterized nuclear strategy as follows:

> military strategy in the conditions of modern war becomes the strat-egy of deep rocket-nuclear strikes in combination with actions by all services of the armed forces, with the aim of simultaneously striking and destroying the economic potential and the armed forces on the whole depth of the enemy's territory for attaining the objectives of the war in a short time.[29]

Sokolovskii argued that although war was not fatally inevitable, it might occur, in spite of the best efforts of the Soviet Union to prevent it. An attack on the Soviet Union or another socialist state might develop into a world war. Such a war would be the decisive conflict between the socialist and capitalist social systems, and would naturally (*zakonomerno*) end in the victory of the progressive communist order over capitalism, which is historically doomed. The guarantee of victory is provided by the real relationship of political, economic and military forces between the two systems, which favours the socialist camp. 'But victory in a future war will not come by itself,' wrote Sokolovskii. 'It must be thoroughly prepared and provided for.'[30] The Soviet Union must have superiority over the probable aggressor in the quantity and quality of arms and military equipment.[31]

Sokolovskii stressed that while a third world war would be a rocket-nuclear war, other forces would play an essential role, and final victory could be attained only by the combined efforts of all services. Nuclear war would be conducted by mass armies. The initial period of the war would have decisive significance for its outcome. Here the main problem was to master 'methods of reliably repulsing a surprise nuclear attack, and also methods of frustrating the aggressive plans of the enemy, by means of a timely shattering blow against him'.[32] But while it was essential to make preparations to try to attain victory over the aggressor in the shortest possible time, it was necessary also to prepare for a protracted war. It was, moreover, vital to make the country as a whole ready by preparing the economy and the population for war, and by providing civil defence.

The Sokolovskii volume, new editions of which appeared in 1963 and 1968, did not remove all the arguments about force structure. The role of the Ground Forces, in particular, remained contentious. In December 1963 Khrushchev said that the government was considering 'the possibility of some further reduction in the numerical strength of our armed forces'. Later in the month Marshal Chuikov, Commander-in-Chief of the Ground Forces, wrote that NATO was now building up its ground forces, and that Western military leaders had abandoned 'one-sided theories' and realized that 'in a future war they will not be able to get along without mass armies'. In September 1964 the post of Commander-in-Chief of the Ground Forces was abolished, and the Ground Forces subordinated directly to the Minister of Defence.[33]

General nuclear war has remained the central concern of Soviet military thought, but after Khrushchev's fall from power in October 1964 attention moved away from exclusive concentration on what Marshal of Tank Forces Rotmistrov called 'one-variant war'. In September 1967, six months after Marshal Grechko's appointment as Minister of Defence, the largescale *Dnepr* manoeuvres in the Western Soviet Union tested the Armed Forces' capacity to conduct non-nuclear operations.[34] This was in answer to NATO's strategy of flexible response, with its view that a European conflict might open with a conventional phase. In the same year Army General Pavlovskii was appointed Commander-in-Chief of the Ground Forces.

At the same time Soviet military thought began to take more interest in local wars. The third edition of *Military Strategy*, published in 1968, warned that the Soviet Armed Forces had to be prepared not only for a world war, but also for local wars that the imperialists might unleash. Soviet strategy, it said, had to study the methods of waging such wars too, in order to prevent them from developing into a world war and to achieve victory over the enemy quickly; for although a world war would most probably start with a surprise attack, it might grow out of a local conflict.[35]

The Sokolovskii volume provided a strategic theory to fit the new doctrine outlined by Khrushchev in 1960. Its publication did not end all disagreement, however, for there were different schools of thought about the forces needed to fight and win a nuclear war. Moreover, Khrushchev seems to have gone further than most military thinkers in believing (though the evidence is not conclusive) that the requirements for fighting and winning a nuclear war did not need to be met, and that war could be prevented through the threat of destructive retaliation. This was at variance with the military insistence that a strategy had to be devised, and the forces provided, for waging and winning a general nuclear war.

Yet Sokolovskii recognized, as had Khrushchev in his 1960 speech, that general nuclear war would be immensely destructive: hundreds of millions of people would perish, not only in the West, but in the Soviet Union and throughout the world.[36] The main aim of preparing for a general nuclear war was to prevent it. Prevention was seen to be a function of preparation for war. Indeed, at the very time that the first two editions of Sokolovskii's book appeared, the Soviet Union was engaged in a bitter dispute with the Chinese leadership in which the issue of nuclear war played a key role. The Soviet leaders were very critical of Mao Zedong, whose statements were taken to imply that he faced the prospect of nuclear war with equanimity. They stressed that such a war would be extremely destructive: 'thermonuclear war will have catastrophic consequences for all peoples, for the whole world. All countries, even those that survive the war, would be thrown back in their development by decades, if not centuries.'[37] The main burden of their argument was that world nuclear war could be avoided, in large measure thanks to the strength of the Soviet Union; that such a war was not necessary for the triumph of socialism; and that only a madman would think that the devastation resulting from a general nuclear war was a satisfactory foundation on which to build socialism.

In this exchange with the Chinese, the Soviet leaders also said that 'there is no doubt, of course, that if the imperialist madmen do unleash a war, the peoples will wipe out and bury capitalism'.[38] Marxist-Leninist theory holds that the world is now in transition from capitalism to socialism, and world nuclear war is viewed, in line with Clausewitz's definition of war as a continuation of policy by other means, in terms of the historic struggle between capitalism and socialism. Soviet leaders have not allowed that world nuclear war might reverse the course of history, and have claimed that such a war would mean the end of capitalism. Soviet theorists, however, have been careful to distinguish between the essence of world nuclear war, and its utility as an instrument of policy.[39] It has been claimed that the Soviet Union and its allies would emerge victorious from such a war, but there is nothing to suggest that the Soviet leaders think that a general nuclear war would be anything other than catastrophic, for the victors as well as the vanquished.

## Catching up

In January 1960, Khrushchev declared that the United States would try to catch up with the Soviet Union in the production of missiles by 1965. But the Soviet Union, he said, would use the time it had gained 'to develop rocket weapons and occupy a leading position in this field until an international agreement on the question of disarmament is reached'. Five years later Khrushchev's ambitions had collapsed. When he was removed from office in October 1964, the Soviet Union lagged very far behind the United States in intercontinental forces. In the early 1960s Soviet policy had given priority to the deployment of the SS-4 MRBM and the SS-5 IRBM, which could strike targets in and around Europe. Nearly 750 of these missiles entered service between 1959 and 1965. But only four of the SS-6 ICBM, which had been flight tested in August 1957, were deployed, and it was not until 1962 that the deployment of the next generation of ICBMs (the SS-7 and SS-8) got under way. Meanwhile, however, the Kennedy Administration had launched a rapid build-up of American strategic forces. By 1965 the Soviet Union, far from maintaining a lead in missile development and production, now faced the task of catching up with the United States.

The build-up of Soviet intercontinental forces proceeded at a rapid rate in the late 1960s: between 1966 and 1969 the Soviet ICBM force grew by about 300 new silo launchers a year, and in 1969 surpassed the number of ICBM launchers in the American force. The chief missiles deployed were the heavy SS-9, which carried a warhead with a yield of 20–25 MT, and the smaller SS-11, which had a 1–2 MT warhead. Development of these systems must have begun in the mid-1950s, but it is not clear when the decision was taken to produce and deploy them. Some ICBM production (mainly of the SS-7 and SS-8) was presumably included in the Seven Year Plan for 1959–65, but it seems likely that the plan was altered in response to the Kennedy Administration's build-up of strategic forces. New decisions may have been taken in 1961, after the magnitude of the American programs had become clear. It is also possible that a major revision of the ICBM program took place in 1963, following the Cuban missile crisis and the failure to install the SS-4 MRBM on the island. Further changes may have come after Khrushchev's removal from office, though the dates of Soviet deployment suggest that the main production decisions were taken before Khrushchev's fall.

The ICBM deployment soon made it clear that the Soviet leaders would not accept a position inferior to that of the United States. They evidently did not regard the possession of an assured destruction capability – the ability to retaliate against the United States in the event of an American first strike – as an adequate guarantee of Soviet security. Such a capability would not satisfy the military requirement for preparing to wage a nuclear war. The ICBM program made it clear that the Soviet Union was intent, at the very least, on matching American strategic power. By the end of the decade the Soviet Union was close to attaining strategic parity with the United States.

This raised an important question for Soviet policy. Should the Soviet Union strive for significant superiority in strategic arms, the better to ensure victory in the event of nuclear war? Or should it accept that mutual vulnerability to devastating retaliatory strikes was the only possible relationship with the United States at the current stage of strategic arms competition? Both the ambition to attain superiority and the recognition of mutual vulnerability were present in Soviet thinking in the 1960s. But a choice became necessary only with the attainment of parity. The choice was not one of principle, for superiority would clearly be desirable. It was forced by the practical consideration that the pursuit of superiority might prove extremely costly, and ultimately unsuccessful.

The choice was posed most sharply by the prospect of a race to deploy anti-ballistic-missile (ABM) systems. In the mid-1960s the Soviet Union began to build such a system around Moscow. Defence against ballistic missile attack fitted well into Soviet military strategy, for it would lessen the destruction caused to the Soviet Union by nuclear war. Moreover, it reflected a desire not to let Soviet security depend on the balance of terror. Major-General Talenskii wrote in 1964 that 'the creation of an effective anti-missile system enables the state to make its defenses dependent chiefly on its own possibilities, and not only on mutual deterrence, that is, on the goodwill of the other side.'[40] In February 1967 Kosygin, the Chairman of the Council of Ministers, told a press conference in London that defensive systems were not 'a cause of the arms race but designed instead to prevent the death of people'.[41] But in September 1967 the United States decided to deploy nationwide ABM defences, and this soon led the Soviet leaders to see these systems in a different light.

In the late 1960s the future course of Soviet strategic arms policy became bound up with negotiations to limit such arms. In 1964 the Soviet Union had rejected President Johnson's proposal for a 'verified freeze' on strategic arms; that would have frozen the Soviet forces into a position of numerical inferiority. In January 1967 the United States made an approach to explore the possibility of negotiations to limit the deployment of ABM systems. During the year the Soviet Union indicated that it might be interested in talks to limit both offensive and defensive arms, and in June 1968 Foreign Minister Gromyko told the Supreme Soviet that the Soviet Union was ready for such talks. In November 1969 SALT (Strategic Arms Limitation Talks) began, after a delay of a year caused by the Soviet invasion of Czechoslovakia and the election of a new President in the United States.[42]

Discussions in the Soviet military press on the eve of SALT showed a clear awareness that each side was vulnerable to massive retaliatory strikes in the event of war. What also emerged was a recognition that this nuclear balance could be upset in one of two ways: either by attainment of superiority in offensive missiles, or by the deployment of effective ballistic missile defences. A leading Soviet theorist, Major-General Zemskov, wrote in 1969 that

> the degree of probability of a particular type of war at each historical segment, of course, does not remain the same, and changes under the influence of a number of political and military-technical factors. Of special importance here can be the disruption of the 'nuclear balance of power'. It is possible, for example, in case of further sharp increase of nuclear potential or the creation by one of the sides of highly-effective means of protection from a nuclear attack of the enemy in conditions when the other side lags considerably in resolution of these missions. In a change of 'nuclear balance of power' in favor of the countries of imperialism, the danger of a nuclear war will increase manyfold.[43]

Zemskov's article reflected the changing Soviet view of ABM systems. It was now accepted that these could play an offensive as well as a defensive role, and that an effective (or comparatively more effective)

American ABM system would disrupt the nuclear balance by enabling the United States to lessen the effectiveness of a Soviet nuclear strike. The Soviet leaders may have feared that their experience with ICBMs would be repeated. The Soviet Union had been the first to test such a missile, but the United States had soon achieved a massive numerical and technological superiority, which the Soviet Union had eliminated only with considerable effort.

These considerations appear to have governed the Soviet approach to SALT. The opening Soviet statement at the negotiations (as summarized by Gerard Smith, the chief American negotiator) declared that

> mountains of weapons were growing, yet security was not improving but diminishing as a result. A situation of mutual deterrence existed. Even in the event that one of the sides was the first to be subjected to attack, it would undoubtedly retain the ability to inflict a retaliatory blow of destructive force. It would be tantamount to suicide for the ones who decided to start war. However, in the Soviet Union view, mutual deterrence did not entirely preclude nuclear war. Each side has its own understanding and interpretation of the numerous factors and complex interactions of the evolving political military situation. This could lead to major miscalculations. The strategic situation by no means excluded the risk of nuclear conflict arising from unauthorized use of nuclear missiles from a provocation on the part of some third power possessing nuclear weapons.[44]

At SALT the Soviet Union insisted on the principle of 'equal security' as if to emphasize that it would not let slip from its grasp the equality it had achieved at such cost.[45]

In 1970 the Soviet Union proposed that a Treaty be concluded on ABM systems alone, thus showing concern about the prospect of a race in defensive systems.[46] The United States insisted, however, that offensive systems be covered too, since one of the main American aims at SALT was to obtain limitations on the deployment of the heavy SS-9 ICBM, which, it was feared, would pose a threat to American ICBM silos. The ABM Treaty and the Interim Agreement on Offensive Missiles were signed in Moscow in May 1972.

The SALT Agreements were a public mark of strategic parity between the Soviet Union and the United States, and the Soviet leaders evidently regarded this as an important achievement. They saw the ABM Treaty as the more significant agreement, which would preclude – for the time being at least – the possibility of a competition in ABM systems. Marshal Grechko, the Defence Minister, claimed that the Treaty prevented 'the development of a competition between offensive and defensive rocket-nuclear weapons'.[47] Nothing as important was claimed for the Interim Agreement, which was intended to last only for five years. It imposed limits on the number of silo launchers each side could deploy, but did not prohibit the modernization of ICBM and SLBM forces. The Soviet Union negotiated the Interim Agreement with great care, so as not to prevent the deployment of a new generation of ICBMs in the mid-1970s. Competition in offensive strategic missiles has continued apace since 1972, in spite of the negotiations to conclude a second SALT Treaty.

In Soviet eyes, the build-up of strategic forces brought important gains. Nuclear war was now less likely because the Soviet Union was stronger, and therefore less likely to be attacked. The American leaders were forced to recognize that they could not win the nuclear arms race, and were thus willing to pursue serious arms limitation talks.[48] At the same time, however, the strategic relationship with the United States was one of mutual vulnerability and this was not, from the Soviet point of view, entirely satisfactory. The Soviet Union was concerned, as its opening statement at SALT showed, about the danger of accidental war, and about the possibility that a third state might provoke a world war. Agreements were signed in 1971 to reduce the risk of accidental war, and to improve the 'hot line' between Moscow and Washington.[49]

The Soviet Union tried to gain American agreement on joint action in the event of a third country's using modern weapons in order to provoke a Soviet–American war. It is not clear what lay behind this proposal, which was turned down by the United States. It may have been prompted by fear of a Chinese provocation, and a desire to reach agreement on how to deal with such an attack. It may have sprung from a desire to create a superpower understanding about third states, and thus to weaken the ties between the United States and the other nuclear weapons states, all of which (Britain, France and China) had better relations with the United States than with the Soviet Union. In any event, the Soviet proposal betrayed anxiety about these other states, and a wish for superpower cooperation in dealing with them. In June 1973 the two governments signed an Agreement on the Prevention of Nuclear War. This commits the two sides to consult whenever there is a danger of nuclear war, and may have given the Soviet Union a little of what it sought from the earlier proposal.[50]

## Managing Parity

In the decade before the SALT Agreements in 1972, Soviet strategic policy was dominated by the drive to catch up with the United States. The Agreements themselves were a public and visible sign of the success of that effort. In the ten years since 1972 the competition in offensive strategic weapons has not stopped, and although each side has committed itself publicly to parity, each has been accused by the other of striving for superiority. The chief American fear has been that for the Soviet Union parity is only a transitional stage in its progress from inferiority to superiority. The continuing development and deployment of strategic missiles, as well as the stress laid in military writings on preparing to wage and win a nuclear war, have been taken as evidence of the Soviet determination to move beyond parity. Soviet writers, for their part, have argued that the American 'military industrial complex' finds parity unpalatable, and that the policy of the United States, and in particular of the Reagan Administration, is to try to regain superiority, and thus to restore to American strategic power the political and military utility it lost as a result of the Soviet build-up of the 1960s and 1970s.[51]

Since the mid-1970s, and in particular since January 1977, Soviet leaders have been at pains to stress that they are not striving for strategic superiority. In a speech in Tula in that month Brezhnev declared that 'the Soviet Union's defense potential must be sufficient to deter anyone from taking the risk of interfering with our peaceful life. Not a policy aimed at superiority in armaments, but a policy aimed at reducing them, at lessening military confrontation – that is our policy.'[56] Marshal Ogarkov, the Chief of the General Staff, has pointed to this as an important statement of military doctrine.[53] At the 26th Party Congress in February 1981 Brezhnev said even more categorically that 'the military and strategic equilibrium prevailing between the USSR and the USA, between the Warsaw Pact and NATO, is objectively a safeguard of world peace. We have not sought, and do not now seek military superiority over the other side. That is not our policy.'[54] Since Brezhnev's Tula speech in January 1977 Soviet leaders, both political and military, have emphasized that their military doctrine is defensive and that the aim of their policy is to prevent attacks on the Soviet Union, not to seek superiority over the United States in order to fight and win a nuclear war. Brezhnev told the 26th Party Congress that 'to try to outstrip each other in the arms race or to expect to win a nuclear war is dangerous madness.'[55] He repeated this statement in October 1981, in response to President Reagan's comment, made at a press conference earlier in the month, that 'the Soviet Union has made it very plain that among themselves they believe [a nuclear war] is winnable'.[56] Brezhnev went on to echo the sentiment expressed in the opening Soviet statement at SALT in 1969, that starting a nuclear war in the expectation of victory would be tantamount to suicide.[57] The emphasis in Soviet statements about nuclear war changed in the late 1970s: superiority has been explicitly rejected as the goal of Soviet policy, and the expectation of victory in nuclear war has been called madness.

Parity is now the official Soviet description of the Soviet–American strategic relationship. Although an imprecise term, parity is not altogether without meaning. It clearly excludes superiority in the sense of an ability to destroy, in a single strike, all the enemy's strategic nuclear forces; and it excludes inferiority in the reverse sense. Parity is, therefore, a relationship in which each side is vulnerable to a retaliatory strike by the other: in which each side possesses the capacity to inflict extensive damage on the other, irrespective of who strikes first. In other words, parity is the relationship normally described in the West as 'mutual assured destruction' or 'mutual deterrence'.

Nevertheless, the Soviet leaders have not accepted that the capacity to inflict assured destruction in a retaliatory strike is sufficient for Soviet security. At the Moscow summit meeting in May 1972 Brezhnev told Nixon that the Soviet Union would press ahead with its programs in those areas not covered by the Interim Agreement.[58] Since 1972 it has deployed a new generation of ICBMs, which possess multiple warheads and greater accuracy. These have replaced older systems within the limits set by the Interim Agreement. New missile-carrying submarines and SLBMs have also been deployed. The strike power of Soviet strategic forces has been considerably enhanced.

American strategic theorists have argued that the new generation of ICBMs gives the Soviet Union – or will soon give it – a significant strategic advantage. They fear that the new missiles will make it possible for the Soviet Union, using only a small part of its ICBMs, to destroy a large part (up to 95 per cent) of the American ICBM force in a first strike. The American President would then be forced either to capitulate, or to retaliate against Soviet cities in the knowledge that the Soviet Union would still be able to destroy American cities after the American strike. While the Soviet leaders might not exploit this vulnerability by launching a nuclear attack, the knowledge that this vulnerability exists will, it is claimed, give them an edge in any crisis, and thus encourage them to pursue an adventuristic foreign policy. This is especially so because, in the prevailing American view, the Soviet leaders believe that they can fight and win a nuclear war.[59]

There are, however, a number of reasons for doubting that the Soviet leaders believe in what has been called the 'window of vulnerability'. To achieve a successful first strike against the American ICBM silos the Soviet leaders would have to assume, first, that the United States has not adopted a 'launch-under-attack' policy and that the missiles would still be in their silos when the Soviet warheads arrived. Second, they would have to calculate that the Soviet ICBMs would function as well as they have done on their best test flights, even though they would be flying over a different part of the earth, where different geodetic effects would be felt. This might affect the accuracy of the Soviet warheads, and the hypothesis about American ICBM vulnerability is highly sensitive to assumptions about that accuracy. Thirdly, the Soviet leaders would have to take the chance that the American President would not retaliate with SLBMs and strategic bombers, which could wreak devastation on the Soviet Union. Marshal Ogarkov, the Chief of the General Staff, has written that American expressions of concern about ICBM vulnerability often leave American SLBMs and bombers (which carry 75 per cent of U.S. strategic warheads) out of account [60] – but Soviet military planners and political leaders could hardly do so. There is little evidence in Soviet thinking of the kind of technological hubris that would be required to launch such a horrendously risky strike. Moreover, the analysis given in this chapter does not suggest that the Soviet leaders contemplate nuclear war as readily as this argument seems to assume. It is hard to see, therefore, that the 'window of vulnerability' appears as promising to the Soviet leaders as it seems threatening to some Americans.[61] (See Appendix I.)

Soviet writers have claimed, however, that the growth of Soviet strategic power has restricted the United States' ability to use its strategic forces in support of its foreign policy, and that it has made nuclear war less likely. One commentator has noted that the United States has been much less ready to put its strategic forces on alert during crises since the Soviet Union attained parity.[62] (See Table 3.1.) Others have argued that American plans for more selective use of strategic weapons – as envisaged, for example, by the Schlesinger doctrine of 1974 and Presidential Directive 59 of 1980 – show that the United States is trying to escape from the restrictions of parity and to restore political utility to its strategic forces. The Reagan Administration's strategic arms policy has been portrayed as an attempt to achieve superiority over the Soviet Union.[63] Brezhnev told the 26th Congress that such attempts were 'absolutely futile'.

## Table 3.1: *Incidents in which U.S. and Soviet strategic nuclear forces were involved*

| U.S. Forces: Incident | Date |
| --- | --- |
| U.S. aircraft shot down by Yugoslavia | November 1946 |
| Inauguration of president in Uruguay | February 1947 |
| Security of Berlin | January 1948 |
| Security of Berlin | April 1948 |
| Security of Berlin | June 1948 |
| Korean War: Security of Europe | July 1950 |
| Security of Japan/South Korea | August 1954 |
| Guatemala accepts Soviet bloc support | May 1954 |
| China–Taiwan conflict: Tachen islands | August 1954 |
| Suez Crisis | October 1956 |
| Political crisis in Lebanon | July 1958 |
| Political crisis in Jordan | July 1958 |
| China–Taiwan conflict: Quemoy and Matsu | July 1958 |
| Security of Berlin | May 1959 |
| Security of Berlin | June 1961 |
| Soviet emplacement of missiles in Cuba | October 1962 |
| Withdrawal of U.S. missiles from Turkey | April 1963 |
| *Pueblo* seized by North Korea | January 1968 |
| Arab–Israeli War | October 1973 |
| | |
| Soviet Forces: Incident | Date |
| Soviet emplacement of missiles in Cuba | October 1962 |

*Sources*

U.S. Forces: Barry M. Blechman and Stephen S. Kaplan, *Force Without War. U.S. Armed Forces as a Political Instrument*, Washington D.C.: The Brookings Institution, 1978, p. 48; Soviet Forces: Stephen S. Kaplan, *Diplomacy of Power. Soviet Armed Forces as a Political Instrument*, Washington D.C.: The Brookings Institution, 1981, p. 54.

*Note*

The list of incidents in which U.S. strategic forces were involved covers those when 'a force, which at the time had a designated role in U.S. plans for strategic nuclear war, took part in one of the political incidents in such context that a nuclear signal of some type could be inferred' (Blechman and Kaplan, p. 47); it does not include incidents in which tactical nuclear forces were used. Fourteen of the nineteen incidents involved Soviet forces, and in at least nine of them American policy-makers saw a serious danger of imminent conflict with the Soviet Union (Blechman and Kaplan, p. 100). The use of nuclear threats was much more common in the early years when the United States had a dominant strategic position. Since the late 1960s, when the Soviet Union attained parity, only two threats have been made. Only during the Cuban missile crisis did the Soviet Union actually raise the alert status of its strategic nuclear forces; no such moves took place on the other occasions when Khrushchev practised missile diplomacy (see Chapter 5). Of course, the alert status of Soviet forces may have been raised during other incidents, but not, apparently, as overt instances of coercive diplomacy.

The Soviet leaders evidently believe that attaining parity has brought them important advantages, and while not entirely happy with the relationship (because it does not entirely preclude nuclear war) they apparently believe that there is at present no alternative to the relationship of mutual vulnerability with the United States. The Soviet Union has, nevertheless, tried to reduce its vulnerability to a nuclear attack by maintaining an extensive civil defence program. It has had such a program since the 1930s: in 1954 this began to take account of nuclear weapons, and in July 1961 it was centralized under Ministry of Defence control. The program was strengthened after 1972. Its chief missions are: to protect the population, to ensure the viability of the economy, and to secure the survival of the state in the event of war.[64]

This program has caused anxiety in the West, where some people fear that the Soviet Union is seeking to escape from its vulnerability to an American retaliatory strike, and thus to upset the existing strategic balance. One American study has claimed that the Soviet Union could reduce its deaths in a nuclear war to about ten million — fewer than the twenty million who died in the Great Patriotic War.[65] The Soviet state survived that war, and the economy recovered. Consequently, the argument runs, the Soviet leaders might regard a nuclear war as tolerable if the United States could be destroyed, while the Soviet Union survived. If the Soviet leaders thought this, the American strategic forces would lose their deterrent effect and, even if this did not lead to war, it might have dire consequences for American foreign policy.

There are serious difficulties with this argument. In the first place, the comparison with the Great Patriotic War is misleading. Stalin did not start the war with Hitler, but did his utmost to avoid it. Moreover, the twenty million lives were lost over a period of four years, not four hours — and this difference in time would greatly increase the social and moral effect of the casualties.

A more serious objection is that uncertainty is inherent in any estimate of casualties in a nuclear war. Such estimates have to make assumptions about targeting, weapons performance, weather conditions, the degree of warning, the effectiveness of civil defence measures, and so on. Besides, the longer-term casualties resulting from the collapse of the infrastructure of health and social services, and from damage to the earth's ecological system, are difficult, if not impossible, to assess. Although one American study has put Soviet deaths in a nuclear war at about ten million, others have reached different conclusions. The U.S. Arms Control and Disarmament Agency estimated in 1978 that if the Soviet Union launched a first strike against the United States, it could expect to lose 100 million people in a retaliatory strike against industries and military sites, if it took no civil defence measures; that 25 to 35 million people would die if the cities had been evacuated; and that 70 to 85 million would be killed if the United States aimed its missiles at the evacuation sites. Other United States government studies have pointed to Soviet casualties of a similar order.[66]

There is no evidence to suggest that the Soviet authorities disagree with these estimates, or that they think that casualties could be reduced to such a level that the Soviet Union could initiate a nuclear war with impunity. The evidence of this chapter suggests, on the contrary, that they believe that a nuclear war would be immensely destructive, for the victors as well as the vanquished. In July 1981 Marshal Ogarkov wrote of a new world war that 'many hundreds of millions of people would be caught up in its maelstrom. In the bitterness and scale of possible destruction it could not be compared with any wars of the past. The very character of modern weapons has become such that, if they are set in motion, the future of all mankind will be at stake.'[67] The Soviet authorities evidently recognize that, with large numbers of warheads on either side, and with no effective defences at present available against ballistic missiles, the consequences of nuclear war would be devastating for all those involved. In April 1981 Soviet physicians took part in a conference organized by International Physicians for the Prevention of Nuclear War, to draw public attention to the consequences of nuclear war. The conference was widely reported in the Soviet press, which stressed the catastrophic effects such a war would have for human life, and quoted the opinion expressed by the head of the Soviet delegation, Dr. Ye. I. Chazov, a Deputy Minister of Health, that in a nuclear war there would be no victors.[68]

Nevertheless, the Soviet authorities apparently believe that civil defence could make some difference to the level of casualties in a nuclear war, and perhaps also to its outcome. The civil defence effort signifies a readiness to think beyond the outbreak of a nuclear war to the measures that might limit damage to the Soviet Union and help the state to survive. It suggests that although the Soviet leaders have committed themselves to parity, they would try to ensure the survival of the state in the event of general nuclear war, and they may think that civil defence would have an even greater role to play in a nuclear war with China. It may be, indeed, that they believe that the Soviet state would survive a nuclear war better than the Western states – Stalin, after all, claimed that victory over Germany proved the superiority of the Soviet state and social order. But it does not follow from this that they would willingly expose their country to such a dreadful test. (See Appendix II.)

The Soviet Union has not been content merely to possess the capability to retaliate in the event of an American attack. It has tried to maximize its own ability to fight a nuclear war, should it come to that. Soviet military science and military strategy stress the importance of preparing for a nuclear war. For example, the entry on military strategy that appeared in the *Soviet Military Encyclopedia* over Marshal Ogarkov's name in 1979 restated the position put forward by Sokolovskii:

> Soviet military strategy proceeds from the fact that if nuclear war is forced on the Soviet Union, then the Soviet people and its Armed Forces need to be ready for the most severe and prolonged trials. The Soviet Union and the fraternal socialist states in that case will, by comparison with the imperialist states, possess definite advantages, conditioned by the just goals of the war, and the progressive character of their social and state order. This creates for them objective possibilities for attaining victory. However, for the realization of these possibilities timely and all-round preparation of the country and the Armed Forces is necessary.[69]

It appears, therefore, that the Soviet Union applies two different principles to its strategic weapons policy. The first, elaborated by Brezhnev, is that parity should be the goal of Soviet policy because the pursuit of superiority would provoke a reaction and thus prove self-defeating. The second, to be found more frequently in the military press, is that the Soviet Union should prepare for nuclear war.

These two principles point in different directions, for unless the pursuit of superiority is very clearly seen as futile, the logical extension of preparing for war is indeed to strive for superiority.[70] In terms of the structure of Soviet military thought, the first principle is more important than the latter because it has been articulated by the Party leadership and expresses a doctrinal position that takes account of the realities of the strategic nuclear balance. Military thinking takes these realities into account too, but focuses on the problem of how to fight and win a war. The Party leaders stress the defensive nature of Soviet military doctrine, but Soviet military strategy gives primary importance to the offensive,[71] and the combination of a defensive doctrine and an offensive strategy has seemed at best ambiguous, at worst threatening, to Western governments.

The tension between the two elements of Soviet thought has had its effect on Soviet policy. At SALT the Soviet Union committed itself to a relationship of parity with the United States, but its negotiating behaviour was strongly influenced by considerations of military strategy. The Soviet Union refused to accept stringent limitations on its ICBMs, although these have caused anxiety in the United States because of the threat they pose to American ICBMs. This refusal was one of the major causes of American opposition to SALT II and of the general American disillusionment with arms control. The SALT II Treaty was signed at the Vienna summit meeting in July 1979, but was not ratified by the U.S. Senate.

In spite of these ambiguities, however, there are signs that Soviet thinking about nuclear war has changed since the mid-1970s. The Soviet leaders have tried to spell out more clearly the rationale for their strategic power. They have argued that their chief aim is to deter a nuclear attack on the Soviet Union. Brezhnev's statements that superiority is not the Soviet goal, and that parity is 'objectively a safeguard of world peace', do introduce a new element into Soviet military doctrine. Moreover, notwithstanding the *Soviet Military Encyclopedia*'s entry on military strategy, the assertion that nuclear war can be won has become much less common. It is not clear, however, that Soviet strategic thought has adjusted completely to the idea that parity is the proper relationship between the Soviet Union and the United States. This new element of doctrine has made aspects of Sokolovskii's *Military Strategy* outdated. A new work is perhaps to be expected that will take the latest doctrinal developments into account.

## Conclusion

Two themes have been stressed in this survey of Soviet thinking about nuclear war: the prevention of such a war, and preparation to wage it. In Soviet thinking these two aspects are not conflicting, but complementary. It is therefore mistaken to draw, as some commentators have done, a sharp contrast between the war-fighting policy of the Soviet Union and the war-deterring policy of the United States. The primary goal of Soviet military preparations is to prevent world nuclear war. At the same time, however, a strong emphasis on the need to prepare to wage such a war has been a distinctive feature of Soviet military thinking in the nuclear age.

There are several reasons for this. Perhaps the most important has been the nuclear relationship with the United States. For most of that relationship, until the end of the 1960s, the Soviet Union lagged behind in the development and deployment of strategic weapons. The Soviet Union could not take the deterrent power of its own forces as much for granted as the United States – hence the attempt to hide Soviet vulnerability; hence also the stress on preparing for war. From the Soviet vantage-point, American policy did not appear to be exclusively one of deterrence. Soviet writers have stressed that the United States made preparations for waging nuclear war, and put its strategic forces on alert during crises in order to put pressure on the Soviet Union. They have claimed that American policy towards the Soviet Union aimed more at intimidation than at deterrence.[72] In the 1970s Soviet leaders evinced greater faith in the deterrent power of their military forces, arguing that their military build-up had caused the danger of nuclear war to recede. They claim that the danger of war has increased once again because the United States has embarked on a drive to achieve superiority.

The influence of this external relationship on Soviet thinking about nuclear war has been reinforced by several important domestic factors. The first of these has been the role of the professional soldiers, who have tried to think about nuclear war as they would about other kinds of war. This was especially clear in the 1950s and 1960s when the new doctrine and strategy were being elaborated. Marshal Sokolovskii's book, for example, is an attempt to think through the problem of how to fight and win a nuclear war, in full awareness of the immense destruction such a war would cause. The prevention of war is seen as the responsibility of the Party leadership, not of the military, except insofar as war is to be prevented by effective military preparations. Military science and military strategy have remained (as far as one can tell) the preserve of the General Staff and the military academies. There is no corps of civilian defence intellectuals such as exists in the United States. Since the late 1960s some Academy of Sciences institutes have devoted serious attention to military-political relations with the West, and the studies they prepare may have some influence on foreign policy, but almost certainly not on strategic planning.

Of course, the notional division of labour between Party and military leaders can hardly exist in such precise terms in the actual process of defining military doctrine. It does appear, however, to have contributed to the structure of Soviet doctrine, with its emphasis on the prevention of war through the preparation for war. In the late 1950s and early 1960s, for example, when the theory of deterrence was elaborated in the United States, and while Khrushchev was trying to exploit Soviet strategic power in support of his foreign policy, Soviet military theorists were concentrating on the study of a future war and how to wage it. Since the mid-1970s the Party leaders have laid more stress on the political side of military doctrine, in an apparent attempt to adapt the doctrine to the relationship of strategic parity with the United States.

Secondly, it has been difficult for the Party to accept that nuclear war could permanently reverse the course of history and lead to the defeat of socialism. The military stress on preparing to fight and win a nuclear war has been reinforced by the ideological belief that, if world nuclear war did take place, it would be the decisive contest between socialism and capitalism, and that socialism would emerge victorious. As the Soviet leaders made clear in their polemics with the Chinese Party, however, the chief aim of their military preparations has been to prevent such a war. Party and military leaders alike have pointed to the terrible destruction it would bring. This does not mean, however, that all preparations to survive a nuclear war should be abandoned, for such a war might take place.

Finally, the memory of 1941 has had a profound effect on Soviet thinking about nuclear war, and in particular about surprise attack. When the issue was raised in the mid-1950s, Soviet military theorists concluded that while surprise would bring huge advantages, it could not be decisive in a war with a country that possessed a strong social and state order – just as it had not been decisive in 1941. Two consequences followed from this. The first was that Soviet forces should be able to retaliate in the event of a surprise attack, and that the country should be prepared to survive a nuclear war. The second was that, because surprise was so important (and because the Soviet Union lagged in strategic weapons), Soviet strategic thought placed considerable emphasis on preemption: if the Soviet Union was sure that the enemy was about to attack, it should strike first in order to break up his forces.

Since the late 1960s, however, strategic thinking has placed less emphasis on the idea of preemption.[73] This may result from the attainment of parity and the acquisition of an assured capability to retaliate in the event of an American attack; preemption is not now seen to be so urgent. Moreover, there may be a link here with the historiography of 1941. Recent writing has shifted away from Khrushchev's view that Stalin was personally responsible for the failure to anticipate the German attack to a view that underlines the complexity of the situation and the difficulties of foreseeing a surprise attack. Perhaps preemption is now seen to be inherently problematical in nuclear war too.

The legacy of 1941 is reflected in a more general way in the determination of the Soviet leaders to build up the power of the state. They have not wanted to be vulnerable to attack, or to expose any vulnerability to the outside world. It is partly for this reason that they have regarded mutual deterrence with suspicion, because it rests on the mutual vulnerability of the United States and the Soviet Union to attack by each other. Since the 1970s, however, they have made it clear that they recognize such vulnerability as a fact of life, for the time being at least. They have disavowed the pursuit of superiority, and have accepted parity as the proper relationship with the United States and NATO. They have elaborated a deterrent and defensive rationale for Soviet strategic power. How military strategy will be affected is not clear, but the factors listed here suggest that emphasis will continue to be placed on preparation for war, even if only within the constraints of parity.

The recent statements of Soviet leaders have evidently been intended to assuage Western fears about Soviet policy, but it would be wrong to dismiss them as worthless for this reason alone. They may also reflect the evolution of military doctrine and its adaptation to the relationship of parity with the United States. Soviet military strategy, with its stress on superiority, provided no criterion for deciding how much military power was enough. The adoption of parity has provided such a criterion, albeit a vague and general one. Parity is given concrete definition through arms control negotiations, which have now become an important instrument of Soviet policy for regulating and managing the strategic relationship with the United States. In contrast to the General and Complete Disarmament proposals of the 1950s, which appear to have had little purpose other than propaganda, Soviet arms control policy in the 1960s and 1970s has pursued specific limitations on the testing and deployment of weapons.

## CHAPTER THREE: APPENDIX ONE. The Soviet – American Strategic Balance

A.　*Strategic balance at key dates, 1964–81.*

|  | USA |  | USSR |
|---|---|---|---|
| 1964: January – Johnson Freeze Proposal; balance on July 1. | 834 | ICBMs | 190 |
|  | 416 | SLBMs | 107 |
|  | 630 | Bombers | 175 |
|  | 1,880 | Total | 472 |

|  | USA |  | USSR |
|---|---|---|---|
| 1967: January – first SALT proposal by U.S. | 1,054 | ICBMs | 500 |
|  | 576 | SLBMs | 100 |
|  | 650 | Bombers | 155 |
|  | 2,280 | Total | 755 |
| 1968: September – SALT due to begin. | 1,054 | ICBMs | 875 |
|  | 656 | SLBMs | 110 |
|  | 565 | Bombers | 150 |
|  | 2,275 | Total | 1,135 |
| 1969: November – SALT begins. | 1,054 | ICBMs | 1,140 |
|  | 656 | SLBMs | 185 |
|  | 525 | Bombers | 145 |
|  | 2,235 | Total | 1,470 |
| 1972: May – SALT Accords signed; balance on June 30.[1] | 1,054 | ICBMs | 1,527 |
|  | 656 | SLBMs | 459 |
|  | 430 | Bombers | 156 |
|  | 2,140 | Total | 2,142 |
|  | 3,858 | Missile IRVs | 1,986 |
|  | 5,700 | Missile + Bomber Warheads | 2,500 |
| 1974: November – Vladivostok Accord; balance on June 30.[2] | 1,054 | ICBMs | 1,567 |
|  | 656 | SLBMs | 655 |
|  | 390 | Bombers | 156 |
|  | 2,100 | Total | 2,378 |
|  | 5,678 | Missile IRVs | 2,222 |
|  | 7,650 | Missile + Bomber Warheads | 2,500 |
| 1979: June – SALT II Treaty signed; balance on September 30.[3] | 1,054 | ICBMs | 1,400 |
|  | 656 | SLBMs | 923 |
|  | 348 | Bombers | 156 |
|  | 2,058 | Total | 2,493 |
|  | 7,274 | Missile IRVs | 5,375 |

| USA | | USSR |
|---|---|---|
| 9,200 | Missile + Bomber | 6,000 |

| 1981: January 1 | 1,052 | ICBMS | 1,398 |
|---|---|---|---|
| | 576 | SLBMs | 950 |
| | 316 | Bombers | 150 |
| | 1,944 | Total | 2,498 |
| | 7,065 | Missile IRVs | 6,375 |
| | 9,000 | Missile + Bomber Warheads | 7,000 |

*Sources*
1964:   *The Military Balance 1977–78*, London: The International Institute for Strategic Studies, 1977, p. 80.
1967, 1968, 1969: Raymond L. Garthoff, 'SALT and the Soviet Military', in *Problems of Communism*, January–February 1975, pp. 22–4.
1972, 1974, 1979: Stockholm International Peace Research Institute, *World Armaments and Disarmament. SIPRI Yearbook 1980*, London: Taylor & Francis, 1980, pp. XLII–XLVI.
1981:   U.S. Secretary of Defense, *Annual Report Fiscal Year 1982*, p. 53.

*Notes*
1.   The SALT I Interim Agreement did not limit bombers, or warheads; the ceilings it set on ICBMs and SLBMs took account of Soviet systems then under construction, as well as of those deployed.
2.   The Vladivostok Accord, which was designed to set a framework for the SALT II Treaty, established a ceiling of 2,400 strategic nuclear delivery vehicles (ICBMs, SLBMs and bombers) for each side.
3.   The SALT II Treaty has not been ratified by the U.S. Senate, but neither side is doing anything to contravene the Treaty.

*Acronym:*   IRV – independently-targetable reentry vehicle.

## B.   The Strategic Balance in the 1980s

(i)   In 1982 the Soviet Union has the theoretical ability to destroy 91 per cent of the U.S. ICBMs in a single strike. This could in theory be done by launching 210 SS-18 ICBMs, each with ten warheads, against the U.S. ICBM silos. Such a strike would result in the destruction of 1,960 warheads, or about 18 per cent of the total number of U.S. warheads.

   The United States, by firing 550 Minuteman III ICBMs, with three warheads apiece, against the 820 MIRVed Soviet ICBMs, could theoretically destroy 4,300 warheads, or about 39 per cent of the Soviet total. This calculation assumes that the planned improvements to Minuteman III guidance and warheads have been carried out.

*Source*
Warner Schilling, 'U.S. Strategic Concepts in the 1970s', in *International Security*, Fall
1981, pp. 71–2, and footnote 33. The assumptions underlying this calculation, and the
method used, are specified there.

(ii)   In his Annual Report for Fiscal Year 1982 Secretary of Defense Harold Brown
presented an analysis of the effects a Soviet–American counterforce exchange would
have on the strategic balance. The basic scenario was as follows: 'The Soviets begin with
an SLBM attack on time-critical bomber bases and $C^3$ [Command, Control and
Communications] facilities and an ICBM strike against U.S. missile silos and shelters,
SSBN bases, and supporting installations. The U.S. retaliates against Soviet bomber
bases, SSBN ports and related nuclear weapon support installations including hardened
$C^3$ facilities, and uses most surviving ICBMs and some bombers against ICBM launch
control centres and ICBM silos themselves in order to deny the Soviets the ability to with-
hold ICBM weapons for later use. The U.S. retaliation is assumed to occur promptly,
without degradation from the Soviet attack on $C^3$.' This scenario was considered in
different variants: (a) *with SALT II* limits in force: the U.S. proceeds with deployment of
the MX ICBM, while the Soviet Union acquires a new 10-warhead ICBM, because that
provides more capability against the MX. (b) *Without SALT II*: This assumes an expanded Soviet missile program, and a modest American reaction (i.e. more MXs). (c) *Day-
to-day alert*: almost all U.S. ICBMs, and about 30 per cent of bombers are available;
over two thirds of SSBNs are at sea and survivable; Soviet ICBM availability rate is
slightly lower than the U.S. rate; it is assumed that Soviet SLBMs and bombers could
raise their alert levels and disperse without providing sufficient strategic warning to
change the U.S. alert posture. (d) A *generated alert* situation: both sides would have all
their on-line strategic forces available, as a result of warning.
   Two important omissions should be noted in this scenario. First, the possibility of an
American first strike is not considered, although Soviet planners would have to take it
into account. The MX ICBM and the Trident II SLBM, which will be able to destroy
hardened missile silos, must look much more threatening to Soviet planners than this
scenario suggests. Second the assumption that $C^3$ facilities will survive intact is crucial,
and almost certainly unwarranted. A nuclear war would hardly be as controlled and tidy
as this scenario suggests.
   An analysis of this scenario led to the following conclusions:

1.   Until about 1987 a counterforce exchange initiated by a preemptive Soviet strike,
     against U.S. forces on day-to-day alert, would leave the Soviet Union with a greatly
     improved relative position in EMT, and would be true both with and without SALT.
     With SALT the EMT ratio would shift in 1982 from 1·5 : 1 in the Soviet favour to
     3 : 1; without SALT it would move to 3·5 : 1. The warhead ratio would shift from
     1·5 : 1 in the American favour to 1 : 0 (with SALT) to 1 : 1·1 (without SALT).
     (These figures are approximate since they are read off a diagram). The United States
     would still possess a 'large residual capability against the Soviet and non-Soviet Pact
     military, leadership and industrial target base'. In a generated alert the post-
     exchange ratios would be more favourable to the United States.
2.   By the end of the 1980s a Soviet attack would 'probably result in a residual balance
     less favourable to them than existed before', as a result of new American strategic
     weapons.
3.   Under SALT constraints the overall picture is more favourable to the U.S. than

without them. This is because it is assumed that without SALT the Soviet Union will significantly increase its forces.

4. Even in the worst case, the retaliatory potential of U.S. forces after a counterforce exchange (i.e. even after the United States has retaliated against Soviet military targets) is considerable.

*Source*
U.S. Secretary of Defense, *Annual Report. Fiscal Year 1982*, pp. 55–8.

*Acronyms*
MIRV – Multiple, independently-targetable reentry vehicle (warhead).
SSBN – Ballistic-missile submarine, nuclear.
EMT – Equivalent megatonnage; megatonnage to the power of two thirds.

## *CHAPTER THREE: APPENDIX TWO. Civil Defence and Soviet Casualties in Nuclear War*

*A.   Statements by Soviet leaders and experts*

1. The toll of nuclear war 'would run not into millions, but into tens and even hundreds of millions of human lives'. (Khrushchev, September 1959)
2. 'According to the calculations of scientists the very first strike [in a thermonuclear war] would destroy between 700 and 800 million people. All large cities, not only in the United States and the Soviet Union, the two leading nuclear powers, but also in France, Britain, Germany, Italy, China, Japan and many other countries would be razed to the ground and destroyed. The consequences of atomic-hydrogen bomb war would persist during the lives of many generations and would result in disease, death, and would cripple the human race.' (Khrushchev, January 1963)
3. The existing stockpiles of nuclear weapons are 'capable of blowing up the entire planet'; World War III would be a 'tragedy the like of which has not been seen in the history of mankind'. (Brezhnev, October 1973)
4. 'Both combatants can not only destroy each other, but can also considerably undermine the conditions for the existence of mankind' (Lieutenant-General P. Zhilin, Chief of the Ministry of Defence's Institute of Military History, November 1973).
6. 'On the basis of scientific facts, it was shown that a nuclear war would have catastrophic consequences, that immediately after its outbreak, hundreds of millions would die, hundreds of millions more would suffer serious injuries, burns, traumas. It will be impossible to render them effective medical aid since 80–90 per cent of the doctors and medical workers would perish, and hospitals, medicines and means of transport would be destroyed. Soon after the outbreak of war serious epidemics would spread ... The participants of the conference came to the unanimous conclusion: if nuclear war breaks out, there can be no winner in it.' (*Meditsinskaya Gazeta* –newspaper of the Ministry of Health – 1 April 1981, commenting on the First Congress of International Physicians for the Prevention of Nuclear War, in which a Soviet delegation took part)
7. 'We considered the results of an all-out nuclear war. Estimates show that it would cause the death of more than 200 million people, and 60 million more would be mutilated.' (Dr. Ye. I. Chazov, Deputy Minister of Health, April 1981)

*Notes*

Further comments can be found in the text of Chapter 3.

1.  Pravda, 19 September 1959. Speech to the United Nations General Assembly, quoted in Arnold L. Horelick and Myron Rush, *Strategic Power and Soviet Foreign Policy*, Chicago and London: Chicago U.P., 1966, p. 78.
2.  Pravda, 17 January 1963. Quoted in Horelick and Rush, *op. cit.*, p. 177.
3.  Speech to the World Congress of Peace Forces. Quoted by Robert L. Arnett, p. 178.
4.  'Soviet Attitudes towards Nuclear War: Do They Really Think They Can Win?' *Journal of Strategic Studies*, September 1979, p. 178.
5.  *Mezhdunarodnaya Zhizn'*, 1973, no. 11, p. 33. Quoted by Arnett, *loc. cit.*, p. 181.
6.  A.A. Grechko, *Vooruzhennye Sily Sovetskogo Gosudarstva*, 2nd ed., Moscow: Voenizdat, 1975, pp. 208–9. Grechko was Minister of Defence at the time.
7.  *Meditsinskaya Gazeta*, 1 April 1981.
8.  *Komsomol'skaya Pravda*, 10 April 1981. Chazov was head of the Soviet delegation to the Congress of International Physicians for the Prevention of Nuclear War.

*B.  Fatalities in a Soviet–American Nuclear War: Results of a Study by the United States Arms Control and Disarmament Agency.*

Near-term fatalities from attack on counterforce, other military targets, and industry (in millions).

|  | U.S. fatalities | | USSR fatalities | |
|---|---|---|---|---|
|  | *Generated* | *Nongenerated* | *Generated* | *Nongenerated* |
| No civil defence | N/A | 105–131 | N/A | 81–94 |
| In place protection, no evacuation | 107–126 | 76–85 | 80–88 | 60–64 |
| In place protection, with urban evacuation | 69–91 | N/A | 23–34 | N/A |
| In place protection, with urban evacuation (direct population attack) | 87–109 | N/A | 54–65 | N/A |

*Source*

U.S. Arms Control and Disarmament Agency, An Analysis of Civil Defense in Nuclear War, December 1978, in U.S. Senate, Committee on Banking, Housing, and Urban Affairs, *Civil Defense*, Hearing, January 8, 1979, Washington, D.C.: USGPO, 1979, p. 105.

*Notes*

These estimates are based on scenarios in which the Soviet Union strikes first against U.S. strategic forces, other military targets and industry. The U.S., having lost most of its ICBMs, SLBMs and bombers, then retaliates against a similar set of Soviet targets. In the first three rows, 10 to 15 per cent of the surviving U.S. weapons are withheld; in the fourth row these weapons are launched against the evacuated Soviet population. Soviet fatalities could be raised to 70–85 million, even with a full civil defence measure, if all U.S. weapons were ground burst (*ibid.*, p. 107).

In row one people are engaged in their normal activities near their homes. In row two people take protection in the best available shelters. In row three 80 per cent of the urban population is evacuated up to a range of 150 km, and the remaining 20 per cent takes refuge in the best available shelters.

The table does not include longer-term fatalities, which would be considerable (*ibid.*, pp. 108–15). According to the table more Americans would be killed, for two main reasons: a) a Soviet first strike is assumed; an American first strike would result in many more weapons falling on the Soviet Union; and b) Soviet weapons have a higher yield, and so result in more fall-out. The Soviet Union's better shelter program does not contribute much to the difference in fatalities (*ibid.*, p. 106).

N/A – not applicable.

*Generated* forces are those on the alert readiness appropriate to times of tension (e.g. more submarines out of port, more bombers on alert) (*ibid.*, p. 101).

*Nongenerated* forces are those on day-to-day alert.

# CHAPTER FOUR

# The Politics of Arms Control: Theatre Nuclear Systems in Europe

In the 1960s and 1970s the Soviet Union engaged in serious negotiations with Western powers and concluded agreements which, although they did not halt arms competition, imposed specific limitations on the testing and deployment of weapons. The most important of these agreements were the Partial Test-Ban Treaty of 1963, the Non-Proliferation Treaty of 1968, the SALT I Agreements of 1972 and the SALT II Treaty of 1979. On 30 November 1981 the Soviet Union and the United States began negotiations in Geneva to limit theatre nuclear systems in Europe.

Arms control is a highly technical affair: weapons have to be defined, balances measured, and methods devised for verifying compliance with any agreement. But it is not only a technical matter. It is deeply embedded in politics. Negotiations take place on the assumption that a common interest exists in reaching agreement to limit arms. But the negotiating states also have conflicting interests and, as a result, each side fears that the other is trying to gain military advantage. Furthermore, arms control can be – and has been – used as a means of pursuing wider political purposes. The Soviet Union has used its arms control and disarmament policy to enhance Soviet prestige, to present itself as a peace-loving state, and to support the more general objectives of its foreign policy.

## The Development of Soviet Medium-Range Forces

In April 1947, at a meeting in the Kremlin, Stalin pointed to the importance of intercontinental rockets: 'Do you realize the tremendous strategic importance of machines of this sort? They could be an effective straitjacket for that noisy shopkeeper Harry Truman. We must go ahead with it, comrades. The problem of the creation of transatlantic rockets is of extreme importance to us.'[1] Ten years later, in August 1957, the Soviet Union conducted the world's first successful flight test of an ICBM. The TASS announcement noted that

> The results obtained show that it is possible to launch rockets to any region of the globe. The solution of the problem of creating inter-continental ballistic rockets will make it possible to reach distant regions, without resorting to strategic aviation, which at the present time is vulnerable to the modern means of air defense.[2]

In October the same rocket, the SS-6, was used to launch Sputnik I. This demonstrated, in a very dramatic way, that the United States could now be attacked by Soviet nuclear weapons, and signalled, as Khrushchev tried to make plain in the coming years, a major change in the strategic relationship of the two countries.

In the mid-1950s the Soviet Union began to acquire, alongside its stockpile of nuclear weapons, the means to deliver them to their targets. These delivery systems were of various ranges. In 1955 the Tu-16 *Badger* medium-range bomber and the SS-3 MRBM (Medium Range Ballistic Missile) began to enter service. In the following year the Long-Range Air Force acquired two intercontinental bombers, the Mya-4 *Bison* and the Tu-95 *Bear*. In 1957 the SS-4 MRBM and the SS-6 ICBM were flight tested. In the same year the Ground Forces began to receive short-range tactical missiles (FROG and SCUD) for use on the battlefield.

In spite of its success in developing intercontinental delivery systems, however, the Soviet Union gave priority to the deployment of medium-range systems that could strike targets around the Soviet periphery, particularly in and around Europe. In the late 1950s, 1,000 *Badgers* entered service, compared with 150–200 *Bisons* and *Bears*.[3] In 1959 deployment began of the SS-4, and in 1961 of the SS-5 IRBM (Inter-mediate Range Ballistic Missile). But only four SS-6s were deployed for operational use; not until 1962 did the next generation of ICBMs start to enter service. By 1965 the Strategic Rocket Forces, which had been set up in December 1959 to take command of land-based strategic missiles (by Soviet definition, those with a range of 1,000 km or more), had 750 medium-range systems, compared with 224 intercontinental missiles.[4]

The Soviet decision to give priority to the deployment of medium-range systems in the late 1950s and early 1960s appears to have been influenced by several different considerations. The first was technological. The early intercontinental bombers suffered from serious deficiencies: the *Bison*, which was a jet bomber, did not have a great enough range for two-way intercontinental missions, while the turboprop *Bear*, which had a greater range, had a lower speed and ceiling and was thus more vulnerable to air defences.[5] The ICBM was, from the Soviet point of view, a much better weapon because it did not require bases close to the United States (which the Soviet Union did not have) or inflight refuelling to be effective; nor could it be brought down by air defences. The first ICBM, however, was not suitable as a military missile because it used a highly unstable, non-storable propellant and needed ground stations for guidance. These drawbacks did not prevent it from being used as one of the main launchers in the space program.[6]

The second consideration was that many of the nuclear forces that could threaten the Soviet Union were based close to the Soviet borders, particularly in and around Europe; other nuclear forces might be redeployed to those regions in the event of war.[7] Soviet military thinking assumed that a world war would inevitably be nuclear. If war came, the Soviet Union would try to destroy the enemy's forces and his capacity to wage war. The most important targets for nuclear strikes were thought to be the enemy's war industry, communications, command and control centres, and his strategic nuclear forces. These were the targets the Soviet Union would wish to strike with its medium-range forces.[8] (Short-range missiles were intended for use on the battlefield against enemy tactical nuclear weapons and troop formations.) It made sense, therefore, to give priority to those systems that could destroy the nuclear forces that posed the most direct threat to Soviet territory.

The third consideration was that the threat of nuclear destruction in Western Europe would help to deter an attack by the United States. In September 1961, during the Berlin crisis, *Izvestia* carried a report of an interview Khrushchev had given the *New York Times*. This said that 'Khrushchev believes absolutely that when it comes to a showdown, Britain, France and Italy would refuse to join the United States in a war over Berlin for fear of their absolute destruction. Quite blandly he asserts that these countries are, figuratively speaking, hostages to the USSR and a guarantee against war.'[9] Khrushchev is reported to have told the British Ambassador during the same Berlin crisis that all Western Europe was at his mercy: six hydrogen bombs would annihilate the British Isles, while nine others would take care of France.[10]

The aim of deterring an American attack by threatening Western Europe with destruction complemented rather than contradicted the interest in war-fighting. Even if the early medium-range systems were targeted against military installations alone (and the missiles were not accurate enough to be wholly suited to this mission) they could not have been used without immense destruction and loss of life. In November 1958 Khrushchev told students graduating from military academies that 'now it is enough to press one button and not only air-fields and the communications of various staffs, but whole cities too will be blown sky-high, whole countries can be destroyed.'[11] In May of the following year he said, when speaking of American missiles based in Italy, that 'if an attack is undertaken against us, we shall try above all to destroy the rocket bases directed against us. And what does it mean to destroy these bases? They are situated not on bare cliffs but there where people live.'[12] Soviet military thought did not then and does not now draw a sharp distinction between weapons intended to strike military targets in the event of war and weapons designed to deter through the threat of destroying cities. The deterrent effect of these weapons was not seen as something separate from their utility in fighting a war.

Deployment of medium-range nuclear forces ended in the mid-1960s and did not begin again until the mid-1970s. In the intervening years these forces faced three major problems. The first was the growing vulnerability of the SS-4s and SS-5s to attack by enemy nuclear missiles. Although Soviet strategic thought at this period seems to have placed considerable importance on preemption, the Soviet leaders tried to ensure that their missile force would be able to retaliate even if attacked first. In January 1960 Khrushchev said that

> we deploy our missile complexes in such a way as to insure duplication and triplication. The territory of our country is vast; we are able to disperse our missile complexes, to camouflage them well. We are creating such a system that, if some means intended for a retaliatory blow were put out of commission, one could always send into action the means of duplicating them and hit the targets from reserve positions.[13]

This statement was made before reconnaissance satellites became operational. These soon made it possible to locate the SS-4 and SS-5 launch sites accurately. Only a small proportion of the missiles were placed in underground silos, and most were thus poorly protected against nuclear weapons blast. This vulnerability was increased by the concentration of the launchers, with three or four to each site.[14] The Soviet Union tried to solve this problem in the mid-1960s by developing new mobile land-based systems, the SS-14 MRBM and the SS-15 IRBM. These missiles were derived from the solid-fuel SS-13 ICBM, but – apparently for technical reasons – they were not deployed in any number.[15]

The second problem was that a discrepancy emerged between the operational characteristics of the SS-4s and SS-5s and Soviet thinking about the course a war might take in Europe. These missiles apparently take from eight to twenty-four hours to make ready for firing. This slow reaction time was a serious drawback, given the Soviet interest in preemption. It became more serious when Soviet ideas about a war in Europe began to change in the late 1960s as a result of NATO's shift towards a strategy of flexible response, which envisages the possibility that war in Europe may begin with a conventional phase. The Soviet Union did not wish to be tied into an inflexible one-variant strategy of its own, and accordingly adjusted its policy to prepare for non-nuclear as well as nuclear operations in Europe. Since a European conflict might go nuclear at any time, flexible weapons, which could be fired quickly, were required. The SS-4s and SS-5s did not meet this requirement.

The third problem was the transformation of the Sino-Soviet dispute into a military confrontation. In the mid-1960s the Soviet leaders decided that the state of their relations with China required a build-up of military forces along the Sino-Soviet border. As part of this build-up they redeployed some of their SS-4s and SS-5s to the Far East.[16] After 1969 they also deployed the new SS-12, an operational-tactical missile with a range of about 800 kilometres, in the area. The confrontation with China now meant that a new element had entered into Soviet calculations of the balance in medium-range nuclear forces.

The Soviet Union responded to these problems by adapting the variable-range SS-11 ICBM for use against targets in the European theatre. By the early 1970s some 120 of these missiles had been deployed in SS-4 and SS-5 missile fields in the western part of the country.[17] Some SLBMs (Submarine Launched Ballistic Missiles) appear to have been assigned to the European theatre too. But in the mid-1970s two new purpose-built systems began to enter service: the Tu-22M *Backfire* bomber and the SS-20 IRBM. Both of these systems are a considerable improvement, in operational terms, over their predecessors.

The *Backfire* can fly at very low altitudes and at very high speeds and thus has a greater capacity to penetrate enemy air defences. It has a greater range and more modern armament than the *Badger* or *Blinder*, and would be more effective against mobile targets. The SS-20 is also a significant improvement over the SS-4 and SS-5. It is a solid-fuel missile, derived from the SS-16 ICBM. It is mobile and therefore less

vulnerable to attack. It can deliver three warheads, and is more effective against military targets, and better suited for a preemptive strike. It
takes an hour to make ready for firing, and is thus more flexible. It also
has a greater range, which allows it to reach more targets in Europe and
China. In the mid-1970s the SS-19 ICBM, which can carry multiple
warheads, began to replace the SS-11s deployed in the SS-4 and SS-5
missile fields.[18]

Development of these systems must have begun in the 1960s, but the
decision to deploy them was probably taken in the early 1970s. By that
time it was clear that medium-range systems would not be covered by
SALT I. The old systems were obsolescent. The case for deployment
must have seemed overwhelming.

## Competition in Strategies

In the 1970s NATO governments became increasingly concerned about
the credibility of the strategy of flexible response. This aims to deter
Soviet aggression by the threat of escalation from conventional to
tactical nuclear, and then to strategic nuclear warfare. This strategy
was devised at a time when the United States had larger strategic forces
than the Soviet Union, and NATO had more tactical nuclear weapons
than the Warsaw Pact; in this way NATO could compensate for the
preponderance it believed the Pact to have in conventional forces. But
when the Soviet Union reached strategic parity, this raised the fear that
the threat to escalate might no longer be credible. The American
nuclear guarantee would not be effective in deterring a Soviet attack on
Western Europe because the Soviet leaders would not believe that the
American President would invite the destruction of his own country by
coming to the aid of his allies. Even without war, the political effect
might be to split Western Europe from the United States. NATO concluded that new American missiles were needed in Europe to strengthen
the ties between the two parts of the alliance. It agreed that these
missiles should have two main characteristics: they should be able to
reach Soviet territory; and they should be ground-launched, so as to be
more visible, in a political sense, than the Poseidon SLBMs at present
committed to SACEUR (Supreme Allied Commander Europe). In
December 1979 NATO decided to deploy 464 GLCMs and 108 Pershing IIs in Europe.[19]

Although the new Soviet medium-range systems are not the primary
cause of NATO's doubts about the strategy of flexible response, they

have contributed to NATO anxieties about Soviet policy. Western governments appear to have regarded the Soviet SS-4s and SS-5s as no more than a stopgap, intended to hold Western Europe hostage until an effective intercontinental force was deployed.[20] Because of this misunderstanding, they did not anticipate the deployment of new systems, now that the Soviet Union possessed powerful strategic forces capable of striking the United States. The new systems, therefore, have been interpreted not as a follow-on to the older ones, but as part of a Soviet attempt to tilt the balance of power in its favour by making NATO strategy unworkable. It is feared that the Soviet Union now has 'escalation dominance' in Europe, and that this makes the NATO threat to resort to nuclear weapons in the event of Soviet attack much less credible, and therefore much less effective as a deterrent. NATO claims that its December 1979 decision was necessary to restore the military balance in Europe.

The Soviet Union, however, claims that parity exists, and that the new missiles are part of an attempt by the United States to regain superiority. From the Soviet point of view, the new American systems are not so much an addition to NATO's theatre forces as an augmentation of American strategic power, and thus a means of upsetting the balance ratified by the SALT Treaties. In a speech to military leaders in June 1980, Marshal Ogarkov, Chief of the General Staff, said that the implementation of NATO's plan 'would not only disrupt sharply the approximate balance of medium-range nuclear systems that has been created in Europe, but would also lead to sharp qualitative changes in the military political situation, since it would create the threat of a surprise suppression of the launches of our strategic nuclear forces.'[21] The Pershing II missile is of special significance in this regard, because it is highly accurate and could reach targets in the Western part of the Soviet Union within four to six minutes of being launched from Western Europe. If the Soviet Union has adopted a launch-on-warning policy, Pershing II's short flight time poses a particular threat because the missile could strike command and control installations in the Western Soviet Union with very little warning. Some Soviet commentators also argue that the GLCM's great accuracy would make it an effective first-strike weapon against missile silos.[22]

Soviet leaders see further evidence of an effort to break out of the relationship of parity in the increasing attention American strategic thought has given to the selective and controlled use of nuclear weapons in war. Soviet commentators have interpreted the idea of selective nuclear strikes as springing from a desire to restore political and military utility to American strategic forces.[23] There is nothing in Soviet military thinking or weapons deployment to suggest that a nuclear war could be controlled, and much to suggest that it could not.[24] Party leaders have been at pains to stress that nuclear war could not be conducted in a limited and selective manner, and they have warned that such ideas increase the risk of war by making it more 'thinkable'. Brezhnev told the 26th Party Congress in February 1981 that 'a "limited" nuclear war, as conceived by the Americans in, say, Europe, would from the outset mean certain destruction of European civilization. And, of course, the United States too, would not be able to escape the flames of war.'[25] It is ironic that while NATO has been worried that the Soviet leaders might doubt the American commitment to its allies, the Soviet leaders have professed anxiety that the United States might make the mistake of thinking that it could conduct a nuclear war in Europe without incurring a nuclear strike on its own territory.

What has been taking place between NATO and the Warsaw Pact is not only a competition in arms, but also – and perhaps more importantly – a competition in strategies. Each side believes that the other is attempting to make its strategy unworkable and thereby to undermine its security. NATO sees Soviet policy as an effort to destroy the credibility of the strategy of flexible response, and thus to give the Soviet Union a military and political advantage through its preponderance of conventional forces. The Soviet Union claims that NATO is attempting to achieve military superiority, in order to be able to deal with the Soviet Union from a position of strength.

## Arms Control

The NATO decision of December 1979 had two parts: to deploy the new American systems and to enter into negotiations with the Soviet Union to limit Long-Range Theatre Nuclear Forces (in Soviet terms, medium-range systems) in Europe. The new systems are to be deployed in Britain, Italy, West Germany, and perhaps also in Belgium and the Netherlands, beginning in 1983. On 30 November 1981 the Soviet Union and the United States opened negotiations in Geneva to limit medium-range systems in Europe.

Medium-range systems are not covered by the main SALT I and SALT II agreements, although they were an important issue during the negotiations. When the talks opened in 1969 the United States proposed that the Soviet SS-4s and SS-5s be included in any agreement. The Soviet side argued that all American nuclear weapons capable of striking Soviet territory, and in particular the 'forward-based systems' (FBS) in Europe, should be counted as strategic systems for the purposes of SALT; the SS-4s and SS-5s should not be so counted, however, since they could not reach the United States. FBS remained a contentious topic at SALT until the Vladivostok Accord of November 1974 deferred them to a future round of negotiations – and even then they re-emerged as an issue at the talks. A Protocol to the SALT II Treaty imposed restrictions on the testing and development of some types of cruise missile, but this lapsed on 31 December 1981. A statement of agreement limited production of the *Backfire* bomber to thirty a year; the United States pressed for this restriction because it feared that the bomber might be used in an intercontinental role.[26]

In October 1979 Brezhnev tried to head off the impending NATO decision by promising to reduce the number of medium-range nuclear delivery systems in the Western part of the Soviet Union if NATO did not go ahead with its plans. He claimed that the number of Soviet medium-range missiles, and the yield of their warheads, had been reduced over the previous ten years, and that the Soviet Union now had fewer medium-range bombers (Western figures support these claims); consequently the Soviet Union was not upsetting the military balance.[27] When, in spite of the Brezhnev proposal, NATO went ahead with its decision, the Soviet Union appeared unwilling to negotiate. In October 1980, however, the United States and the Soviet Union began preparatory talks in Geneva.

These talks were soon cut short by the election of a new President in the United States. But they lasted long enough to show that the two sides were far apart in their approaches to negotiation. The United States argued that negotiations should concentrate on medium-range missiles and their warheads, that an agreement should give each side the same ceilings and rights, and that it should be adequately verifiable. The Soviet Union, for its part, insisted that talks about missiles had to be 'organically linked' with discussions about American FBS, and they proposed that launchers be limited rather than warheads.[28]

The two sides have continued to disagree about the state of the military balance and the scope of the negotiations. In an interview with *Der Spiegel* in November 1981, Brezhnev asserted that the Soviet Union had 975 medium-range systems in Europe, compared with NATO's 986.[29] Two weeks later Reagan claimed that the Soviet Union had a six-to-one lead.[30] Table 4.1 shows how these figures are arrived at. The

Table 4.1:    *Soviet and U.S. views of the balance of medium-range nuclear forces in Europe, November 1981*

*United States view: USSR leads by 6 to 1*

|  | USA | USSR |
|---|---|---|
| *IRBM* | 0 | 250 SS-20 |
|  |  | 350 SS-4/5 |
|  |  | 100 SS-12/22 |
| *SLBM* | 0 | 30 SS-N-5 |
| *Bombers* | 164 F-111 in W. Europe | 45 *Backfire* |
|  | 63 FB-111 in USA | 350 {*Blinder* / *Badger* |
|  | 265 F-4 | 2,700 {Su-17 / Su-24 / MiG-27 |
|  | 68 A-6/7 |  |
|  | 560 Total | 3,825 Total |

*Soviet View: USSR and NATO in balance*

|  | USA + NATO | USSR |
|---|---|---|
| *IRBM* | 18 French | 243 SS-20 |
|  |  | 253 SS-4/5 |
| *SLBM* | 80 French | 18 SS-N-5 |
|  | 64 British |  |
| *Bombers* | 65 US FB-111 | 461 {Backfire / Blinder / Badger |
|  | 172 US F-111 |  |
|  | 246 US F-4 |  |
|  | 240 US A-6/7 |  |
|  | 46 French Mirage IVA |  |
|  | 55 British Vulcan |  |
|  | 986 Total | 975 Total |

*Source*
Jane M.O. Sharp, 'Four Approaches to an INF Agreement', in *Arms Control Today*, March 1982, p. 2.

table makes it clear that the chief disagreement is not how many weapons of each type the two sides have, but rather which systems to weigh in the balance.

The Soviet balance includes British and French systems on the Western side: the Soviet Union does not wish to negotiate limitations on these systems at Geneva, but it does argue that they should be taken into account in assessing the state of the balance. The Soviet tally also counts all the A-6 and A-7 planes on the aircraft carriers that could be deployed to the European theatre. No tactical aircraft are included on the Soviet side, however. The American balance, as presented by Reagan, excludes British and French systems. It also excludes the Pershing 1A, although a comparable Soviet missile, the SS-12, is included. All Soviet Frontal Aviation aircraft are counted; these are nuclear capable, though it is often assumed that only one quarter or so would be available for nuclear roles.[31] Not all nuclear-capable aircraft are included on the American side. Apart from these differences over what to count, there are two major discrepancies in the table. The Soviet figure for Soviet medium-range bombers is higher than the American, for reasons which are not apparent. The Soviet figure for SS-4s and SS-5s is lower than the American, and this reflects disagreement about the rate at which the older systems are being dismantled.[32]

Neither presentation of the balance includes the Poseidon SLBMs assigned to SACEUR, or the Soviet SS-11 and SS-19 ICBMs that appear to be intended for the use in the European theatre. These systems are already covered by the SALT II Treaty. Nor do the balances take account of Chinese nuclear forces, which certainly affect Soviet requirements. This factor is likely to cause problems in the negotiations, because some SS-20s are deployed in such a way as to be able to strike targets in Europe and China. The United States will seek global ceilings, while the Soviet Union, under the principle of equal security, will want allowance made for its military confrontation with China.

Both sides have publicized their conceptions of the existing balance of forces, and their views about what would constitute an equitable agreement. The Soviet Union claims that parity exists, and that all that is needed to maintain parity is for NATO to reverse its decision of December 1979. The United States claims that a major imbalance exists, and has proposed that the Soviet Union dismantle its SS-4s, SS-5s and SS-20s. In return the United States would refrain from deploying Pershing IIs and GLCMs in Europe.[33]

Both the United States and the Soviet Union have responded to the rise of the anti-nuclear movement in Western Europe by trying to present themselves as the champions of peace and arms limitation. The Reagan Administration adopted this tone only after ten months of bellicose rhetoric. Soviet policy, however, has always given an important place to 'peace forces'. In 1952, Stalin, evidently in response to views expressed in the Soviet Union, warned that the peace movement in Western Europe would not be able to prevent war. But in 1956 Khrushchev pointed to the important role of 'peace forces' when declaring that war should no longer be considered fatalistically inevitable. In the late 1960s and early 1970s the Soviet Union made a renewed effort to mobilize Western public opinion in support of its own conception of detente.[34] The most notable of many activities was the Congress of Peace Forces held in Moscow in 1973 and addressed by Brezhnev. The Soviet Union welcomed the rise of the peace movement in Western Europe in 1980 and 1981, and encouraged it to try to stop the deployment of the new NATO missiles.

The Western European peace movement is certainly not the creature of Moscow. It grew in response to several important international events: the NATO decision of December 1979, and the growing American interest in limited nuclear war; the worsening of Soviet–American relations after the Soviet intervention in Afghanistan; the failure of the United States to ratify the SALT II Treaty, and the growing awareness that twenty years of arms control talks had not succeeded in slowing down the nuclear arms race. The peace movement, which embraces a very wide range of groups and political positions, has criticized Soviet nuclear weapons policy and the deployment of the SS-20. Nevertheless, its chief target has been the new NATO systems, perhaps because the NATO governments are more amenable to popular pressure than the Soviet Union.

In spite of its rhetorical support, the Soviet Union has done little to encourage the peace movement by limiting its own weapons deployment. The Brezhnev offer of October 1979 would not have restricted deployment of the SS-20 while the SS-4s and SS-5s were being withdrawn from service. (He announced at the same time the withdrawal of 20,000 troops and 1,000 tanks from East Germany, but this had no effect on the nuclear balance, and was too small to change the conventional balance in a substantial way.) At the 26th Party Congress Brezhnev proposed a moratorium on the deployment of medium-range systems in Europe, to take effect once negotiations began. NATO rejected this on the grounds that it would merely ratify Soviet superiority, and would not limit systems capable of striking Europe from east of the Urals.[35] In November 1981 Brezhnev took this proposal a step further, during his visit to Bonn, saying that if there were a moratorium, the Soviet Union would cease deployment of the SS-20 and reduce unilaterally its medium-range systems in the European part of the Soviet Union.[36] This offer was not taken up by NATO. In March 1982 Brezhnev said that the Soviet Union would not deploy any new medium-range nuclear systems in the European part of the Soviet Union before an agreement was reached, unless NATO began practical preparations for the deployment of the Pershing 2 and the GLCM.[37] NATO has not changed its policy in response to this.

The Soviet position has evolved, and this may indicate an interest in reaching a serious agreement. But it is conceivable that a more imaginative Soviet gesture in October 1979 – for example, a unilateral decision to stop deployment of new medium-range systems – might well have affected the NATO decision, since some West European governments were reluctant to go ahead with it. A similar move later on might have strengthened the peace movement, and increased its pressure on Western governments. In fact, however, deployment of the SS-20 has continued after December 1979, until December 1981, apparently at a faster rate than before.[38] It is not clear why the Soviet leaders have been unwilling to take unilateral steps of this kind, but several explanations are possible. First, it may be that they intend to have a large missile force targeted on Europe, irrespective of whether or not the NATO deployment goes ahead. This interpretation is supported by the military rationale that appears to have underpinned the decision to deploy the SS-20. According to this logic, the NATO deployment will call for some further countervailing action. The Soviet leaders have indeed made it clear that they see the NATO decision as an attempt to upset the existing balance of forces in Europe, and that they will respond.

Second, the Soviet stress on parity reinforces the belief that every concession must be reciprocated: nothing is to be given away for nothing. After many years of lagging behind the United States in nuclear forces, the Soviet leaders are likely to think that strength consists in not appearing amenable to pressure, whether from foreign governments or from Western public opinion. They may fear that any concession would reveal too great an eagerness to forestall the NATO decision, and be taken as a sign of weakness.

Third, it may be objected that the Soviet leaders calculate that the NATO deployment will be stopped in any event, and that concessions are therefore unnecessary. Perhaps that is so. But it is more likely that they refuse to make major concessions because they place more trust in their own military power than in the peace movement as a guarantee of Soviet security. They may indeed believe that the peace movement is too disorganized and elemental a force, and too far removed from Moscow's control, to have much reliance placed on it; that concessions would only encourage further demands; and, moreover, that it is precisely because the Soviet Union is so unresponsive to public opinion that more pressure is directed against Western governments. They may also think that there are currents in the peace movement – nationalist elements in West Germany, for example, or those opposed to the bloc structure in Europe – that they do not wish to encourage beyond the point of seeing Western governments embarrassed.

Finally, it may be that the Soviet leaders are more interested in seeing NATO split than in providing a concession great enough to allow it to make an orderly retreat from its December 1979 decision. Western Europe now occupies a key place in Soviet policy. Since 1978 the Soviet leaders have felt themselves threatened by a hostile quasi-alliance between the United States, China, Japan and Western Europe. Western Europe has been the weakest link, and therefore the primary object of Soviet attention. The Soviet Union may feel that disagreements between the United States and Western Europe enhance Soviet security by weakening the cohesion of this potential alliance.

## Conclusion

There are those in the West who think that the driving force of the arms race is the Soviet pursuit of superiority, and that if the Soviet Union would commit itself wholeheartedly to parity, the arms race could be brought to a halt. Similarly, the Soviet leaders have argued that it is the American striving after superiority that fuels the arms race, and that if the United States would abandon that ambition, the arms race could be ended. The United States and the Soviet Union see each other as accepting parity only under duress, and each fears that the other is seeking to gain superiority. The United States argues that the Soviet Union enjoys superiority in theatre nuclear forces in Europe. The Soviet Union, for its part, claims that parity exists in medium-range nuclear forces in Europe and that the United States is trying to break out of the relationship of parity by deploying the new systems in Europe.

The absence of an agreed standard of measurement for nuclear forces makes it difficult to define parity unambiguously. This has emerged clearly from the public arguments that preceded the opening of the Geneva negotiations. The Soviet Union and the United States have differed over the categories of weapons to be considered in the balance. They have stressed different units of measurement: the United States is concerned to limit warheads, while the Soviet Union has put more emphasis on launchers. The United States would like to see limitations on Soviet medium-range systems east of the Urals. The Soviet Union would like to confine agreement to Europe, so as not to restrict its military policy in the Far East.

The problems of measurement are compounded by the asymmetries between the two sides in terms of force of structure, geography, technology and military strategy. Soviet medium-range forces are very different in structure from those of NATO countries. Their development has been shaped by geography – the proximity of American bases in Western Europe, and the confrontation with China; by technology – in particular by the early successes of the rocket development program; and by military strategy – the stress on preparing to fight war. All these factors greatly complicate the problem of defining parity precisely in terms of the levels of arms on either side.

The dynamism of military technology makes it difficult to give a stable definition of parity. New weapons may upset the balance, and it is not always clear in advance what those will be. At SALT I the head of the Soviet delegation dismissed American proposals for the limitation of cruise missiles. The head of the American delegation, Gerard Smith, writes that

> Semenov analogized cruise missiles to prehistoric animals of the Triassic period. I recalled that a Soviet Ambassador Tsarapkin had argued at the Geneva Conference on Disarmament as early as 1964 that all bombers were obsolete, but now the Soviets were placing great stress not only on heavy bombers but also on lighter delivery aircraft (FBS). If Semenov was right their FBS position was really an attempt to summon up ichthyosaurs. Semenov closed out the conversation by saying, 'A nightingale to one is an owl to another.' Now the Soviet owl has become a nightingale, and in the SALT II negotiation they pressed very hard for limitations on cruise missiles.[39]

The modern cruise missile, with its greatly improved guidance system, now poses a threat to the Soviet Union, and will no doubt, once the Soviet Union has developed the technology, pose a similar threat to NATO. Moreover, the cruise missile presents formidable problems for arms control. Because it is small and mobile, limitations on deployment will be difficult to verify.

All these factors point towards the conclusion that defining parity in specific terms is not a technical, but a political problem. Where there are so many disagreements, and no agreed technique for resolving them, the only solution is a political one. Only negotiation – whether formal or informal – can provide an agreed definition of parity in terms of the numbers of arms on either side. The process of negotiation presents difficulties of its own, however, apart from those already discussed. Weapons may be developed and produced as bargaining chips, or agreements may direct interest towards technologies that are not limited. In this way arms control negotiations may actually stimulate competition. Moreover, tough negotiating (and what government wants to negotiate flabbily?) may draw out the process, to the point where the agreement is overtaken by the development of new weapons technologies.

Arms control is not isolated from politics, but is deeply rooted in the East – West political relationship. It is at once an arrangement for pursuing the cooperative objective of regulating the competition in arms, and an arena in which the two sides try to further their competing interests. In the prelude to the Geneva negotiations both the Soviet Union and the United States declared their interest in controlling the arms race, and tried to present themselves as more armed against than arming. It is not clear whether, in view of the great differences that divide them, they can translate their professions of interest in arms limitation into an effective agreement.

# CHAPTER FIVE

# Military Power and Foreign Policy

The external function of a socialist army (as opposed to its function of repressing the revolution's enemies at home) was described as follows in a Soviet work on 'War and the Army', published in 1977:

> In modern conditions the external function of the socialist army is naturally becoming broader and deeper. This is explained by huge socio-political changes on the international arena.
>
> Firstly, . . . before the socialist state and its army stands the task of defending, together with other socialist states and their armies, the whole socialist system, and not only its own country.
>
> Secondly, . . . it is the international duty of the socialist states to provide support and help to the liberated countries in cutting off the imperialist export of counterrevolution.
>
> Thirdly, . . . the task of all progressive forces consists in deterring the aggressors, in denying them the possibility of bringing mankind to a new nuclear war. This can be done above all by counterposing to imperialism a mighty military force, by creating a situation in which aggression will unavoidably meet retaliation. It is primarily the states of the socialist community that are called upon, and are in a position, to do this.
>
> . . . The external function of the socialist army . . . takes different forms. It can take the form of direct military actions in defense of the socialist Fatherland or deterrence (*sderzhivanie*) of aggressors by means of a constant strengthening of the combat preparedness of the army in the context of peacetime.[1]

Soviet thinking about the uses of military power is rooted in the official Marxist-Leninist ideology of the state. This asserts that the world is moving from capitalism to socialism, and that this transition began with the October Revolution. The Soviet people, under the leadership of the Communist Party, have built a socialist society, and are now engaged in constructing a communist one. Between the wars the Soviet Union stood alone against hostile capitalist powers. Victory over Germany laid the foundation on which a socialist camp could be built. More recently the socialist camp has grown in size, and has been joined by countries of 'socialist orientation' such as Angola and Ethiopia. In Soviet eyes these changes signify that since 1917 the 'correlation of forces' in the world has been moving in the direction of socialism.

The 'correlation of forces' is the term used in the Soviet Union to describe the power relationship between capitalism and socialism. It is a broader concept than the 'balance of power', for it embraces not only military, but also political, economic and moral elements: it is not always clear, however, what weight is being given to the different elements in the relationship. The Soviet concept differs also from the 'balance of power' idea in that it does not imply that equilibrium is a good thing, or that efforts should be made to correct imbalances. The object of Soviet policy is to further the movement of the correlation of forces towards socialism, not to maintain a balance of power between socialism and capitalism.[2]

In Soviet theory it is not Soviet actions that move the world from capitalism to socialism, but the contradictions inherent in capitalism itself. These contradictions give rise to revolutionary and national liberation movements, which struggle to overthrow the capitalist states and destroy their network of imperialist domination. Armed struggle may be necessary in some cases if the forces of reaction use the repressive agencies of the state to resist change. But the transition to socialism can take place without violence in individual countries, and on a world scale the ultimate triumph of socialism can be secured without world war.

The functions of military power are presented, in Soviet writings, in this context. The main function is to prevent a world war by deterring a nuclear attack through the threat of certain retaliation. The second is to defend the socialist community and its individual member states. The third is to aid national liberation movements and newly independent states to resist the forces of imperialism. The growth of Soviet military power is seen to contribute to all these purposes by weakening the ability of the imperialist states to use their military power to stop the movement of the correlation of forces toward socialism.

These uses of military power are all explained in terms of the conflict between socialism and capitalism. In an article on 'Local Wars and Their Place in the Global Strategy of Imperialism', Army General I.

Shavrov, Chief of the General Staff Academy, writes that local conflicts are the 'epicentres of that acute struggle which is taking place on a global scale'.[3] The imperialist countries, he says, have pursued a strategy of local wars precisely because they know that a direct attack on the socialist countries would lead to a nuclear war which would have devastating consequences for capitalism. This became clear in the late 1950s, and explains why Western military theory became particularly interested at the time in limited and local wars. Shavrov sees a definite relationship between the strategic nuclear balance and the incidence of local wars. Although he says that there is a danger that such wars will grow into nuclear war, his analysis of imperialist strategy implies that Soviet military power is effective in deterring a direct attack on the Soviet Union.

Shavrov, whose article appeared in 1975, argues that the strategy of local war was experiencing a crisis by the mid-1970s, and claims that between 1971 and 1975 'the forces of world reaction did not succeed in gaining one major victory through the application of military force'[4]. This failure, he says,

> serves as a reflection of the further process of change in the correlation of forces on the world arena in favour of the forces of progress and socialism, of the ever more sharply emerging contradiction between the 'position of strength' policy conducted by imperialism and its [imperialism's] real possibilities, as proof of the triumph of the Soviet foreign policy course directed at detente.[5]

Shavrov, like other Soviet commentators, identifies two major shifts in the correlation of forces in the post-war years, the first in the late 1950s, the second in the late 1960s and early 1970s. Growing military power is not the only reason given for these shifts, but it is seen as important in each case. In the late 1950s the Soviet Union began to acquire a strategic missile force that was capable of striking first Western Europe, and then the United States. In the late 1960s and early 1970s the Soviet–American strategic relationship became clearly established as one of parity.

Shavrov argued in 1975 that because the strategy of local wars was failing, militant circles in the imperialist countries were trying to develop new military strategies, and to devise new and more effective methods of expansion. The deterioration of East–West relations since the late 1970s has been portrayed in the Soviet Union as resulting from Western efforts to regain military superiority and to reverse the movement of the correlation of forces.

*Peaceful Coexistence and Missile Diplomacy*

The belief that the correlation of forces was moving in favour of the Soviet Union allowed Khrushchev to declare in 1956 that war was no longer inevitable. The growing power of the socialist camp, and in particular its growing military power, made it less likely that the West would attack the Soviet Union or its allies. The idea of peaceful coexistence between states with different social systems now acquired new meaning, for it could be envisaged as a permanent relationship rather than as a breathing-space before the next world war. This did not mean that preparation for war should cease. War might break out, and in any event the best method of preventing it was to prepare for it. Nor did peaceful coexistence mean that political, economic and ideological competition between socialism and capitalism was at an end. Khrushchev espoused the idea of peaceful competition, and argued that the transition to socialism would be furthered by peaceful coexistence with the capitalist world.

Soviet nuclear forces, it was claimed, contributed to peaceful coexistence by making a Western attack less likely. They also seemed to offer the opportunity for political gains. Khrushchev tried to exploit this opportunity by pursuing a more active foreign policy. In a series of crises from 1956 to 1962 he tested the political possibilities of the new military relationship by pointedly drawing attention to the ability of the Soviet Union to destroy Western countries with nuclear weapons. In November 1956, during the Suez crisis, he wrote to the British and French governments to tell them that they were reckless to start a war against Egypt when the Soviet Union could literally destroy their countries.[6]

The Soviet success in testing an ICBM and launching Sputnik I in 1957 seems to have confirmed Khrushchev in his belief that the correlation of forces was moving rapidly in the Soviet favour. He now made exaggerated claims about the size of the Soviet intercontinental missile forces. In September 1958, during the Taiwan Straits crisis, he promised to support China with nuclear weapons if the United States attacked. In June 1959 he told Averell Harriman that '"Your generals talk of maintaining your position in Berlin with force. That is bluff. If you send in tanks, they will burn and make no mistake about it. If you want war, you can have it, and remember it will be your war. Our rockets will fly automatically. . . ." And his colleagues echoed like a chorus, "Automatically."'[7] In 1961 he once again rattled Soviet missiles in an attempt to win concessions from the West over Berlin.

Khrushchev's policy was based, in significant measure, on bluff. Strategic parity hardly existed, let alone the superiority he sometimes claimed. He seems to have thought, however, that political gains could be made on account, as it were, even before the Soviet Union possessed a powerful intercontinental force. He was careful in most instances not to risk making a specific threat that he might have to carry out. In the offshore islands crisis of 1958, for example, it was only when it was clear that 'there was no possibility that a nuclear war would break out and no need for the Soviet Union to support China with nuclear weapons',[8] that Khrushchev expressed his support for China. He may have believed, nonetheless, that his missile diplomacy was effective, for example in securing the collapse of the Suez operation. In his memoirs he wrote that the message he sent to the British government 'evidently influenced them. Previously they had apparently thought that we were simply bluffing when we openly said that the Soviet Union possessed powerful rockets. But then they saw that we really had rockets. And this had its effect.'[9] Similarly, he may have believed that it was the threat of Soviet involvement in Cuba that made Kennedy break off the Bay of Pigs invasion in April 1961.[10]

In September 1961 the Kennedy Administration began to make it known that earlier American estimates of Soviet missile strength had been wrong, and that the Soviet Union had, not 200 ICBMs, but fewer than 50. (In fact, later reports indicate that the Soviet Union had only four ICBMs deployed in 1961.)[11] If there was a missile gap, it now favoured the United States. The Kennedy Administration did indeed claim that the United States had more strategic forces than the Soviet Union. This may have been one of the reasons why Khrushchev tried to deploy medium-range nuclear systems in Cuba in October 1962. This deployment would have increased, at a stroke, the number of Soviet nuclear systems capable of reaching American territory. But the attempt failed, and Khrushchev's forced withdrawal of the missiles meant that in the short term the strategic balance would deteriorate sharply from the Soviet point of view. Strategic weapons production plans may have been revised in consequence. The Cuban missile crisis was a severe setback for the Soviet Union, and Kennedy's promise not to invade Cuba if the missiles were withdrawn could not hide that fact. The Chinese leadership, some months after the crisis, accused Khrushchev of adventurism for putting the missiles in Cuba, and of capitulationism for taking them out.[12]

Khrushchev's missile diplomacy was a failure. He did not win major concessions, nor did he succeed in forcing the United States to accommodate itself to Soviet interests. He tried to exploit a relationship of strategic equality (sometimes he claimed superiority) that, although in the process of being formed, had not yet come into existence. His claims about Soviet missile strength contributed to the missile gap scare and thus helped to justify the Kennedy Administration's massive build-up of strategic forces in the early 1960s. After the Cuban missile crisis Khrushchev abandoned missile diplomacy. In 1963 a period of detente began. The Soviet Union and the United States signed the Hot Line Agreement and – along with Britain – the Partial Test Ban Treaty.

When Khrushchev was removed from office in October 1964, the Soviet Union lagged very considerably behind the United States in strategic nuclear forces, and was engaged in a bitter open dispute with China. The new leaders, who had after all been close colleagues of Khrushchev, continued to build up Soviet strategic forces. They also adopted a more flexible military posture by strengthening the Ground Forces and preparing for non-nuclear as well as nuclear operations in Europe. They pursued a cautious policy towards the West, for they evidently felt that Khrushchev's policy had been dangerous as well as ineffective.

The new leaders made a brief effort to improve relations with China, but once that failed they began to strengthen their forces along the Chinese frontier. In 1966 they concluded a defence pact with Mongolia and stationed several divisions in that country. From 1967 they increased Soviet forces along the border; the number of divisions rose from fifteen in 1968 to thirty in 1970 and over forty in 1973. Soviet nuclear forces in the area were also strengthened.[13]

Khrushchev's successors apparently felt that his military policy had not provided adequate support for Soviet foreign policy. The Soviet Union had been forced to choose between risky challenges to the West, on the one hand, and passivity on the other. The new leaders must have felt that their policy towards China lacked a firm military basis. The build-up of forces along the Chinese frontier provided the Soviet Union with a powerful instrument of pressure, and an effective fighting force in the event of war.

## Detente

Between 1969 and 1971 the Soviet Union embarked on a policy of detente towards the West. The new policy was a response to major changes in world politics and in the Soviet position in the world.

The first important impetus for the new policy was provided by the Sino–Soviet clashes of 1969, which helped to push China out of the self-imposed isolation of the Cultural Revolution. In March Soviet and Chinese frontier forces skirmished along the River Ussuri, where there was disagreement about the exact line of the border. In the following months the Soviet Union put pressure on China, by both military and diplomatic means, to settle the border dispute and, on this basis, to agree to an all-round improvement in relations. In the autumn the Soviet leaders increased the pressure by letting it be known that they were thinking about a nuclear strike against China. There is no evidence to suggest that they were seriously contemplating a nuclear attack, that this was more than an attempt at intimidation. In the event the pressure worked, for negotiations about the border were resumed between the two countries in October. But the long-term consequences were far less beneficial for the Soviet Union. Soviet military pressure reinforced China's fear and hostility, and prompted it to end its diplomatic isolation by seeking friends elsewhere.[14]

China's emergence from isolation offered the United States an important diplomatic opportunity. The Nixon Administration now began the intricate exercise of improving relations with China, in order to push the Soviet Union towards a more accommodating policy with the United States. The Nixon Administration wanted better relations with the Soviet Union for several reasons. It hoped that the Soviet Union would help the United States to extricate itself from Indochina. It wished to pursue agreement on strategic arms limitation. It sought to devise a framework for the conduct of Soviet–American relations and thus encourage growing Soviet power to adapt to the existing international system.[15]

The high point of Soviet–American detente came between 1972 and 1974. But before that a major political settlement took place in Europe, as a result of the *Ostpolitik* of the West German government under Chancellor Brandt. This took office in September 1969 with a firm desire to settle outstanding disputes with the Soviet Union and the Eastern European countries. The political climate in Europe was transformed by the 1971 Four-Power Agreement on Berlin, which ended the city's role as the focus of East–West tension, and by treaties between West Germany, on the one hand, and Poland, the Soviet Union and East Germany on the other. These political changes did not lead, however, to a reduction in the level of military confrontation in Central Europe.

These developments in international politics coincided with two major changes in the Soviet position in the world. The first was that the build-up of strategic forces was now creating a relationship of parity with the United States. This raised new questions for Soviet defence policy: whether to pursue superiority or parity, and whether to try for serious arms control agreements. The second question was economic. The Czechoslovak crisis in 1968 set back the cause of economic reform in the Soviet Union because it seemed to show that such reform would create pressure for political change. The Soviet leaders now put greater stress on acquiring foreign technology as a way of improving economic performance.[16]

Soviet leaders claimed that East–West detente followed from an increase in Soviet power and a shift in the correlation of forces towards socialism. The Soviet attainment of strategic parity would prevent Western governments from trying to deal with the Soviet Union from a position of strength, and would encourage them to adopt more 'realistic' policies. These policies in turn would lead to a relaxation of tension and to a reduction in the risk of war. Arms control talks would help the Soviet Union to manage the relationship of strategic parity, and to restrain any attempt by the United States to regain superiority as it had done in the early 1960s. Detente would also lead to better trade relations with the West, and thus to greater access to Western credits and technology. Finally, by pursuing a policy of detente towards the West, the Soviet Union hoped to forestall too close a rapprochement between China and the United States.

In Soviet eyes, therefore, detente not only resulted from growing Soviet power, but provided a favourable context in which to pursue Soviet objectives, some of which entailed cooperation with the West, and some of which entailed conflict. The Soviet leaders did not see a contradiction between growing military power and detente. On the contrary, the one was seen to provide the basis for the other. Soviet military expenditures continued to grow in the 1970s, alongside the arms control negotiations. Nor was the military burden affected by the effort to improve economic performance.

At the 24th Party Congress, early in 1971, Brezhnev outlined a Peace Program, which signified the opening of a Soviet 'peace offensive'. Soon thereafter the Soviet Union took decisions that made progress possible at SALT, and opened the way to negotiations on force reductions in Central Europe, which began in Vienna in 1973, and to the Conference on Security and Cooperation in Europe, which led to the Helsinki Agreement in 1975. These decisions, as well as Soviet anxiety about growing Sino–American ties, laid the basis for the Moscow summit meeting of May 1972, at which the SALT I Agreements were signed. Brezhnev and Nixon decided also to conclude a trade agreement, and signed a document setting out the Basic Principles of Relations between their two countries.[17]

The SALT Agreements provided an outward and visible sign of strategic parity between the two countries. The Basic Principles stressed that they should conduct their relations on the basis of equality, reciprocity, mutual accommodation and mutual benefit. The Soviet Union had pressed for a document of this kind, presumably in order to signify that the United States recognized not only strategic parity, but also Soviet equality as a superpower. The Soviet leaders evidently regarded this as an important achievement. In the late 1920s the Party had adopted the historic mission of catching up and overtaking the advanced capitalist powers. The same goal had been espoused once again after the war. Khrushchev had claimed strategic and political equality. In one of his letters to Kennedy during the Cuban missile crisis, Khrushchev had rather plaintively asked why the United States was demanding withdrawal of the Soviet missiles from Cuba when it had missiles in countries close to the Soviet borders: 'How then does the admission of our equal military capabilities tally with such unequal relations between our great states? This cannot be made to tally in any way.'[18] The Cuban debacle had shown that Khrushchev's claims to equality were premature. Now at last, however, the Soviet Union had attained strategic parity, and had forced the United States to recognize that fact. The Soviet leaders evidently hoped that strategic equality would lead to a recognition of overall equality and thereby bring political and economic gains for the Soviet Union.

At the June 1973 summit meeting in Washington and San Clemente, Brezhnev and Nixon signed the Agreement on the Prevention of Nuclear War. This was perhaps the high point of the Soviet–American detente. The October 1973 war in the Middle East strained relations, because there were those in the United States who thought that the Soviet Union should have warned the United States that Egypt was planning to attack Israel.[19] Such a warning would have been quite remarkable, for the United States would almost certainly have told Israel, and Soviet influence as a superpower protector in the Middle East would have been destroyed. In fact Soviet policy before the war, and in its early stages, was restrained, showing clearly that the Soviet Union did not want a disruption of detente. When it looked as though Israel would achieve a crushing victory, the Soviet Union moved to help Egypt and Syria by resupplying them with arms and by threatening unilateral intervention if Israel did not comply with the ceasefire adopted by the U.N. Security Council. The United States responded by raising the alert status of its strategic forces. The war showed that the elements of conflict in the Soviet–American relationship could threaten the elements of cooperation. Brezhnev later claimed, however, that without detente the confrontation might have been much worse.[20]

In 1974 and 1975 further obstacles emerged to block the improvement of Soviet–American relations. The first was the Soviet failure to obtain agreement from the United States to pursue a joint policy towards China. The Soviet leaders feared a rapprochement, and ultimately a military alliance, between the United States and China. Nixon did not agree, however, to Brezhnev's idea of a Soviet–American Treaty, and this must have lessened Soviet interest in pursuing better relations with the United States.[21]

The second setback came in January 1975 when the Soviet Union abrogated the Trade Agreement with the United States, after the Senate had adopted an amendment linking Soviet–American trade to Jewish emigration from the Soviet Union. The Soviet leaders were not willing to tie their domestic policies to their foreign policy in such an overt way. Such linkage ran counter, in their mind, to the very idea of political equality.

The third strain in Soviet–American relations came later in 1975 when the Soviet Union delivered large supplies of arms to the MPLA in Angola and provided support for the Cuban forces fighting there. Soviet and Cuban help was decisive in securing MPLA victory in the Angolan Civil War. The Ford Administration saw the Soviet action as a sign of a more assertive and expansionist Soviet policy, and as a blow to any hope of agreeing to a framework within which to conduct superpower rivalry.

In 1975 the Helsinki Final Act ratified the post-war political settlement in Europe, and marked the end of a period of major political change. But Soviet–American detente had run into serious difficulties.

## Expansion and Encirclement

The Soviet intervention in Angola was the first sign of a more active Soviet policy in the Third World in the late 1970s. Several different factors combined to encourage the Soviet leaders to take a greater interest in the use of military power in Africa and Asia. First, they may well have felt that the Soviet status of political equality with the United States gave them (in the words of one Soviet official) an 'equal right to meddle in Third Areas'.[22] As the Defence Minister, Marshal Grechko, put it – less succinctly – in 1974:

> at the present stage the historic function of the Soviet Armed Forces is not restricted to their function in defending our Motherland and the other socialist countries. In its foreign policy activity the Soviet state purposefully opposes the export of counter-revolution and the policy of oppression, supports the struggle for national liberation, and resolutely resists imperialist aggression in whatever distant region of our planet it may appear.[23]

The Soviet leaders now claimed full equality with the United States and evidently felt that it was their right to exercise their power on a global scale.

Second, the North Vietnamese victory over the United States showed that small states could defeat the largest Western power. Shavrov claimed in 1975 that the Western 'strategy of local wars' was going through a crisis. The Soviet leaders may have felt that a more active military policy on their part could further weaken Western positions in the Third World, for, as Shavrov had argued, Soviet aid could be a most important factor in determining the outcome of a local war.[24] The Soviet Union's ocean-going navy and growing airlift capability could be used increasingly to support Soviet allies and inhibit Western intervention in local conflicts.

Third, the setbacks to Soviet–American detente in 1974 and 1975 may well have encouraged the Soviet leadership to pursue a more active policy in the Third World. There was now less to be gained from restraint. In any event, Brezhnev told the 25th Party Congress in February 1976 that 'detente does not in the slightest abolish and cannot abolish or alter the laws of the class struggle. Some bourgeois leaders affect surprise over the solidarity of Soviet Communists, of the Soviet people, with the struggle of other people for freedom and progress. This is either outright naivete or more likely a deliberate befuddling of minds.'[25] It was clear that Soviet and American conceptions of detente were different. The United States had hoped to restrain Soviet expansion by offering the Soviet Union cooperation in areas of mutual interest. The Soviet leaders, on the other hand, saw detente as a relationship of both cooperation and conflict. They rejected the American concept of linkage, arguing that cooperation in such areas as arms control and trade was mutually beneficial, and that therefore the Soviet Union should not be expected to pay an extra price by changing its political system or modifying its foreign policy to conform to American ideas about the norms of international behaviour. Moreover, whatever prospects may have existed in 1972 and 1973 that the Soviet Union would modify its foreign policy in order to improve relations with the United States had diminished by 1976, for most of the incentives for such modification had vanished.

The Soviet leaders were encouraged to pursue a more active policy in the Third World by the feeling that they had attained a new international status, and a new ability to influence events around the world. They have used arms transfers, military advisers and Cuban troops to help governments and movements that they supported; only in Afghanistan have Soviet combat troops been used on a large scale. But Soviet actions should not be seen merely as the result of a single policy decision, for contingent factors have played an important role. The collapse of three empires – the Portuguese (1974), Ethiopian (1974) and Iranian (1979) – created opportunities the Soviet Union felt able to exploit. Moreover, Soviet policy has been guided not only by the desire to assert Soviet status as a global power, but also by more specific objectives: the security of its own frontiers, the containment of China, the restriction of Western power and influence. Soviet policy has to be interpreted not merely in terms of Soviet ambitions, but in the context of the regions where it intervenes. The Soviet Union is indeed an important actor on the international stage, but it does not devise the plot, write the script, set the scene and direct the play as well.

In 1977 the Soviet Union airlifted arms and sent military advisers to help the revolutionary government in Ethiopia. Ethiopia had been invaded by Somalia, which was trying to seize the province of Ogaden, and faced rebellion in other parts of the country, notably in Eritrea. The Soviet intervention included the airlift of Cuban troops, who fought under Soviet command to push the Somalis out of the Ogaden. As in Angola, the intervention by the Soviet Union and Cuba was decisive in ensuring the victory of the forces they supported.[26]

Both of these interventions stimulated pressure in the United States for a tougher foreign policy. The Soviet Union was increasingly seen as a global power, willing and able to use military force around the world to further its political ambitions. Since it was a major aim of American policy to restrain Soviet expansion by linking cooperation in arms control and trade to Soviet behaviour abroad, Soviet activities in Africa inevitably undermined American faith in cooperation. Carter's national security adviser Zbigniew Brzezinski later noted that the SALT II Treaty lay 'buried in the sands of the Ogaden'.[27]

As Soviet relations with the United States deteriorated, so American ties with China grew stronger. After Mao's death in 1976 the Soviet Union put out feelers to see whether the new leadership was ready for an improvement in relations. But it was soon clear that, in spite of major changes in domestic affairs, hostility towards the Soviet Union would remain a feature of Chinese policy. The new Chinese leaders were determined to make China a modern industrial state by the year 2000 and sought closer contact with the United States, Western Europe and Japan.

In August 1978 China and Japan signed a Treaty of Peace and Friendship, which included an 'anti-hegemony' clause that, in spite of disavowals, was clearly directed against the Soviet Union. The Soviet government denounced the Treaty as 'a threat to stability in Asia'.[28] In November of the same year Vietnam (within weeks of signing a Treaty of Friendship and Cooperation with the Soviet Union) invaded Kampuchea, which was allied to China, and installed a pro-Vietnamese government there. In December the United States and China announced that they had reached agreement on the position of Taiwan and would now proceed to establish normal diplomatic relations. In February 1979 China invaded Vietnam in order to 'teach it a lesson' for its invasion of Kampuchea, but withdrew its forces within a month. The Soviet Union both gained and lost from this flurry of invasions and Friendship Treaties. Vietnam and the Vietnamese-backed government in Kampuchea were now firmly allied with the Soviet Union against China. But in June 1978 Brezhnev had warned the United States not to play the 'China card' against the Soviet Union, declaring that this was a 'short-sighted and dangerous policy' which its architects might bitterly regret.[29] Six months later Japan, China and the United States had drawn much closer together.

By the end of 1978 it was clear that a potential or quasi-alliance, based on anxiety about the growth of Soviet power and the assertiveness of Soviet policy, was being formed between the Soviet Union's chief adversaries. The Soviet intervention in Afghanistan gave further impetus to this realignment, for it was interpreted by the United States and China as further evidence of Soviet expansionism. President Carter abandoned the now hopeless effort to have the SALT II Treaty ratified by the Senate. He imposed economic sanctions on the Soviet Union, and continued to move towards closer ties with China. In January 1980 Congress granted Most Favored Nation trading status to China (the Soviet Union had lost the chance of such status by abrogating the trade agreement in 1975). In the same month the Secretary of

Defense said, after a visit to Beijing, that the two countries shared similar strategic assessments and would broaden their military contacts. The United States has gradually eased restrictions on the technology – including military technology – that can be sold to China (and announced in 1978 that it would not oppose the sale of arms to China by its Western European allies). In spite of difficulties over Taiwan, Sino–American ties seem likely to become closer.[30]

The view that the Soviet Union is now being threatened by a new encirclement, similar to the capitalist encirclement of the 1930s, was forcefully expressed by Marshal Ogarkov in a speech to military leaders in June 1980:

> A serious threat to peace is presented by the strengthening military-political rapprochement of the USA, China and Japan, the attempts to form a unified anti-Soviet front in which the military might of the USA and the European countries of NATO in the West would be united with the manpower resources of China and the industrial potential of Japan in the East. By widening military contacts with China, and increasing deliveries of military machinery and equipment, the Western powers are calculating on pushing Beijing into open aggressive actions against our country and the states of South East Asia. In fact what is happening is the creation of a military alliance between the USA, China and Japan similar to the 1930s Rome–Berlin–Tokyo 'axis' of sad memory.[31]

Ogarkov claimed that it was now the policy of the United States to undermine, by any means possible, the growing influence of the Soviet Union and the socialist community, and to achieve a crushing military superiority over them. The ultimate goal of imperialist policy was 'to change the correlation of forces in favor of imperialism'.[32]

This new encirclement must be set against Soviet successes in the Third World. It has been a serious setback; and Soviet efforts to forestall it have been clumsy and ineffective. In February 1978, for example, the Soviet Union tried to head off the Sino–Japanese Treaty by publishing a draft treaty on 'Good Neighbourly Relations and Cooperation' with Japan. But the draft made no reference to the four Kurile islands whose jurisdiction is in dispute between the two countries, and so angered the Japanese government. Japan claims these islands as its own, but the Soviet Union has held them since the end of World War Two. The Soviet leaders were unwilling to make any concession on this issue to prevent a Sino–Japanese rapprochement. Perhaps they felt that a concession would be taken as a sign of weakness and provoke claims from other governments, in particular from China.

It would be wrong, however, to place too much stress on the threat that this potential alliance poses to the Soviet Union. China faces formidable problems in achieving its modernization program and, for all its warnings about the Soviet threat, is concentrating on industrial development rather than on a military build-up. Notwithstanding their common interest in opposing the Soviet Union, China and the United States are divided on the important question of Taiwan, which has become more contentious since Reagan took office. Japan, in spite of anxiety about Soviet policy and prodding from the United States, has not yet raised its military expenditures above one per cent of GNP.

Most significantly perhaps, major differences exist within NATO. The Western European reaction to the Soviet intervention in Afghanistan and to the military crackdown in Poland was not as sharp as the American. The achievements of detente have been more tangible in Europe: trade with the Soviet Union has become important for the Western European economies; the benefits of detente for individuals and families have been greater, especially in West Germany. Detente in Europe has had its setbacks: the Helsinki Agreement of 1975 did not create a new pattern of international relations in Europe; nor have the negotiations on force reductions in Central Europe, which have been taking place in Vienna since 1973, borne any fruit. But there nevertheless exists in Europe a much clearer sense than in the United States that detente did bring significant changes which should not be lightly reversed, and that, in spite of disappointments, detente is a sound basis for relations with the Soviet Union.

Yet, for all these qualifications, the Soviet Union's chief adversaries have drawn closer together during the decade of detente, and this must be considered a major failure of Soviet policy.

## *Afghanistan and the End of Soviet–American Detente*

The Soviet intervention in Afghanistan, and the American response to it, marked the end of Soviet–American detente. Most of the substance had gone from that relationship by 1976, but the Soviet action was seen by the Carter Administration as a particularly egregious example of Soviet expansionism. The American reaction – the non-ratification of the SALT II Treaty and the imposition of economic sanctions – clearly indicated that one chapter in Soviet–American relations had been closed.

Close observers of politics in Afghanistan foresaw in 1979 that the Soviet Union might feel impelled to send combat troops to save the government, which had seized power in April 1978. That coup, which appears to have been neither planned nor instigated by the Soviet Union, brought to power a pro-Soviet Marxist-Leninist government that was bitterly divided by factional politics. The new government provoked widespread rebellion by launching far-reaching reforms in a brutal and disorganized way. By the summer of 1979 there were 7,000 Soviet military and civilian advisers in Afghanistan, and the government had called for further Soviet military aid to repress the insurgents.[33]

In an effort to restore stability in Afghanistan the Soviet leaders urged President Taraki to remove his Prime Minister, Hafizulluh Amin, to form a more broadly-based government and to moderate his policies. This plan was thwarted by Amin, who appears to have been forewarned of Taraki's intention. He eliminated Taraki and took over power himself in September 1979. The Soviet leaders apparently regarded Amin as untrustworthy (as he no doubt regarded them) and feared that he might take Afghanistan out of the Soviet sphere of influence. On December 24 the Soviet Union began to airlift troops into Kabul, claiming that it was responding to an appeal from the government to suppress a counter-revolution which was being fomented from outside the country. On 28 December Kabul Radio broadcast a speech by Babrak Karmal announcing that Amin had been deposed and that he had taken power. Babrak Karmal had been in the original post-coup government, but had fallen victim to factional in-fighting and had been 'exiled' to the ambassadorship in Prague. He was in the Soviet Union at the time of the intervention but was soon brought to Kabul and installed as President; Amin was killed in the early stages of the intervention.[34]

In the event, the Soviet occupation appears to have stiffened resistance to the government in Kabul, which has lost control of large parts of the country. The Afghan Army dwindled as a result of desertions, and efforts to rebuild it have not been successful. During 1981 Soviet forces were increased from about 85,000 to over 100,000. By the end of the year Soviet casualties were estimated at 5,000 to 6,000 killed and 12,000 to 15,000 wounded.[35] The Soviet forces are in no danger of being defeated, but they have found it difficult to deal with the insurgents. They have not extended their control much beyond the main towns and roads. The Soviet Union has not moved to try to secure a quick victory; neither is it so embarrassed or troubled by the resistance as to seek a face-saving way of withdrawing its forces. It has insisted that any settlement of the international crisis over Afghanistan must be based on recognition of the existing government in Kabul, and it is on this point that the European Communities' initiative for a peace conference foundered in July 1981.[36]

The Soviet claim that it acted in response to appeals from the Afghan government for help in countering external aggression is correct in one respect, but misleading in others. Taraki and Amin had indeed requested Soviet military aid, and Amin apparently believed when the Soviet troops started to arrive that they were coming to help him. But the Soviet version omits to say that Amin was killed and replaced by Babrak Karmal's rival group, with the aid of Soviet forces; it makes the unbelievable charge that Amin was a CIA agent all along; and it ignores the domestic roots of unrest in Afghanistan, placing the blame for this on external forces.[37] Nor are these aspects of the Soviet version explained by the Soviet Union's claim that it acted out of a sense of socialist internationalism.

Brezhnev told the 26th Party Congress that the situation in Afghanistan posed 'a direct threat to the security of our southern frontier'.[38] The Soviet leaders evidently feared that an anti-Soviet government would emerge in Afghanistan, whether under Amin, or following his defeat by the rebels. Soviet intervention under the guise of an invitation for aid would forestall such a possibility, and would certainly be easier than invasion if Afghanistan did acquire a hostile government. The Soviet Union did not resort to military force at the first opportunity; it tried to stabilize the situation there by political means. When that failed, it sent in its forces. Soviet decisions appear to have been taken in response to events in Afghanistan, rather than as a part of a broader strategy towards the Middle East.

The Soviet action was interpreted by the Carter Administration as a step towards Soviet domination of the Persian Gulf. In 1979, 25 per cent of the United States', 66 per cent of Western European, and 75 per cent of Japanese oil imports passed through the Strait of Hormuz. The collapse of the Shah's regime had already weakened the Western position in the region. The Soviet intervention in Afghanistan brought Soviet forces closer to the Strait and demonstrated Soviet willingness to use combat troops outside Eastern Europe. On 23 January 1980 Carter warned that 'an attempt by any outside force to gain control of the Persian Gulf region will be regarded as an assault on the vital interests of the U.S.A., and such an assault will be repelled by any means necessary, including military force.'[39] The Soviet action gave new impetus to the creation by the United States of a Rapid Deployment Force, ready to intervene in distant areas of the globe, and in particular in the Persian Gulf.

The Soviet leaders evidently believed that intervention would prevent Afghanistan from being added to the chain of encirclement. They may also have calculated that a military presence there would give them a stronger position in an unstable area. Poor American relations with Iran and with Pakistan (over Pakistan's nuclear program) precluded any military reaction from outside. American opposition to ratification of SALT II and the NATO decision to deploy American missiles in Europe indicated that little was to be gained from restraint. Occupation of Afghanistan would also contribute to the strategy of surrounding China with Soviet allies.

There is some evidence that the whole operation misfired, and that the killing of Amin was not planned; perhaps the Soviet leaders expected to carry it off with fewer political repercussions. In any event the Soviet Union found itself isolated to an unprecedented degree at the United Nations and subjected to severe criticism, not only from Western governments, but also from Islamic and Third World countries: it did nothing to endear the Soviet Union to the revolutionary regime in Iran. Western governments imposed economic sanctions, and the United States and China drew closer together. The Soviet intervention had harmful consequences for Soviet foreign policy as a whole, and for Soviet policy in South-West Asia. But Soviet leaders have traditionally given more weight to physical guarantees of security than to the less tangible factor of international opinion, and the former may well prove more durable in this case than the latter.

The Soviet intervention may have sprung in part from anxiety about the security of Soviet frontiers, but it appears also to have reflected a sense of power and a feeling that superpowers have rights that smaller states – mere pawns in a larger game – do not. The Soviet leaders may have wanted to make it plain that if the West had, as the United States was claiming, special interests in the Persian Gulf region, so too did the Soviet Union. In November 1978, when the Shah's regime was in trouble, Brezhnev warned against military intervention in Iran, declaring that it would be regarded by the Soviet Union as a matter affecting its security interests.[40] In December 1980 Brezhnev proposed an international treaty on the Persian Gulf, but this was rejected by the United States on the grounds that it would legitimate Soviet interference in the region. The United States did not wish Soviet influence to be extended, either by force of arms or by international treaty.

## The Polish Crisis

The central preoccupation of Soviet military thought has been a world nuclear war with the United States. The aspect of Soviet policy that has most alarmed Western governments in recent years is military intervention in the Third World. But it is in its relations with other socialist states that the Soviet Union has most often used its military forces on a large scale.

After the invasion of Czechoslovakia in 1968, the Soviet Union formulated the Brezhnev Doctrine. This states that a threat to socialism in one country is the concern of all socialist countries, which have the right – and the duty – to take the necessary action to remove the threat. In September 1968 an article in *Pravda* put it as follows:

> every Communist Party is responsible not only to its own people but also to all the socialist countries and to the entire Communist movement. Whoever forgets this in placing sole emphasis on the autonomy and independence of communist Parties lapses into onesidedness, shirking his internationalist obligations . . .
>
> The sovereignty of individual socialist countries cannot be counterposed to the interest of world socialism and the world revolutionary movement . . . [41]

This doctrine provides a theoretical justification for intervention in socialist countries, by force of arms if necessary. The practical basis for such intervention in Eastern Europe is provided by the Warsaw Pact, which organizes the armed forces of the non-Soviet members in such a way as to ensure that they have a very limited capacity to resist Soviet intervention.[42]

The crisis in Poland in 1980–1 fell into the curious cyclical pattern of crisis in Eastern Europe. In 1956 Soviet forces put down the Hungarian Uprising. In 1968 the reform movement in Czechoslovakia was crushed by Soviet and other Warsaw Pact forces. The Soviet Union appears to have come close to using its own forces in Poland in December 1980 and in March 1981. But, as in other Eastern European crises, the threat of force (as opposed to its use) did little to arrest the process of political change.[43] In the end it was the Polish authorities who repressed the movement for political renewal by declaring a state of war and imposing martial law, on 13 December 1981.

The movement for political renewal in Poland gave the Soviet leaders considerable anxiety. They viewed the emergence of Solidarity with concern, for the very idea of an independent trade union is fundamentally anti-Leninist. The Polish Party lost control of events in the country and thereby became incapable of performing the basic role of a Leninist Party, of acting as the 'leading and directing' force in society. The Party leadership, however, remained loyal to Moscow, and only reluctantly acceded to the pressure for reform. By the summer of 1981 the Party itself had been affected by the process of change: one-third of the Party's three million members were also members of Solidarity. In June the Soviet leaders warned their Polish counterparts that the situation in the Polish Party had 'recently become a subject of special alarm'.[44] The Extraordinary Party Congress in July was much more open and disorganized than is customary for a Leninist Party.

The political and economic aspects of the Polish crisis have been inseparable. The movement for political change was sparked off by strikes protesting against food price increases. The political institutions lacked the authority to take measures to revive the economy, and so it appeared that political reform would have to precede economic revival. It seemed for a time in 1980 and 1981 that the state would acquire authority through the process of political renewal. But the political leaders found themselves in a difficult position, and needed the support of two constituencies: the Soviet Union and the Polish people. In the event they proved unable, or unwilling, to satisfy both.

Long before the military crackdown of December 1981, events in Poland had reached the point at which, on past experience, the Soviet Union might have been expected to intervene with force. By speaking of the 'onslaught of the internal counterrevolution, which relies on the support of imperialist subversive centers abroad'[45] the Soviet authorities had provided themselves with as much justification as they usually have for intervening with military force. It seemed, however, in the summer of 1981 that they were willing to accept some change in Poland. Polish socialism has always had special features: the Party-State has not been able to dominate society as completely as in other Eastern European countries; the Church has provided a powerful focus of loyalty and national identity; Polish agriculture remains largely in private hands; and popular unrest has been a significant factor in Polish politics, precipitating changes in the Party leadership in 1956, 1970 and 1980.

The swiftness of General Jaruzelski's crackdown on 13 December 1981 gave him the initiative and took Solidarity by surprise. Active resistance was difficult since the movement's leaders were rounded up and interned, and communications were cut. Besides, active opposition might lead to civil war and to a bloody Soviet intervention. The precise role of the Soviet Union in the decision to impose martial law is not clear, but it is evident that the Polish authorities' decision was a response to Soviet pressure to take tough measures. The Soviet leaders were evidently very reluctant to use their own forces, perhaps because they feared that they would meet resistance. The repression imposed by the Polish government was the best outcome they could hope for. They have played down their own involvement and presented General Jaruzelski's action as an internal Polish affair.

General Jaruzelski has destroyed, at least for the time being, the movement for political renewal, but the long-term consequences of his action are not apparent. The economy is in a critical state, with falling production, food shortages and a huge foreign debt, and it is not evident that the repressive rule of a demoralized population is going to make things better. The state still faces powerful social forces, to which the Church can give some expression, and it is not clear that it can achieve accommodation with them, or rule without such accommodation. Jaruzelski appealed not to socialism but to order and patriotism in support of his action.[46] It is difficult to see, however, that these will provide his rule with legitimacy, since martial law was so clearly imposed in response to Soviet pressure.

In spite of these difficulties, however, the Soviet leaders may feel that the crisis has been restored, in the short term, with the least possible damage to their own interests. Although Jaruzelski's action has become an issue in East–West relations, the international repercussions are less severe than they would have been if the Soviet Union had intervened directly. This was doubtless a factor in Soviet thinking, in view of the part that Western Europe now plays in Soviet foreign policy. The Western governments have condemned the crackdown and have imposed some sanctions on Poland and the Soviet Union. But Western European governments have not broken trade relations with the Soviet Union, and even the United States, which wanted to make a tougher response, has not gone as far as imposing a grain embargo or suspending the talks on medium-range nuclear weapons in Europe.

## Conclusion

It is not surprising that the Soviet leaders see military power as one of the main guarantees of Soviet security, and of the Soviet position in the world, for it is in the creation of military power that they have come closest to 'catching up and overtaking' the capitalist countries. Since the late 1960s the Soviet Union has had a relationship of strategic parity with the United States, and has acquired a growing capacity to project its military power around the world. The Soviet leaders evidently hoped that they could gain, on the basis of their military equality, acceptance of political equality with the United States, and also create the conditions in which Soviet economic performance could be improved. The attempt to do this through detente has not been successful.

Soviet theory does not give primary importance to military power in the 'correlation of forces', but the very success of the Soviet military effort means (in accordance with the law of comparative advantage) that the military instrument plays a major role in Soviet foreign policy. The Soviet Union conducts its relationship with the West from a position of military parity but economic backwardness. It has maintained its dominant position in Eastern Europe through the use, or the threat of the use, of military force. It has used arms transfers and military advisers as major instruments of policy in the Third World. Two of the most important foreign policy conceptions – peaceful coexistence and detente – are direcly linked, in Soviet eyes, to the growth of Soviet military power.

Yet the Soviet use of military force must be viewed in perspective. Compared with American, British and French forces, Soviet troops have seen little combat since 1945: before Afghanistan, Soviet forces had engaged in nothing comparable to the Korean or Vietnamese wars. The Soviet leaders have sought to avoid a major conflict with the West, and – with the partial exception of Khrushchev – have used their military power circumspectly. Khrushchev's successors realized that his policy was flawed because he claimed to have forces that did not exist. They seem to have accepted that it was flawed in another sense too: even if he had had the forces he claimed, his attempts at missile diplomacy would have been just as dangerous, because they would still have run the risk of starting a nuclear war. Although the Brezhnev leadership claims that parity has brought the Soviet Union important political gains, it has not brandished its new strategic power in a threatening way during crises.

Since Stalin's death most of the Soviet Union's major military actions have been directed against other socialist states. In Eastern Europe the Soviet Union has used the Warsaw Pact as much to maintain its own position in the region as to prepare for a possible war with NATO. The Soviet relationship with China has degenerated into military confrontation, marked by periodic border clashes. As fissures have developed within the socialist camp, so military power has played an important role in Soviet relations with other socialist states.

Since the late 1960s – in particular since the Six Day War in June 1967 – the Soviet Union has come to use its forces more actively in the Third World. The extended deployment of the Soviet Navy, which was intended primarily to counter Western ocean-going forces that threaten the Soviet homeland (missile-carrying submarines and aircraft carriers), has provided a major instrument for this purpose. The growing Soviet airlift capability has allowed the Soviet Union to intervene quickly in local conflicts. It is not to be supposed, of course, that, because the Soviet Union can now intervene more readily, Soviet policy is always the cause of such conflicts, or that it always benefits from them. But its increased ability to project its military power (and to use such allies as Cuba and the GDR) has made the Soviet Union a more important actor on a global scale.[47]

The uses of military power outlined here are roughly the same as those given in the Soviet work quoted at the beginning of this chapter. There the functions of military power were described in terms of the transition of the world from capitalism to socialism. But at another level these uses of military power acquire their legitimacy (in Soviet eyes) from the victory over Germany. That war has had a profound influence on Soviet thinking about nuclear war and nuclear deterrence. It has also affected Soviet thinking about Eastern Europe. After the invasion of Czechoslovakia in August 1968 the Czechoslovak leaders were taken to Moscow. In the presence of the Soviet Politburo Brezhnev explained to them why the Soviet Union had resorted to military force. According to Zdenek Mlynar, who was there, part of the explanation was couched in the following terms:

> Brezhnev spoke at length about the sacrifice of the Soviet Union in the Second World War: the soldiers fallen in battle, the civilians slaughtered, the enormous material losses, the hardships suffered by the Soviet people. At such a cost, the Soviet Union had gained security, and the guarantee of that security was the postwar division of Europe and, specifically, the fact that Czechoslovakia was linked with the Soviet Union, 'forever'. According to Brezhnev, this was a logical and justifiable result of the fact that thousands of Soviet soldiers sacrificed their lives for Czechoslovak freedom as well, and Czechs and Slovaks should therefore honor their graves, not defile them. Our Western borders were not only our own borders, but the common borders of the 'socialist camp'. The Soviet Politburo had

no right to allow the results of that war to be jeopardized, for it had no right to dishonor the sacrifices of the Soviet people.[48]

Similar arguments were advanced in the Soviet press during the Polish crisis of 1980 and 1981. No matter how unjust it is to the people of Eastern Europe, this line of thought helps to explain why the Soviet leaders think they have a right to dominate the region, and why they were so anxious to have the post-war territorial boundaries in Europe ratified by the Helsinki Agreement.

The Soviet Union's global aspirations too were reinforced by the Great Patriotic War. When Foreign Minister Gromyko told the 24th Party Congress in 1971 that 'today there is no question of any significance which can be decided without the Soviet Union or in opposition to it', this was taken in the West as an assertion of a new Soviet global status.[49] But Gromyko was echoing very clearly what Molotov had said in February 1946:

> The USSR ranks today among the most authoritative of the world powers. Important problems of international relations cannot nowadays be settled without the participation of the Soviet Union or without heeding the voice of the country. The participation of Comrade Stalin is regarded as the best guarantee of the successful solution of complicated international problems.[50]

The Soviet leaders felt that their victory over Germany had earned them the right to take part in shaping the post-war international order. But for most of the post-war period they were excluded from the exercise of this right. In the 1970s they began to exercise this right more assertively, with the aid of their military power. When Stalin had told Kurchatov to build the atomic bomb as quickly as possible, he had remarked that Hiroshima had destroyed the balance of power. The attainment of strategic parity restored to the Soviet Union the equality that it felt it had earned in 1945.

It would, however, be wrong to look for permanent rules of Soviet behaviour, because the context in which the Soviet Union exercises its military power is changing. When the build-up of Soviet nuclear forces began in the mid-1950s, the Soviet Union and the United States were the two most important centres of power in the world. The growth of Soviet military power altered the Soviet–American relationship by eliminating American superiority and creating a rough parity between the two countries. But since the 1950s new forces have emerged to transform and complicate international politics. The new states of

Africa and Asia have provided an additional arena for East–West rivalry and introduced a new element into world politics. Major changes have taken place in the Eastern and Western blocs. By the late 1960s, when the Soviet Union attained strategic parity with the United States, Japan and Western Europe had become major centres of economic power, while the Sino–Soviet dispute had become a military conflict too.

Soviet opportunities to use military power in support of foreign policy have grown most notably in the Third World. Here the Soviet Union has had important successes. It helped Egypt to avoid a crushing defeat in the October 1973 war. It helped North Vietnam to defeat South Vietnam and the United States. It helped the MPLA to win the civil war in Angola. It has sustained the revolutionary government in Ethiopia. In 1978 it cemented its ties with Vietnam and the Vietnamese-backed government in Kampuchea. The Soviet leaders evidently feel that they have acquired a new international stature, and the capacity to carry out a global policy. But they have suffered setbacks, as for example in Egypt and Somalia, which both expelled their Soviet advisers. After the 1973 war the Soviet Union found itself excluded, by American diplomacy, from the Middle East peace process, and reduced to hindering American policy rather than shaping the politics of the region. Moreover, Soviet intervention has not always helped governments to establish themselves firmly in power, as events in Ethiopia and Afghanistan show.

The greatest danger the Soviet Union faces is that its major adversaries will combine against it. This has happened to some degree, in part as a reaction to growing Soviet military power. The fact that a potential alliance has emerged against the Soviet Union is a major failure of Soviet detente policy, which was in large measure designed to prevent precisely such an alliance from forming. Soviet detente policy failed in other respects too. Foreign technology has not reinvigorated the economy; relations with the United States are worse than at any time since the early 1960s; a major new round of the arms race is now underway. Although we know in principle that East–West relations are not a zero-sum game, that one side's loss is not necessarily the other's gain, in practice we tend to forget it and to assume that because the world now appears more dangerous for the West it must be safer for the Soviet Union. But that is not so, and the failure of detente in the 1970s was a major setback for the Soviet Union.

Soviet foreign policy in the 1970s can be seen as a move away from isolation towards greater involvement in the international system:

foreign trade was given greater weight in economic policy; security was seen to depend not only on Soviet efforts, but also on cooperation with potential enemies; Soviet power was asserted more actively throughout the world. None of these aspects of Soviet policy was wholly new, but taken together they raised the question of the Soviet Union's place in the world in a new way. Four different tendencies can be identified in Soviet thinking about this question.[51] The first is an autarkist tendency, which urges reliance on the Soviet Union's own resources to ensure economic development and provide security. This is based on a deep suspicion of involvement in the rest of the world: anxiety about the dangers of dependency on foreign grain and technology, fear of cooperative arrangements for security, and worry about the costs and risks of using military force in the Third World. A second tendency stresses the importance of detente with the West as a way of slowing down the arms race, reducing the risk of war and furthering Soviet economic development. The third – 'activist' or 'internationalist' – tendency points to the opportunities for expanding Soviet power and influence and increasing Soviet security by restricting the power of the major Soviet adversaries. The fourth and most ambitious tendency – the 'globalist' – looks beyond the expansion of Soviet power to the creation of a new world order.

Soviet policy-making should not be seen as a struggle between groups representing these different schools of thought; the influence of these ideas and sentiments is more diffuse than that. Moreover, policy can draw on different tendencies at the same time. Nevertheless it can be useful to think of Soviet policy in these terms. In the mid-1970s a shift of emphasis took place from detente to activism. This prompts the question: might Soviet policy have developed differently if the West, and in particular the United States, had pursued detente more vigorously, giving the Soviet Union more to hope for from cooperation (and perhaps also more to fear from conflict)? The question cannot be answered on the available evidence, but the existence of different currents in Soviet thinking makes it worth asking.

Soviet policy has shown a great fear of dependency, and events in the late 1970s and early 1980s have increased that fear. One Soviet economist has written that the Soviet Union drew two conclusions from the sanctions imposed by the United States after the intervention in Afghanistan: that no important sector of the Soviet economy should become dependent on imports of machinery from the capitalist countries, but that, at the same time, the Soviet Union should not forego the benefits of international economic and scientific-technical collaboration.[52] The fear of dependency can only have been strengthened by the Polish crisis and the immense foreign debts incurred by Poland. The Soviet Union has not shown the same disillusionment with arms control as the United States, perhaps because it never shared the same illusions. The Soviet Union has continued to advance arms control proposals, but recent Soviet statements show an awareness that effective arms control is going to become more difficult to achieve because of the way in which military technology is developing. Marshal Ogarkov's parallel between the Rome–Berlin–Tokyo axis and the present relationship between the United States, China and Japan may suggest that the Soviet Union can guarantee its own security only through its own efforts, and not through cooperative arrangements with potential enemies.[53]

Alongside the fear of dependency there exists a great ambition to create a new world order. Soviet globalists argue that the postwar order created by the United States has now collapsed, and that a new international order – economic, political, and military – must be created. They maintain that there are global problems that require international cooperation for their solution, but that at present these problems are a source of conflict between East and West. A solution can be found only through a restructuring of international relations. Because of growing Soviet power, a new order cannot be created without the participation of the Soviet Union; and the creation of a new world order provides a goal for Soviet power to pursue. Soviet writings do not give a clear picture of such an order, but they do indicate a more subtle vision than is provided by the pattern of domination in Eastern Europe.[54]

The Soviet position in the world presents a contradictory picture: expanding power, linked to ambitions to play a global role and even to create a new world order; foreign policy setbacks and the fear of a new encirclement. The 26th Party Congress in February 1981 did not, however, initiate a major change of course: it reaffirmed the policy of detente and presented the Soviet Union as the champion of peace in a troubled world. The worsening state of international relations was noted more in sorrow than in anger. Brezhnev declared the Soviet Union ready for dialogue with the United States, and spelt out more clearly the defensive rationale for the build-up of Soviet military power. He also advanced a wide range of proposals for arms limitation, and for regional security negotiations – affecting most areas of the globe. The present Soviet leaders apparently believe that their foreign policy problems are manageable, and that they can rely on

Soviet power to ward off any dangers. They have an almost Burkean conception of politics, seeing it as a compact between the present generation, past generations and generations yet to come. They seem intent on passing on to the next generation of leaders a powerful and secure state, and leaving to them any major choices about the direction of policy.

# CHAPTER SIX

# The Defence Economy

The Soviet state was born in revolution and civil war; and after twenty years of social and political upheaval it was subjected to the test of a terrible war with Germany. Stalin claimed in 1946 that victory over Germany proved that his policies of collectivization and industrialization had been correct, and he proceeded to build up the power of the state again, arguing that it would take at least until 1960 for the Soviet Union to be ready for 'all contingencies'. In 1960, however, the Soviet Union adopted a new military doctrine for the nuclear age and in the years since then has built up its forces to prepare for the contingencies of nuclear war, and to support its foreign policy.

## The Central Policy-Making Bodies

Control of defence policy rests in the hands of the Party leaders. It is in the Politburo that the main lines of policy are determined, the major resource allocation decisions taken, and the most difficult issues resolved. The Politburo normally meets once a week, but in the early 1970s it met in special session on several occasions to consider American arms control proposals.[1] Its role in foreign and defence policy was strengthened in 1973 when the Ministers of Defence and Foreign Affairs and the head of the KGB were included as full members.

The main specialized body for defence policy-making is the Defence Council, which, according to the 1977 Constitution, is a state and not a Party institution. It appears to consist of a handful of Politburo members, including the Minister of Defence; other military and political leaders may be called to attend when necessary. Like the Politburo, the Defence Council is chaired by Brezhnev, who claimed to speak with the authority of that office when he said in October 1979 that the number of medium-range nuclear delivery systems in the Western part of the

Soviet Union had not been increased over the previous ten years. The Defence Council's responsibilities are wide: it deals with 'questions of military development and of strengthening the might and combat readiness of the Soviet Armed Forces'.[2]

The precise relationship between the Defence Council and the Politburo is not clear. The Defence Council may handle detailed matters of policy for which the Politburo has not time, while leaving major issues to that body. Alternatively, it may consider all major issues and make recommendations to the Politburo, in which case it may be an effective instrument for ensuring Brezhnev's domination of defence policy. The constitutional status of the Council, and Brezhnev's position as Chairman of the Presidium of the Supreme Soviet – which decides on the composition of the Council – suggests that the latter role is possible. But there is no reason to suppose that the balance of influence between the Politburo and the Defence Council always remains the same.

The Politburo's work is supported by the apparatus of the Central Committee Secretariat. This has three departments that deal with defence matters. The Main Political Administration, which is a directorate in the Ministry of Defence, and also has the rights of a Central Committee Department, is concerned primarily with the moral and political state of the Armed Forces; the Administrative Organs Department deals mainly with personnel matters; the Department of Defence Industry has responsibility for military production. The Central Committee Secretariat appears to have no department to oversee the work of the Ministry of Defence and the General Staff on professional military matters; in this respect, defence policy differs from other areas.

The Party leadership dominates the defence policy-making arrangements, but the military, by virtue of their professional expertise, play a crucial role too. The Minister of Defence (who was from 1955 to 1976 a professional soldier) sits on the Defence Council, and also chairs the Main Military Council, or Collegium, of the Ministry. This consists of the Minister and his deputies: the Chief of the General Staff, the Commander-in-Chief of the Warsaw Pact, the Chief of the Main Political Administration, the First Deputy Minister for General Affairs, the Commanders-in-Chief of the military services, the Inspector General, the Deputy Ministers for Armament and Electronics, the Chiefs of the Rear Services and Civil Defence, and the Deputy Minister for Construction. The Main Military Council coordinates the activities of the different elements of the Armed Forces, and probably has considerable power in the day-to-day running of the military establishment.[3]

The General Staff is the main repository of professional military expertise, and by Soviet tradition, the 'brain of the Army'. Strategic planning for future operations is the responsibility of the General Staff. According to an article in the General Staff journal *Military Thought*, 'the most important task of the General Staff in preparing for a modern war is the detailed planning of the employment of nuclear weapons by all services of the Armed Forces.'[4] The General Staff also controls military intelligence, organizes the training of the Armed Forces and ensures their combat readiness. It directs the development of military theory through its Military Science Administration, which was set up in the early 1950s. The General Staff is also the main agency through which the political leadership commands the Armed Forces.[5] It may serve in peacetime as the secretariat of the Defence Council. The exact divisions of responsibilities between the General Staff and the main administrations of the Ministry of Defence is not clear. The appointment as Minister of Defence of Ustinov, whose career has been in defence production rather than in the military profession, suggests that the Ministry may concentrate on administration of the military system as a whole.

The role of the Council of Ministers appears to be confined mainly to the planning and management of military research and development (R & D) and production, in line with the general policy laid down by the Politburo. One of the Council's Deputy Chairmen (i.e. a Deputy Premier), L.V. Smirnov, is head of the Military-Industrial Commission, which oversees weapons development and production, but the Commission may in effect be an executive arm of the Defence Council. The Commission does not seem to duplicate the activities of Gosplan (the State Planning Commission), which has a special military department, and may concentrate more on coordinating large-scale military programs than on detailed planning. It probably includes representatives from the Ministry of Defence, Gosplan, the nine defence production ministries and the Central Committee Secretariat.

The development of the Armed Forces has been governed by long-term plans (usually for five years, but sometimes for longer), which define the numbers and types of equipment to be acquired, changes in the organizational structure of the Armed Forces, the missions and roles of the Armed Forces in war, the creation of stocks of arms, *matériel* and other stores, and the training of military manpower and command personnel. These plans appear to be drawn up as follows: the Party leadership gives guidelines for the development of the Armed Forces; in line with these the General Staff coordinates the plans and reconciles the claims of the different branches of the Armed Forces;

the Main Military Council reviews the plans, and the Defence Council or the Politburo makes a final decision.[7]

This process naturally involves a great deal of consultation. It also requires that military and economic plans be coordinated. According to a Soviet textbook,

> coordinating the planning and development of the Armed Forces with military production in the national economy has exceptionally great significance. The appropriate military bodies, together with the agencies of national-economic leadership, work out the principles of a unified military-economic and military-technical policy, coordinate the plans for rearmament and material-technical supply with the plans for the delivery of output by industry and so on. In this the military bodies concentrate their attention on presenting orders to the national economy in good time, on control over the course of fulfilment of the orders, and – in the event of a change in requirements – on rapid correction of the orders.[8]

Gosplan and the other economic agencies must work with the Ministry of Defence and the General Staff in planning defence production. These plans will then be implemented by the production ministries responsible for developing and producing the arms and equipment.

The formal policy-making structure is not very different now from what it was under Stalin, especially during the war with Germany. The Defence Council is modelled on the State Defence Committee, which exercised supreme power in the state during the war, and it may be intended to play a similar role in the event of war. The Main Military Council of the Ministry of Defence would provide the basis for the *Stavka*, the Headquarters of the Supreme High Command, while the General Staff would serve as the chief instrument of command and control.

But the style of policy-making has changed in important ways since Stalin's rule. Stalin dominated, in a ruthless fashion, the Party-State bureaucracy his policies helped to create. His authority in military matters was unquestioned in the latter part of his rule. He took advice, but could ignore it when he wished. He took a detailed part in all aspects of defence policy-making. After the war, for example, he saw Kurchatov almost every day to discuss nuclear weapons development, and played a major part in making decisions about other weapons programs. He also controlled the discussion of military strategy, and barred any assessment of the impact of nuclear weapons on the conduct of war, just as he prevented any critical study of the events of 1941.

Khrushchev's style was different, for even at his most powerful he did not control the policy-making process in the way that Stalin did. Ultimate authority for defence policy still rested with the Party leadership. In his memoirs Khrushchev reports several discussions of specific matters in the Politburo; for example: rejection of a plan from Admiral Kuznetsov (Commander-in-Chief of the Navy) for warship construction; a decision to scrap the Mya-4 *Bison* bomber; and a decision to convert the Tu-95 *Bear* bomber into the Tu-114 civil airliner.[9] But the confused politics of the early 1960 suggests that Khrushchev did not always get his way, as for example in the case of the manpower cuts he proposed in January 1960. Moreover, Stalin's death led to more open discussion about nuclear weapons and the history of the war. Although Khrushchev tried to turn these discussions to his own advantage, he was not always able to impose his own views.

The Brezhnev Politburo has adopted a style of policy-making that is apparently more responsive to the advice of the different elements in the Party-State bureaucracy. Power has been diffused at the centre, and more effort made to base policies on the support of the relevant bureaucracies. In the Soviet Union this change has been described as a shift towards a more scientific form of leadership – an approach that recognizes the claims of professional competence and special expertise. This appears to give professional advice a greater role in decision-making, in military as in other affairs. The greater role for expertise results in part from the increasing complexity of decisions. During the May 1972 summit meeting in Moscow, Brezhnev showed that he had not completely mastered the characteristics of Soviet missiles. And at the final stage in negotiating the Interim Agreement, Smirnov, the head of the Military-Industrial Commission, was brought in to settle the technical details.[10]

A great deal remains unclear about the arrangements for defence policy-making. The existence of the Defence Council was revealed only in May 1976, when Brezhnev was given the rank of Marshal of the Soviet Union; his position as Chairman of the Council was made public at the same time. In October of the following year an article in *Voennyi Vestnik*, the journal of the Ground Forces, mentioned in passing that Brezhnev was Supreme Commander-in-Chief of the Armed Forces; this is the only reference the Soviet press has made to his holding this office.[11]

It is not clear how long the Defence Council has existed, or how long Brezhnev has been Supreme Commander-in-Chief. These arrangements may go back to the late 1960s, or to the early 1970s; or the fact of

Table 6.1:  *Soviet defence expenditure: estimates in billions of rubles*

| | 1955 | 1960 | 1965 | 1970 | 1975 | 1979 | 1980 |
|---|---|---|---|---|---|---|---|
| 1. Official defence budget (current rubles) | 10·7 | 9·3 | 12·8 | 17·9 | 17·4 | 17·2 | 17·1 |
| 2. Official science outlays (current rubles) | | 3·9 | 6·9 | 11·7 | 17·4 | 20·2 | |
| 3. SIPRI (current rubles) | 23·3 | 21·8 | 30 | 42 | 45·4 | 48 | |
| 4. Lee (current rubles) | | | | | | | |
|    (1955 rubles) | 13·5–14·5 | 15·5–16·5 | 25·5–26·5 | 42·5–49 | 66·5–76 | | |
|    (1970 rubles) | 13·5–14·5 | 15·5–16 | 25–26 | 42·5–49 | 71–81 | 99–115 | 108–126 |
| 5. CIA (1970 rubles) | | | | 40–45 | 50–55 | | |
| 6. China (current rubles) | | 19·5 | | 49 | 79 | | |
| 7. British (current rubles) | | | | | 79 | 76–81 | 81–86 |

*Sources*

1.  *Narodnoe Khozyaistvo SSSR*, Moscow: Statistika, various years.
2.  *Ibid.*
3.  Stockholm International Peace Research Institute, *World Armaments and Disarmament. SIPRI Yearbook 1980*, London: Taylor & Francis, Ltd., 180, p. 25. This is a compromise figure, which corresponds neither with the official Soviet figure, nor with the CIA estimate.
4.  W.T. Lee, *The Estimation of Soviet Defense Expenditures 1955–75*, New York: Praeger Publisher, 1977, pp. 78, 115. The 1979 and 1980 figures are taken from U.S. Congress, Permanent Select Committee on Intelligence, House of Representatives, *CIA Estimates of Soviet Defense Spending*, Hearings, September 3, 1980, Washington D.C.: USGPO, 1980, p. 22.
5.  CIA: National Foreign Assessment Center, *Estimated Soviet Defense Spending: Trends and Prospects*, SR 78–10121, June 1978, p. 1. Defence spending is defined to be comparable with U.S. accounts.
6.  *Peking Review*, 28 November 1975, p. 9. The 1975 figure is taken from *Peking Review*, January 1976, as quoted in *The Military Balance 1977–1978*, London: The International Institute for Strategic Studies, 1977, p. 11.
7.  *Statement on the Defence Estimates 1981*, Cmnd 8212, London: HMSO, April 1981, p. 4.

their being announced in 1976 and 1977 may indicate that Brezhnev and the Defence Council were given new responsibilities at the time. Such disclosures are rarely accidental in the Soviet Union. It may therefore be significant that Brezhnev was made Marshal of the Soviet Union, and that his chairmanship of the Defence Council was revealed, less than a month after the death of Marshal Grechko and his replacement as Minister of Defence by Ustinov. Since then the Party's dominant position in defence policy-making has been strongly emphasized, and the defensive rationale for Soviet military power spelled out.

## Soviet Military Expenditures

Apart from some manpower figures quoted by Khrushchev in 1960 and some data made available in connection with arms control negotiations, the Soviet authorities have provided no information about the size of their military effort for any year since 1945.[12] Each year a single figure for the defence budget is published, but this cannot be taken as an indication of what the Soviet Union spends on defence, because it is not clear what this budget heading covers; nor is it clear that it has always covered the same items of expenditure. It is, in any event, far too low to pay for the men and arms that Western governments estimate the Soviet Armed Forces to have. In 1980 the official Soviet defence budget figure was 17·1 billion rubles; the British government estimated Soviet defence expenditure to be between 81 and 86 billion rubles in the same year.[13]

In the absence of trustworthy Soviet figures, Western studies have used two broad approaches to try to estimate the level of Soviet defence spending. The first is to derive a figure from published Soviet economic statistics. Some researchers have taken the Soviet defence budget figure as the basis of their estimates, and have added to it figures from other parts of the budget (e.g. from the 'science' heading) to cover items that may not be included under the 'defence' heading. This procedure may have been valid at one time, but has become less so as the composition of the 'defence' allocation appears to have changed. In the 1970s the Soviet 'defence' heading declined, even though Soviet military power continued to grow, and this suggests that the 'defence' heading has not covered even a specific part of the defence effort in a consistent way.[14]

A different method of using published Soviet statistics is to derive expenditure on weapons procurement by subtracting various items (producer and consumer durables, intermediate products etc.) from the total output of the Machine Building and Metal Working sector; the residual is then taken to be equivalent to military procurement. Other items of military expenditure are estimated from the 'defence' and other headings in the budget. There is nothing to suggest that this approach is wrong, although the actual calculation of the Machine Building and Metal Working residual is fraught with difficulty.[15]

The second main approach to estimating Soviet defence spending is known as the 'direct costing' or 'building block' method. This starts from the physical elements of the Soviet Armed Forces – weapons, manpower, buildings, supplies, operations and maintenance and so on. Where ruble prices are not available, these basic elements are priced in dollars, which are then converted into rubles, if a ruble estimate is desired. For example, the ruble cost of the basic part of a Soviet naval vessel is estimated by first calculating what it would cost to produce that ship in the United States; this dollar cost is then converted into rubles by applying a ruble-to-dollar ratio based on the relative estimated efficiency of Soviet and American shipbuilding.[16]

This approach is open only to Western governments whose intelligence services can provide them with the necessary information. One of its advantages is that it avoids the difficulties associated with Soviet statistics and makes it possible to take account of all defence activities, whether financed from the 'defence' heading or not. Nevertheless, although this approach may be a sound one, it still leaves room for a wide margin of error, particularly in the calculation of ruble-to-dollar ratios. In 1976 the CIA produced revised dollar and ruble estimates of Soviet defence expenditure which raised its earlier estimates from approximately 25 billion rubles to 50 to 60 billion, and from 6–8 per cent of GNP to 11–13 per cent.[17] The CIA revised its estimates for several reasons, one of them being, apparently, that it had covertly obtained information from the Soviet Defence Ministry showing that Soviet spending on weapons procurement in 1970 was between 17 and 18·5 billion rubles, three times as high as the CIA had estimated.[18] The CIA said that one of the chief reasons for its increased estimate was a new assessment of the efficiency of the Soviet defence industry: 'analysis carried out over the past two years . . . clearly indicates that the ruble costs of Soviet weapons and equipment are far higher than previously estimated'.[19] The CIA concluded, for example, that the real ruble costs of producing a major naval vessel were twice as great as had been calculated before.[20]

The CIA's revision of its estimates has not silenced criticism. Some economists have argued that, although the CIA may have the right figure for 1970, it has underestimated the cost of qualitative improvements in Soviet weapons, and that in consequence, its estimate of Soviet defence expenditure in 1980 was too low. These critics contend that there is a consistent downward bias in the CIA's estimates, which springs from the methods used.[21] Other critics have argued that in fact there is an upward bias in the CIA figures, which results in part from not giving due weight to American technological superiority, and that this results in Soviet military expenditure being portrayed as greater than it really is.[22]

When the CIA revised its estimates of Soviet defence spending in 1976 it did not change its assessment of the size and capability of the Soviet Armed Forces; these forces were now seen to cost the Soviet Union twice as much as had previously been thought. Similarly the CIA's critics do not disagree about the size of the Soviet Armed Forces; they lack any independent evidence on the matter. The main disagreement concerns the cost of those forces to the Soviet Union. The technical and methodological aspects of making estimates cannot be examined here. But it should be borne in mind that there must be a wide margin of uncertainty in any of the estimates; the Soviet authorities are successful in hiding their defence expenditures. At the same time, however, this uncertainty cannot obscure the fact that most estimates, derived by whatever means, show Soviet military spending rising since the late 1950s. The estimates of Soviet military spending as a percentage of GNP suggest also that the proportion was lowest in the 1950s. The CIA estimates show this proportion to have remained fairly stable during the 1970s, but other estimates suggest that it has risen.

## The Defence Industry

The basic organizational form of the defence industry – as of the Soviet economy as a whole – was established in the 1930s, during the industrialization drive. At first armaments were produced in enterprises of the People's Commissariat (Ministry) of Heavy Industry. In 1936 a Commissariat of the Defence Industry was established, and in 1939 this in turn was divided into four separate commissariats – for ammunition, armaments, ships and aircraft. Since the war, new ministries have been set up to take charge of the science-based branches of military production. The Ministry of Medium Machine Building was created in 1953, with responsibility for the nuclear weapons program.

Table 6.2: *Western estimates of Soviet defence expenditure as a proportion of GNP (per cent)*

|  | 1955 | 1960 | 1965 | 1970 | 1975 | 1980 |
|---|---|---|---|---|---|---|
| 1. Bergson (current ruble factor cost) | 10·3 |  |  |  |  |  |
|     (1950 ruble factor cost) | 10·7 |  |  |  |  |  |
| 2. Lee (1970 rubles) | 11·5 | 9 | 10 | 12 | 14–15 | 18 |
| 3. CIA (1970 rubles) |  |  |  | 11–13 | 11–13 | 12–14 |

*Sources*
1. A. Bergson, *The Real National Income of Soviet Russia Since 1928*, Cambridge, Mass.: Harvard University Press, 1961, p. 245.
2. William T. Lee, *The Estimation of Soviet Defence Expenditures, 1955–75. An Unconventional Approach*, New York: Praeger Publishers, 1977, p. 98. The figure for 1980 is taken from Lee's testimony in U.S. Senate, Committee on Armed Services, *Soviet Defense Expenditures and Related Programs*, Hearings before the Subcommittee on General Procurement, Washington D.C.: USGPO, 1980, p. 9.
3. CIA: National Foreign Assessment Center, *Estimated Soviet Defense Spending: Trends and Prospects*, SR 78–10121, June 1978, p. i; the 1980 figure is taken from Joint Economic Committee, U.S. Congress, *Allocation of Resources in the Soviet Union and China – 1980*. Hearings before the Subcommittee on Priorities and Economy in Government, Part 6, Washington D.C.: USGPO, 1981, p. 136.

The Ministry of the Radio Industry was set up in 1954 and from it two further ministries have been hived off: those for the Electronics Industry (1961) and for the Communications Equipment Industry (1974). The Ministry of General Machine Building, which is responsible for the development and production of strategic missiles, was established in 1965.

According to the U.S. Defense Intelligence Agency, there are '134 major final assembly plants involved in producing Soviet weapons as end products'.[23] Twenty-four of these produce ground forces *matériel*, twenty-four naval *matériel*, thirty-seven aircraft *matériel*, and forty-nine missile *matériel*. Another 3,500 'individual installations that provide support to these final assembly plants' have been identified.[24] Most of these plants and installations will come under the nine ministries that have primary responsibility for weapons research, development and production. The plants of these ministries also turn out goods for civilian use, and military goods are produced in the factories of ministries not in this group; consequently the defence industry as defined by output is not coextensive with the ministries in the defence industry group. In 1971 Brezhnev told the 24th Party Congress that 42 per cent of the output of defence industry was for civilian purposes, but it is not clear whether he was referring to the defence industry group as a whole, or to the Ministry of the Defence Industry, which is responsible for the production of army *matériel* such as tanks, armoured vehicles, and artillery.[25] According to CIA estimates, one-third of ship-building and aircraft production was civilian in the 1970s.[26]

The defence sector is both an integral part of the Soviet economy, sharing many of its general characteristics, and the highest priority sector in Soviet industry, with special features of its own. Like other production ministries, those in the defence industry have their own research institutes, design bureaus and production plants, and their output is planned and coordinated by higher economic agencies. But the high priority of the defence sector has helped to make it different from the rest of Soviet industry. It has tended to receive the best machinery and instruments. Pay is higher than in civilian production, and the defence industry can offer its workers more benefits – for example, in housing and medical care; the quality of the workers may therefore be higher. High priority is reflected also in the arrangements for day-to-day management. Defence plants have the power to commandeer what they need from civilian industry, and this must be an important advantage in an economy where supply problems are chronic. Economic planning agencies will deal more quickly with requests and orders from the defence industry, and this too must be an advantage in a system where bureaucratic delays can be considerable.[27]

The priority system was established, and remains in existence, to shield the defence industry from shortcomings in the rest of the economy. One consequence of this attempt to protect the defence industry has been, ironically, to encourage a tendency that is found elsewhere in the economy: the pursuit of autarky by ministries, through the creation of supply industries under their own control. This tendency appears to be very strong in the defence industry group. In the 1930s the defence industry commissariats had their own metallurgical base and machine-tool production. In the early 1960s, 90 to 95 per cent of all aviation production (airframes, aeroengines, instruments, avionics) was concentrated in the enterprises of the Ministry of the Aviation Industry. In the mid-1970s the Ministry of the Electronics Industry had to produce hundreds of materials and components it needed because it could not rely on outside suppliers (i.e. on other ministries) to meet its quality requirements.[28] This pattern may show that the defence industry has high priority, since it has been given its own supply industries. But it also shows that the priority system is not wholly effective in ensuring

Table 6.3:   *Ministries in the Defence Industry group*

| Ministry of: | Output |
| --- | --- |
| Aviation Industry | Aircraft and aircraft parts |
| Defence Industry | Conventional Army *matériel* |
| Shipbuilding Industry | Ships |
| Electronics Industry | |
| Radio Industry | Electronic components and equipment |
| Means of Communication | |
| Medium Machine Building | Nuclear weapons |
| General Machine Building | Strategic missiles |
| Machine Building | Ammunition |

*Sources*

Andrew Sheren, 'Structure and Organization of Defense-Related Industries', in Joint Economic Committee, U.S. Congress, *Economic Performance and the Military Burden in the Soviet Union.* A Compendium of Papers Submitted to the Subcommittee on Foreign Policy, Washington D.C.: USGPO, 1970, pp. 123–32. Michael Agursky, *The Research Institute of Machine-Building Technology,* The Hebrew University of Jerusalem: The Soviet and East European Research Center, Soviet Institutions Series Paper No. 8, September 1976, p. 6.

that other branches supply the defence industry with what it needs — otherwise it would not need its own supply industries.

The powerful position of the customer is another important feature of the defence industry. The Ministry of Defence takes part in planning the programs of weapons development and production, and it also exercises considerable control over the execution of those programs. One instrument of Ministry supervision is the system of military representatives in design bureaus and production plants. These have three major functions: to prevent production bottlenecks by speeding up the supply of materials and parts; to supervise the pricing of military products; and to ensure that military production meets quality standards. These representatives give the Armed Forces a degree of consumer power unusual in the Soviet Union.[29]

## Defence Production

The Soviet Union has published no figures for its arms production since 1945. Data have, therefore, to be taken from Western sources, and these are particularly poor for the years from 1945 to 1960.

After the war the Soviet Union made a determined effort to overcome its backwardness in advanced military technologies. It also developed new conventional arms and equipment, and motorized the Ground Forces; by 1954 the cavalry had been disbanded. In the mid-1950s the Armed Forces began to acquire nuclear weapons and other advanced systems as a result of the postwar development programs. Conventional arms production appears to have declined at the same time, alongside cuts in military manpower. Most estimates of Soviet military outlays show the mid-1950s as the period of lowest expenditure. Recent figures from the U.S. Department of Defense suggest that between 1952 and 1958 there was a 25 per cent drop in the estimated dollar cost of Soviet defence activities.[30] (In ruble terms the drop would be smaller because in estimating the dollar cost Soviet troops are costed as though they receive American pay.) But before the end of the decade an upturn took place in defence production. The Seven Year Plan, which began in 1959, included provision for the production of strategic missiles, and perhaps also for an increase in conventional arms production.[31]

The Khrushchev years were a period of upheaval in Soviet military policy. In 1960 a new doctrine was adopted for the nuclear age, and in the 1960s the Soviet Union acquired a large strategic missile force. But major differences of view existed about the forces needed to fight a nuclear war: in particular, there was disagreement about the role of the Ground Forces, and about the kinds of equipment they should have; about the role of bombers – whether, indeed, they had a role; about surface warships. Khrushchev did not think that conventional forces would have a large role in nuclear war.[32] But the available figures do not make it possible to say how far the production of conventional weapons was affected in the early 1960s.

Since 1965 Soviet military policy has enjoyed greater stability, and many of the contentious questions about force structure – for example, about the role of the Ground Forces – were settled by 1967. The major developments in military policy since 1965 have been the attainment of strategic parity with the United States; the build-up along the Chinese frontier; and the more extensive use of military power in the Third World. Soviet forces in Europe have also been extensively modernized. All these developments have required new *matériel*. Table 6.4 gives some figures for weapons production from 1965 to 1980. Production levels have not remained constant for each type of equipment. Annual tank production rose in the late 1960s to a peak of 4,250, and then fell to under 2,500 in 1975, only to rise again to 3,000 in 1980. Fighter

Table 6.4:  *Production of basic types of armament,
1966–1980*

|                                              | 1966               | 1970               | 1975                 | 1980      |
|----------------------------------------------|--------------------|--------------------|----------------------|-----------|
| Tactical aircraft                            | 900[1]             | 850[1]             | 1,250[1]             | 1,300[2]  |
| Helicopters                                  | 350[1]             | 700[1]             | 1,400[1]             | 750[1]    |
| Tanks                                        | 3,100[1]           | 4.250[1]           | 2,250[1]             | 3,000[2]  |
| Armoured vehicles                            | 2,800[3]           | 4,000[3]           | 4,000 +[3]           | 5,500[2]  |
| Artillery                                    | 1,100[3]           | 1,600[3]           | 1,600[3]             | 1,450[2]  |
| Naval shipbuilding (tons displacement)       | annual average[4] 150,000 | | | |

*Sources*
1. Joint Economic Committee, U.S. Congress, *Allocation of Resources in the Soviet Union and China – 1978,* Hearing before the Subcommittee on Priorities and Economy in Government, Pt. 4, Washington, D.C.: USGPO, 1978, pp. 225, 227. The figures in these charts have been deleted for security reasons, but can be filled in with the help of the information given in the sources named in notes 2 and 3 below.
2. Joint Economic Committee, U.S. Congress, *Statement of Maj. Gen. Richard X. Larkin, Dep. Director and Edward M. Collins, Vice Director for Foreign Intelligence, Defense Intelligence Agency,* before the Subcommittee on International Trade, Finance and Security Economics, 8 July 1981, pp. 86–7.
3. *Annual Defense Department Report. FY 1978,* Washington D.C., 1976, p. 27, Chart V-2.
4. *NATO Review,* December 1976, p. 12; for 1966–75.

production was 800 to 900 a year from 1965 to 1970. From 1970 to 1975 it rose to 1,200 a year, and in 1980 it reached 1,300. Yet in spite of fluctuations the overall picture to emerge from U.S. estimates of Soviet weapons production is one of expansion over the fifteen-year period.[33]

This picture of expanding weapons production fits in with the pattern of rising military expenditure to be found in Table 6.1. That is not surprising in the case of the CIA estimates, since they are based, in part, on the figures for weapons production. The cost of arms and equipment is related not only to their quantity, however, but also to their quality. Soviet writings on defence economics acknowledge that the Soviet defence industry, like its counterparts in other countries, faces the problem of rising intergenerational costs. One Soviet textbook lists the reasons for this as follows:

First, the use of critical, costly raw materials, advanced expensive equipment, and large amounts of increasingly expensive electrical energy and electronic equipment; second, the high relative share of expenditures for scientific research and experimental design work, which entails the hiring of a large number of skilled workers and the onetime production of the equipment necessary for these projects; third, the production of military products in small series in peacetime; and fourth, the necessity of putting out the needed type of product in a very short time.[34]

A steady level of military production will become increasingly costly as more complex and expensive systems are produced.

## Arms Transfers

Not all Soviet military production goes to the Soviet Armed Forces. In the 1970s foreign sales came to absorb an increasingly substantial part of the output of the Soviet defence industry. These sales go to two major groups of countries. The first group is the members of the Warsaw Pact and other close allies of the Soviet Union such as Vietnam, North Korea, Mongolia and Cuba. The second group consists of non-Communist 'Less Developed Countries' (LDCs) such as Algeria, Libya and Syria. The Soviet Union has always been the major supplier of arms to the Warsaw Pact countries; in the 1970s its sales to LDCs grew rapidly as the world arms market expanded.

The Soviet Union publishes no data about its arms exports, so that here again foreign estimates have to be used. According to the U.S. Arms Control and Disarmament Agency, between 1974 and 1978 the Soviet Union transferred arms valued at $27 billion, of which $8·5 billion went to the Pact and to other close Soviet allies, and $18 billion went to LDCs.[35] The most striking feature of Soviet arms transfers in the 1970s was the expansion of sales to LDCs. According to CIA figures, the value of Soviet military agreements with LDCs amounted between 1955 and 1959 to $690 million; between 1960 and 1966 to $3,830 million; between 1967 and 1973 to $8,665 million; and between 1974 and 1979 to $34,155 million.[36] Three major developments contributed to this rapid growth: the 1967 and 1973 Middle East Wars, which made it necessary for the Arab countries to reequip their armed forces; Israel's deep penetration raids into Egypt in 1970, which prompted the Soviet Union to start supplying modern weapons to Egypt, and later to other customers; the rise in oil prices in 1973–4, which led the Soviet Union increasingly to seek commercial and financial returns from its arms exports.[37]

From 1974 to 1978 Soviet arms sales (to all customers) amounted to

Table 6.5:   *Production and export of basic types of armament, 1976–mid 1981*

|  | Production | Export | Export/Production |
|---|---|---|---|
| Tanks and SP Assault guns | 17,975 | 7,877 | 44% |
| Field artillery | 7,150 | 17,093 | 239% |
| APC and armoured cars | 28,250 | 9,678 | 34% |
| Naval ships:<br>  major combatants | 64 | 34 | 53% |
| Naval ships:<br>  minor combatants | 292 | 134 | 46% |
| Submarines | 64 | 7 | 11% |
| Combat aircraft | 6,950 | 3,172 | 46% |
| Helicopters | 4,725 | 1,067 | 23% |
| SAMs | 265,000 | 16,041 | 6% |

*Sources*
The production figures are taken from Joint Economic Committee, U.S. Congress, *Statement of Maj. Gen. Richard X. Larkin, Dep. Director and Edward M. Collins, Vice Director for Foreign Intelligence, Defense Intelligence Agency*, before the Subcommittee on International Trade, Finance and Security Economics, 8 July, 1981, pp. 86–7. The figures given there are for 1976–1980. One half of the 1980 production total has been added to make the figures compatible with those for arms exports, which cover 1976 to mid-1981. The export figures are from the U.S. Defense Intelligence Agency, and were released by the office of Congressman Les Aspin.

*Acronyms:*
SP – self-propelled.
APC – armoured personnel carrier.
SAM – surface-to-air missile.

between 12 and 15 per cent of Soviet exports, and were therefore an important element in Soviet foreign trade.[38] But the significance of arms exports for the defence industry can be assessed in more specific terms. U.S. government estimates of Soviet defence spending and arms transfers suggest that from 1974 to 1978 the value of arms exports (measured in domestic rubles) was equivalent to between 16 and 20 per cent of Soviet expenditure on the procurement of weapons for the Soviet Armed Forces. Perhaps one-sixth of total Soviet weapons production in that period was for export or for replacement of equipment that had already been exported.[39]

Exports to LDCs have been absorbing an increasingly high proportion of the output of the Ministry of Defence Industry, which produces tanks, armoured vehicles and artillery, and of the Ministry of the

Aviation Industry. A substantial part of the output of the Ministry of the Shipbuilding Industry is also sold abroad. Between 1967 and 1980 the number of combat aircraft exported to LDCs was equal to one-third of the number produced by the Soviet Union. The same is true of tanks. The figure for artillery is much higher, while that for armoured vehicles is lower, and that for helicopters is much lower.[40] These figures should not be taken to indicate that exports are drawn from current production. It is not possible to tell from the available data what numbers of which models have been exported. Western studies do indicate, however, that in the 1970s the Soviet Union sold its modern weapons to LDCs, whereas in the 1950s and 1960s it had exported mainly older models; in some cases the LDCs have received the latest Soviet models before the Warsaw Pact forces.[41]

The Soviet Union has come increasingly to insist on payment in hard currency. Although Soviet weapons appear still to be comparatively cheap, this marks a change from the practice of the 1950s and 1960s when the Soviet Union offered large discounts, repayment periods of ten years at 2 per cent interest, and accepted local commodities in repayment. The change in policy has come partly in response to the increased revenues of the oil-producing states, some of which – Iraq, Libya and Algeria – have been among the largest Soviet customers.[42] But even Ethiopia, which is not a wealthy state, was, it seems, asked to pay for its Soviet arms in hard currency.[43] The net result of this policy has been to improve the Soviet balance of trade. It has been estimated that between 1971 and 1980, 65 per cent of Soviet arms sales to LDCs were for foreign currency, and brought in $21 billion in hard currency.[44] Hard currency earnings may continue to grow, given the big jump in the volume of agreements concluded between 1974 and 1979.

Soviet arms transfers to LDCs may be primarily political in purpose, but they do have two economic advantages, and one military one, for the Soviet Union. First, they reduce the unit cost of some types of equipment by making possible longer production runs, and they keep productive capacity employed. Second, they have become an increasingly important source of hard currency at a time when hard currency earnings from other sources, e.g. from oil exports, may be about to decline (though only in 1973 did they amount to more than 10 per cent of Soviet hard currency earnings). Third, equipment that is exported may be used in battle and thus provide information about its performance in combat conditions. It is not clear how far the defence industry has been adapted to meet the demand for arms sales, though overall production plans must take account of the export market as well as of the needs of the Soviet Armed Forces. Recent expansion of tank and aircraft production facilities may be partly a response to the increase in arms transfers to other countries.[45]

## Security and Secrecy

The organs of state security have played an important role in the Soviet defence economy. In the 1930s they were responsible for the security of plants producing military equipment, and towards the end of the decade they helped to run the special shops that were set up to prepare the way for military production in civilian industry. The secret police also ran a network of design bureaus in which prisoners, condemned as enemies of the Soviet state, designed and developed weapons for the defence of that state. Beria, as we have seen, was in charge of nuclear weapons development, and between 1945 and 1953 half of atomic energy research was done in special prison institutes.[46]

The secret police's scientific empire was disbanded after Beria's fall in 1953. The KGB still plays an important role in the defence sector, however. It is responsible for the security and secrecy of military R & D and of production (and also for the handling and storage of nuclear weapons). The KGB controls communications within and between institutions engaged in military R & D and production. Each closed institution has a 'first department' which is run by the KGB. This checks on the reliability of all employees, and controls access to all classified information.[47]

No one who tries to examine the Soviet defence economy can fail to be struck by the secrecy in which it is shrouded. This secrecy is justified by the need to prevent hostile powers from gaining information about the Soviet military effort. No doubt it helps to serve this end. But the secrecy must be understood in its domestic context too. In 1939 Stalin defended the activities of the 'punitive and intelligence' organs of the Soviet state by referring to the need to defend the Soviet Union against the capitalist states.[48] But the activities of those organs from 1936 to 1938 greatly weakened the ability of the Soviet Union to defend itself. The purge of the military, weapons designers and defence industry managers can hardly be explained by reference to the external threat, since it actually weakened the Soviet ability to meet that threat. The same point can be made about the secrecy of the post-Stalin years. The fact that a great deal of information about the Soviet military effort which is available abroad (mainly from Western intelligence services) is not allowed to be published inside the Soviet Union, suggests that it is not only the desire to keep foreign governments in ignorance that lies at the basis of Soviet secrecy.

The high degree of secrecy is to be explained by reference not only to the foreign threat, or to the traditions of Russian secrecy (strong though those are), but also to the priority given to defence. Weber remarked that 'every bureaucracy seeks to increase the superiority of the professionally informed by keeping their knowledge and intentions secret'.[49] The General Staff is anxious to protect its claim to professional expertise by discouraging civilian institutions from discussing details of current policy; in this way reasoned criticism can be kept to a minimum. Secrecy helps the General Staff to maintain its monopoly of expertise. (The military have also complained about the tendency of Party leaders to acquire distinguished but retrospective military careers for themselves, since these have been used to bolster their claims to military expertise.)[50]

The secrecy that surrounds defence production helps to buttress its priority by preventing criticism of the efficiency of the defence industry. Khrushchev complained in 1963 that 'because the production of defence industry enterprises is secret, shortcomings in the work of such enterprises is closed to criticism . . . The defence industry is coping successfully with creating and producing modern weapons. But these tasks could have been carried out more successfully and at a lower cost.'[51] Secrecy makes it possible for the defence industry to fend off claims from civilian industry for scarce materials and products. Resources can be commandeered from civilian industry merely by saying that they are needed for defence purposes; secrecy will make detailed justification unnecessary. Finally, the compartmentalization of knowledge and information in the defence sector reinforces the centralized system of policy-making, because only those at the top have a full picture of what is going on, and hence the power of control and initiative.

Secrecy is not merely an accidental feature of the Soviet defence economy, but an inherent element in its mode of operation.

## Conclusion

The evidence of this chapter suggests the following picture of what has come to be known as the 'Soviet military build-up'. Military expenditures have risen steadily since 1959, after a period in which they had dropped or held steady. This rise started with the Seven Year Plan for 1959 to 1965. 1959 was the year in which deployment of the SS-4 MRBM began and the Strategic Rocket Forces were established as a separate service. By 1965 about one thousand strategic missiles (nearly 750 M/IRBMs, 224 ICBMs and 100 or so SLBMs) had been deployed. In 1960 Khrushchev announced that he would reduce the Armed Forces by one-third, and indicated that he wished to curtail the development and production of some kinds of conventional weapons; perhaps he hoped in this way to restrain the rising trend of military expenditure.

Before October 1964, however, an expansion of ICBM deployment appears to have been planned, in response to the Kennedy Administration's strategic weapons program, and to the collapse of Khrushchev's missile diplomacy in the Cuban missile crisis. It is not clear exactly when the decision was taken to embark on the major ICBM build-up, but it may have coincided with the economic reorganization that took place in March 1963. This reorganization was evidently forced on Khrushchev by his colleagues. It was at this time that Khrushchev complained about inefficiency of the defence sector.[52]

After Khrushchev's removal from office in October 1964, the Soviet Union pressed ahead with the strategic arms build-up. It also decided to increase its forces along the frontier with China. The military effort in the Far East grew rapidly until 1972, then levelled off, only to rise again in about 1978. According to the CIA, the Soviet forces facing China absorbed an average of 10 per cent of Soviet military expenditure (in rubles) each year from 1966 to 1979.[53]

By 1967 many of the strategic issues that had preoccupied Soviet military thought in the early 1960s were resolved. The role of the Ground Forces was clarified: in 1967 a new Commander-in-Chief was appointed (the post had been abolished in 1964), and the Ground Forces began to prepare for non-nuclear operations in Europe. The invasion of Czechoslovakia in 1968 demonstrated the role of the Ground Forces in maintaining the Soviet position in Eastern Europe. Similarly, by 1967 it was accepted that bombers, armed with air-to-surface missiles, did have a role, especially in attacking mobile targets which missiles could not easily strike. By 1967 it was accepted that the surface Navy had an important role to play as an instrument of Soviet foreign policy. The June War of 1967 marked the beginning of a new and more active phase in the Soviet use of military power as an instrument of diplomacy. When Marshal Grechko took over as Defence Minister in April 1967, Khrushchev's hopes of matching the growth of nuclear arms with a

Table 6.6: *Comparisons of NATO and Warsaw Pact expenditure and manpower*

|  | NATO | | Warsaw Pact | |
|---|---|---|---|---|
| **1. IISS (millions of current dollars)** | *1975:* | | | |
| | USA – | 88,983 | USSR – | 124,000 |
| | Other NATO – | 60,471 | Other Pact – | 7,937 |
| | Total | 149,454 | Total | 131,937 |
| | China – | n.a. | | |
| | Japan – | 4,620 | | |
| | *1980:* | | | |
| | USA – | 142,700 | USSR – | 214,050 |
| | Other NATO – | 98,186 | Other Pact – | 16,670 |
| | Total | 240,886 | Total | 230,720 |
| | China – | 56,941 | | |
| | Japan – | 8,960 | | |
| **2. SIPRI (millions of 1978 dollars)** | *1976:* | | | |
| | USA – | 110,229 | USSR – | 99,800 |
| | Other NATO – | 74,699 | Other Pact – | 10,530 |
| | Total | 184,928 | Total | 110,330 |
| | China – | 40,300 | | |
| | Japan – | 7,899 | | |
| | *1979:* | | | |
| | USA – | 110,145 | USSR – | 105,700 |
| | Other NATO – | 81,728 | Other Pact – | 12,256 |
| | Total | 191,873 | Total | 117,956 |
| | China – | 44,200 | | |
| | Japan – | 9,516 | | |
| **3. Men under arms** | *1975:* | | | |
| | USA | – 2,130,000 | USSR | – 3,575,000 |
| | Other NATO | – 2,944,300 | Other Pact | – 1,064,000 |
| | Total | 5,070,300 | Total | 4,639,000 |
| | *1980:* | | | |
| | USA | – 2,050,000 | USSR | – 3,663,000 |
| | Other NATO | – 2,847,000 | Other Pact | – 1,101,000 |
| | Total | 4,897,200 | Total | 4,764,000 |

*Sources*
1. *The Military Balance 1981–1982*, London: The International Institute for Strategic Studies, 1981, pp. 112, 113.\*
2. Stockholm International Peace Research Institute, *World Armaments and Disarmament. SIPRI Yearbook 1980*, London: Taylor and Francis Ltd., 1980, pp. 19, 21.
3. *The Military Balance 1981–1982*, pp. 112, 113.

\* The IISS uses the CIA estimate of Soviet defence expenditure.

reduction in conventional arms had been dashed. The need for balanced forces has been a major theme in Soviet military writing since the late 1960s.[54]

According to Western estimates, Soviet military expenditure continued to grow during the early 1970s, the most intense period of detente. This should not be surprising, perhaps, in view of the Soviet argument that detente resulted from the growth of Soviet power, including military power. Soviet strategic weapons programs continued after the SALT Agreements of 1972, within the limits allowed by the Interim Agreement. Forces in Eastern Europe were increased, not reduced, perhaps to make it clear that the Soviet determination to dominate Eastern Europe would not weaken as a result of detente. From the mid-1970s the Soviet Union began to pursue a more active policy in the Third World. There seems to have been some slackening of the rate of growth of military expenditure in 1976 and 1977, the first two years of the Tenth Five Year Plan, but it is not clear whether this was a sign that policy was changing, or merely a result of the timing of weapons procurement programs.[55] In any event, Soviet expenditure began to rise again in 1978. Since then the Soviet Union's military-political environment has begun to look more threatening, and expenditures have continued to rise.

Two general points are suggested by this broad outline of the Soviet military build-up. The first is that it cannot properly be considered in isolation from the changing military-political environment. The build-up initiated in 1959 has not been a single, undifferentiated process. The nuclear build-up has been supplemented by other elements: the military confrontation with China; the changes in strategic thinking and the role of conventional forces; the increasing use of military force as an instrument of diplomacy. In other words, several different elements have overlaid one another in this build-up.

Secondly, the standard comparison made in the West between Soviet and U.S. expenditure is not an appropriate one for understanding how the Soviet leaders view the situation. The United States's allies in NATO are economically and militarily more powerful than the Soviet allies in the Warsaw Pact. Western sources that claim that the Soviet Union outspends the United States by 50 per cent (in dollar terms) on defence also show that NATO has been spending more than the Warsaw Pact, and that NATO has had more men under arms. Moreover, since 1966 the Soviet leaders have directed a part of their defence effort (15–20 per cent in dollar terms, according to the CIA) towards strengthening their position vis-à-vis China. The choices that face the Soviet leaders can be understood only in this broader context.

CHAPTER SEVEN
# Military Technology

Engels wrote in *Anti-Dühring* that

> nothing is more dependent on economic conditions than the army and
> navy. Armament, military structure and organization, tactics and
> strategy, depend primarily on the existing level of production and on
> communications. It is not the 'free creations of the intellect' of gener-
> als of genius that have revolutionized things here, but the invention of
> better weapons and changes in the human material, the soldiers; at the
> very most, the part played by generals of genius is limited to adapting
> methods of fighting to the new weapons and fighting men.[1]

In the same work Engels went on to note how the advent of gunpowder
and firearms had revolutionized the methods of warfare and the relationships of political power; yet these innovations, he wrote, were 'a
step forward in industry, that is, an economic advance'[2], thus illustrat-
ing how warfare could be transformed by technological change.

From the history of infantry Engels drew the moral that 'the whole
organization and method of warfare, and along with these victory and
defeat, prove to be dependent on material, that is, economic conditions; on the human material and the armaments material, and therefore on the quality and quantity of the population and on technical
development.'[3] Nor was Engels alone in this view, for Marx, after read-
ing the article 'Army' that Engels had written for the New American
Cyclopedia, wrote to him that the history of the army brought out
more clearly than anything else the dependence of social relations on
the productive forces. And some years later he exclaimed in a letter to
Engels: 'Is our theory that the *organization of labour* is determined by
the *means of production* confirmed anywhere more splendidly than in
the man-slaughtering industry?'[4] Lenin wrote that 'military tactics
depend on the level of military technology – Engels was the first to
chew over this truth and put it in the mouths of Marxists.'[5]

## The Military R & D Effort

Engels's comments in *Anti-Dühring* were much quoted in the late 1920s when the Soviet Union began to build the economic foundation of its military power. Starting from a weak base, the Soviet Union soon achieved considerable success. Before the war with Germany, large numbers of weapons were produced, some of which – the T-34 tank, for example – were of high quality. But the designers had to take account of the technological level of Soviet industry in creating new weapons. The aircraft designer Tupolev said that 'the country needs aircraft like black bread. You can offer pralines, cakes and so on, but there's no point – there aren't the ingredients to make them out of.'[6] If Soviet aircraft lagged in quality behind their Western counterparts, this could be compensated for by producing them in quantity: 'to hell with it', said Tupolev, 'we'll take them in quantity'. Tupolev did urge, however, that experimental work be done on aircraft which would represent major technological advances.[7]

The war with Germany reinforced the lesson that what were important were designs that were easy and cheap to produce in mass quantities. The war also showed that military technology was changing, and that was why Stalin set up the programs to develop nuclear weapons, rockets, radar and jet propulsion. The results of these programs became evident in the 1950s and ushered in the 'contemporary revolution in military affairs' – the Soviet term for the changes in technology, strategy, force structure and training caused by the development of rockets and nuclear weapons.

In the 1930s and 1940s, the Soviet Union acquired a good deal of military technology from abroad.[8] In the early 1930s models of foreign weapons were imported and used as the basis for Soviet designs. Technical assistance agreements were concluded with foreign companies to help develop the defence industry. Between 1941 and 1945 the Soviet Union received a major infusion of foreign technology from its allies and, more importantly, from defeated Germany. It is difficult to say precisely what contribution foreign technology has made to Soviet military power, but it is clear that it was important for the weapons development programs Stalin launched at the end of the war. Since the late 1940s the opportunities for obtaining foreign military technology have been reduced by the export restrictions adopted by Western governments. Technical information can be acquired from the foreign press, and by espionage, but these channels are likely to be less efficient at transferring technology than imports or technical assistance

Table 7.1: *Estimates of Soviet military R & D outlays (billions of rubles)*

| | 1960 | 1965 | 1970 | 1975 | 1980 |
|---|---|---|---|---|---|
| 1. Total 'science' outlays (current rubles) | 3·9 | 6·9 | 11·7 | 17·4 | 20·2 (1979) |
| 2. Nimitz (current rubles) | 1·6−2 | 2·6−3·3 | 3·3−4·8 (1968) | | |
| 3. CIA (1970 rubles) | | 7−10 (1967) | 8−11·25 | 10−13·75 | 10·6−14·5 (1977) |
| 4. Lee (1970 rubles) | 2·9−4·6 | 4·7−7·7 | 7·5−12·4 | 11·3−18·6 | 14·1−23·2 |
| 5. British (current rubles) | | | | | 16·2−17·2 |

*Sources*

1. L. Nolting, *Sources of Financing the Stages of the Research, Development and Innovation Cycle in the USSR*, Foreign Economic Reports no. 3, US Department of Commerce, Washington D.C., 1973, p. 10; *Narodnoe Khozyaistvo SSSR*, Moscow: Statistika, various years. These figures cover both current and capital expenditure.
2. N. Nimitz, *The Structure of Soviet Outlays on R & D in 1960 and 1968*, R−1207−DDRE, Santa Monica: Rand Corporation, June 1974, p. vii. The figures cover defence and space R & D; they do not cover capital investment.
3. CIA: National Foreign Assessment Center, *Estimated Soviet Defense Spending: Trends and Prospects*, SR 78 10121, June 1978, pp. ii, 1, 2. The figures are derived as follows: the lower end of the range is one-fifth of the lower end of the estimate for overall defence spending; the higher end is one-quarter of the higher estimate of defence spending. I have used here only defence spending as defined for comparison with U.S. accounts.
4. William T. Lee, *The Estimation of Soviet Defense Expenditures, 1955−75. An Unconventional Approach*, New York: Praeger Publishers, 1977, p. 294. The 1980 figure is taken from Permanent Select Committee on Intelligence, U.S. House of Representatives, *CIA Estimates of Soviet Defense Spending*, Hearings, 3 September 1980, Washington D.C.: USGPO, 1980, p. 22. The higher estimates are derived by adding 30 per cent to estimated Soviet R & D expenditures to allow for suspected understatements in the figures. Lee's estimates cover military and space R & D. They also cover capital investment in R & D plant.
5. *Statement on the Defence Estimates 1981*, Cmnd. 8212, London: HMSO, April 1981, p. 4.

agreements. Consequently the Soviet Union has been forced to rely more on its own efforts.

The Soviet Union does not reveal what resources it devotes to military R & D. The output of the military R & D effort can be seen in the new and improves weapons that are developed, but the inputs are a closely guarded secret. The first problem is to estimate total R & D expenditures; here there are difficulties in deciding precisely what the

Soviet figures cover. A further problem arises in establishing the proportion of the total effort that goes to military purposes. Estimates range from 40 to 80 per cent. The latter figure appears too high in view of the scale of Soviet civilian R & D. 50 per cent seems a more plausible figure, though that may have changed over time, with the military proportion falling as civilian R & D has expanded.[9]

Some estimates of Soviet military R & D expenditure are given in Table 7.1. It is clear from the range of estimates that there is considerable uncertainty about the size of the military R & D effort. The CIA estimates that between 1967 and 1977 Soviet military R & D accounted for 20 to 25 per cent of defence spending, and was equal to 40 to 50 per cent of outlays on military equipment.[10] In the United States these proportions are about half: 10 to 12 per cent of the total military budget, and 25 to 30 per cent of the funds available for acquisition. Even with the Soviet stress on the importance of science and technology, these seem to be very high proportions to sustain over such a long period. The CIA acknowledges that its figures for military R & D are the least reliable part of its estimate of Soviet defence spending.

Perhaps the most that can be said is that the Soviet military R & D effort is large, and that it has expanded greatly since the war – just as the overall R & D effort has done. From 1955 to 1960 the number of scientists and engineers engaged in R & D grew at a rate of 9·6 per cent a year; from 1960 to 1965 the rate of growth was 11·7 per cent a year. The rate of growth dropped to 2·1 per cent a year from 1975 to 1978. By 1978, according to the best Western estimate, 828,100 scientists and engineers were engaged in R & D in the Soviet Union.[11] It is possible that as many as half of these were working to develop new weapons and military equipment. The rate of growth of R & D spending shows a similar pattern. That too has slowed down considerably, and it seems likely, therefore, that the rapid expansion of the military R & D effort has come to an end too.

## The Level of Technology

Borrowing from the West was a rational policy for the Soviet Union to pursue in the 1930s, but it carried two dangers: that the country might fall into dependence on the capitalist world, or that it might find itself merely imitating the weapons designs of other countries. Neither dependence nor imitation were acceptable innovation strategies for the Soviet Union. Soviet military-technological policy has been offensive in the sense that (until recently, at any rate) its declared goal has been to attain military-technical superiority over potential enemies. According to the entry on 'military-technical superiority' in the *Soviet Military Encyclopedia*, 'Soviet military doctrine . . . gives a program of actions for ensuring military-technical superiority over the armed forces of probable enemies.'[12] But this goal has not been easy to attain, and in practice Soviet policy has often (though not always) been defensive, in the sense of countering or assimilating innovations made elsewhere. The rhetoric of Soviet innovation is important insofar as it expresses a determination not to be caught in a relationship of inferiority to potential enemies. But this rhetoric should not be taken in isolation from actual performance.

Most studies show that the technological level of Soviet industry is lower than that of Western industry. The most comprehensive analysis of Soviet technology, which looked at a range of technologies from the early 1950s to the early 1970s, found that 'in most of the technologies . . . studied there is no evidence of a substantial diminution of the technological gap between the USSR and the West in the past 15–20 years, either at the prototype/commercial application stages or in the diffusion of advanced technologies.'[13] The Soviet Union tended to perform better in traditional areas such as electric power transmission, and in the iron and steel and machine-tool industries. Soviet performance was less good in the more advanced, science-based branches such as computers, chemicals and industrial process control instruments.

A similar picture of Soviet technological backwardness emerges from the most recent assessments of the U.S. Department of Defense. In 1980 the United States was held to lead the Soviet Union in fifteen of 'the twenty most important basic technology areas', and to be equal in the other five. In 1982 the United States was estimated to lead in fourteen of these areas, to tie in four, and to lag in two. (The areas are not identical in the two years – see table 7.2). The methodology behind these assessments is not clear, but the general picture to emerge both from the most comprehensive open study and from official U.S. assessments is that the Soviet technological base is weaker than that of the United States, and of the West in general.

The picture is somewhat different when one turns to military technology. The two case studies of tanks and ICBMs in the survey of Soviet technology from the early 1950s to the early 1970s offer some support for the view that in the Soviet Union military technology is at a higher level than civilian technology.[14] In the traditional field of tanks, Soviet performance was not markedly better than in traditional civilian

Table 7.2:  *Relative US/USSR standing in the most important basic technology areas (US DOD assessment)*

| Basic Technologies | 1980 US Superior | 1980 US–USSR Equal | 1980 USSR Superior | 1982 US Superior | 1982 US–USSR Equal | 1982 USSR Superior |
|---|---|---|---|---|---|---|
| Aerodynamics/fluid dynamics | | X | | | X | |
| Automated control | X | | | X | | |
| Conventional warhead (including chemical explosives) | | | | | | X |
| Computer | ←X | | | X | | |
| Directed energy | | X | | | X | |
| Electro-optical sensor (incl. IR) | X | | | X→ | | |
| Guidance and navigation | X→ | | | X→ | | |
| Hydro-acoustic | X | | | | | |
| Intelligence sensor | X | | | | | |
| Manufacturing/ production | X | | | X | | |
| Materials (light weight, high strength) | X→ | | | | ←X | |
| Microelectronic materials and integrated circuit manufacture | ←X | | | X | | |
| Non-acoustic submarine detection | | X | | | | |
| Nuclear warhead | | X | | | X | |
| Optics | X→ | | | X→ | | |
| Propulsion (aerospace) | X→ | | | X→ | | |
| Power sources (mobile) | | | | | | X |
| Radar sensor | X→ | | | | X | |
| Signal processing | X | | | X→ | | |
| Software | X | | | X | | |
| Stealth (signature reduction technology | | | | X | | |
| Submarine detection (including silencing) | | | | X→ | | |
| Telecommunications | X | | | X | | |

industries. In ICBM development, however, the Soviet Union does appear to have done better than in the advanced, science-based civilian technologies. Soviet designers have been able, working from a lower technological base, to create powerful and effective weapons. This suggests that the processes of innovation are more effective in the defence sector than in civilian industry, but does not support the view that the defence sector turns out technology of a qualitatively different level.

At the same time, the two case studies suggested that the level of military technology is not as high as in the advanced capitalist countries, when measured in terms of major technological innovations and their diffusion through the stocks of weapons. These studies did not support the view that the Soviet Union has been catching up steadily with the United States in military technology. A more complex picture emerges in which weapons development on each side is influenced by what the other is doing.

Two case studies cannot give a picture of the whole field of military technology, which, after all, accounts for about 50 per cent of Soviet R & D as a whole. But the results are compatible with the conclusions of studies done by United States government agencies. In 1976 the CIA told Congress that 'although some Soviet weapons systems have capabilities that exceed those of U.S. systems in such things as range, these are the result of design choices and do not reflect a higher state of

*Notes*

1. This table is intended to provide a valid vase for comparing *overall* US and USSR *basic* technology, not the technology level in deployed military systems.
2. The technologies selected have the potential for significantly changing the military balance in the next 10 or 20 years. The technologies are not static; they are improving or have the potential for significant improvement.
3. The arrows denote that the relative technology level is changing significantly in the direction indicated.
4. The judgements represent averages within each basic technology area.

*Sources*

The table for 1980 is taken from *The FY 1981 Department of Defense Program for Research, Development and Acquisition*. Statement by the Honorable William J. Perry, Under Secretary of Defense Research and Engineering to the 96th Congress, Second Session, 1980, in US House of Representatives, *Research and Development. Title II*, Hearings before the Committee on Armed Forces, Washington D.C.: USGPO, 1980, p. 82. The 1982 table is taken from *The FY 1983 Department of Defense Program for Research, Development and Acquisition*. Statement by the Honorable Richard D. DeLauer, Under Secretary of Defense, Research and Engineering, to the 97th Congress, Second Session, 1982, p. II–21.

Table 7.3:    *Relative US/USSR technological levels in Deployed Military Systems (US DOD assessment)*

| Deployed system | 1980 | | | 1982 | | |
|---|---|---|---|---|---|---|
| | US Superior | US–USSR Equal | USSR Superior | US Superior | US–USSR Equal | USSR Superior |
| *Strategic* | | | | | | |
| ICBM | | X | | | X | |
| SSBN/SLBM | X→ | | | | | |
| SSBN | | | | | X | |
| SLBM | | | | X→ | | |
| Bomber | X→ | | | X | | |
| SAMs | | | X | | | X |
| BMD | | | X | | | X |
| Anti-Satellite | | | X | | | X |
| Cruise missile | | | | X | | |
| *Tactical Land Forces* | | | | | | |
| SAMs (including naval) | | X | | | X | |
| Tanks | | | ←X | | X | |
| Artillery | X→ | | | | X | |
| Infantry combat vehicles | | | X | | | X |
| Anti-tank guided missiles | | X | | | X | |
| Attack helicopters | X→ | | | | X | |
| Chemical warfare | | | X | | | X |
| Theatre ballistic missiles | | X | | | X | |
| *Air Forces* | | | | | | |
| Fighter/attack aircraft | X | | | X→ | | |
| Air-to-air missiles | X | | | X | | |
| PGM | X | | | X→ | | |
| Airlift | X | | | X | | |
| *Naval forces* | | | | | | |
| SSNs | | X | | | X | |
| Anti-submarine warfare | X→ | | | X | | |
| Sea-based air | X→ | | | X | | |
| Surface combatants | | X | | | X | |
| Cruise missile | | X | | | X→ | |
| Mine warfare | | | X | | | X |
| Amphibious assault | X→ | | | X | | |

Table 7.3 (Cont.)

| Deployed system | 1980 | | | 1982 | | |
|---|---|---|---|---|---|---|
| | US Superior | US–USSR Equal | USSR Superior | US Superior | US–USSR Equal | USSR Superior |
| $C^3I$ | | | | | | |
| Communications | X→ | | | | X | |
| Command & control | | X | | | X | |
| Electronic counter measures | | X | | | X | |
| Surveillance and reconnaissance | X→ | | | X→ | | |
| Early warning | X→ | | | X→ | | |

*Notes*
1. These are comparisons of system technology level only, and are not necessarily a measure of military effectiveness. The comparisons are not dependent on scenario, tactics, quantity, training or other operational factors. Systems farther than one year from IOC (Initial Operational Capability) are not considered.
2. The arrows denote that the relative technology level is changing significantly in the direction indicated.

*Sources*
As for table 7.2, pp. 83 and II–22.

*Acronyms:*
ICBM – Intercontinental Ballistic Missile
SSBN – Ballistic Missile Submarine, Nuclear
SLBM – Submarine-Launched Ballistic Missile
SAM – Surface-to-Air Missile
BMD – Ballistic Missile Defence
PGM – Precision Guided Munition
SSN – Submarine, Nuclear
$C^3I$ – Command, Control, Communications and Intelligence

technology'.[15] In the following year the Director of the CIA testified that 'while virtually all of the Soviet inventory weapons fall within U.S. production technology, the Soviets simply do not have the technology required to produce many of the U.S. weapons nor could they produce close substitutes'.[16] In the same Hearings, the CIA Director made an ambiguous remark which implied that as much as 30 per cent of American military technology was beyond the technological capacity of the Soviet Union to produce.[17]

A similar picture emerges from the Department of Defense assessment of the relative US/USSR technological level in Deployed Military Systems (Table 7.3). Here the United States is shown to enjoy a general lead, although the lead is smaller than in the comparison of basic technology areas. This points to the success of the Soviet acquisition process in creating effective weapons on the basis of a generally lower technological level in industry.

## The Weapons Acquisition Process

The two main elements in the weapons acquisition process are the defence industry ministries, which design, develop and produce the equipment, and the Ministry of Defence, which places orders, supervises development and production, conducts acceptance trials, and assimilates the final products. The whole process takes place under the direction of the central policy-making bodies which have played, as we have seen, a crucial role in initiating and expediting high-priority weapons programs.[18]

Like other industrial ministries in the Soviet Union, each of the defence industry ministries controls production plants where weapons, subsystems and components are produced; research institutes which engage in applied research both in weapons and in production technology; and design bureaus which design and develop weapons and major subsystems, as well as production technology. The research institutes and design bureaus are administered by a technical administration which is responsible for overall R & D policy in the ministry. A scientific-technical council, which includes the ministry's leading scientists, engineers, administrators, and perhaps consultants from outside (for example, from the Academy of Sciences), advises the minister on R & D policy.

From the point of view of weapons development, the important institutions are the research institutes and the design bureaus. The former are often large, well-equipped organizations, with a considerable reputation and directed by leading scientists; a good example is the Central Aerohydrodynamics Institute (TsAGI) of the Ministry of the Aviation Industry. Applied research in the relevant areas is concentrated in such institutes. The design bureaus, like the institutes, specialize in either weapons or production technology. In some cases, especially in such traditional areas as artillery and armour, the bureaus are attached to series production plants. In other fields, notably aerospace, they are independent organizations with factories of their own for producing prototypes. In very advanced or new areas of technology the research institutes and design bureaus may be joined together in one organization with production facilities of its own. The pattern of organization is thus not uniform throughout the defence sector.

In spite of this lack of uniformity, some general features can be pointed to in the standard operating procedure of the weapons acquisition process. First, applied research is by and large institutionally separate from design and development. The funding of applied research does not appear to depend directly on specific equipment orders, although it will depend in a more general way on the importance that a particular area is seen to have for weapons development. Similarly, military production seems not to be as subject to fluctuations as in the West, so that the design bureau is supported by a steady applied research effort, and in turn serves a steady rate of military production. This stability is relative, of course, and does not appear to have existed during the turbulent years from 1955 to 1965.

Second, the role of the designer is crucial, for it is his task to try to match foreign weapons while working from a lower technological base. The importance of the chief designers is underlined by the fame they enjoy (for example, Yakovlev, Mikoyan, Tupolev, the aircraft designers, and Korolev and Yangel', the rocket designers) – though sometimes their names have remained secret during their lifetimes. The work of the designers is constrained in a number of ways: by design procedures which the research institutes lay down in handbooks; by the norms that the ministry sets for the use of scarce materials and the control it exercises over their allocation; and by the Ministry of Defence, which has representatives in the bureaus to see to it that the requirements which have been agreed upon are adhered to. These constraints will encourage standardized design procedures.

Third, the designer, when faced with a new requirement, is likely to try to meet it with what is to hand (though that may, of course, not prove possible). There are various reasons for this. It may be too troublesome to try to remove the constraints imposed by other agencies. Because supply problems are chronic in the Soviet economy (even if less severe in the defence sector), a design that depends on completion of a new or difficult order by another ministry may well expose itself to the risk of failure. In this way commonality in the use of subsystems and components will be encouraged. The designer may well be innovative in his use of existing technologies (for example, in applying the 'cold launch' technique in ICBMs), but he is unlikely to want to push for major innovation in component technologies, unless absolutely necessary. The separation of applied research from development suggests that the designer will turn to the research institute and take what is available, rather than wait for something new; because development programs are not the way in which funds are acquired for applied research, there is no incentive to go for fancy designs. These factors may help to explain the practice of getting a design into production and then modifying it as new components and subsystems become available (hence the proliferation of different models). They might also be thought to encourage evolutionary rather than revolutionary change from one generation to the next. If, however, a large applied research effort is under way, it may provide the basis for major intergenerational changes in design and technology.

Fourth, competition between design bureaus has been a common, though by no means universal, practice in the development of new weapons, especially of aircraft and missiles. Two or more design bureaus may be given the same requirements and asked to produce designs; the Ministry of Defence then selects the best design for development. This gives the customer a degree of choice unusual in the Soviet economy. In a limited number of cases, competition may extend to the development of prototypes, with the choice made only after weapons trials. In some instances weapons that appear to be competitive developments have gone into production. It may be, however, that the redundancy here is more apparent than real, and that the weapons designs either started with different missions or acquired new missions during the acquisition process.

The arrangements of the defence industry impose a certain pattern on Soviet weapons development. But the role of the Ministry of Defence is crucial too. The Ministry issues requirements, requests design proposals, agrees on development contracts with the design bureaus, supervises development, conducts prototype trials, places orders for production, supervises production, and assimilates new equipment. The Ministry possesses the institutional arrangements and the technical competence to perform these tasks. The General Staff has a scientific-technical committee which helps to devise R & D policy, and this presumably calls on outside advice and expertise to help identify promising lines of R & D and to check proposals put forward by the designers or the military services. Since 1947 there has been a Deputy Minister of Defence either for armament or electronics (from 1964 to 1970 a deputy Chief of the General Staff) with responsibility for supervising development and production programs. Since 1978 there appear to have been two such Deputy

Ministers, one each for armament and electronics, just as there were for a while in the mid-1950s. These men are the successors to Tukhachevskii, who was Chief of Armament from 1931 to 1936 and had a key role in the technological transformation of the Red Army. None of them, however, has enjoyed the authority or influence that Tukhachevskii did. Nevertheless, the postwar deputy ministers have played an important part in stimulating innovation and in encouraging the development of new industries. Chief Marshal of Artillery M.I. Nedelin directed, from the military side, the development of the early ballistic missiles and then became the first Commander-in-Chief of the Strategic Rocket Forces. He was killed in a rocket accident in 1960. Engineer-Admiral A.I. Berg, who from 1953 to 1957 was Deputy Minister for Radar and Radioengineering, played an important role in the development of the electronics industry in the Soviet Union. Col. Gen. N.N. Alekseev, one of the Soviet delegates at SALT I, later became Deputy Minister for Armament.[19]

At a lower level, the military services have technical administrations and scientific-technical committees which deal directly with their suppliers, issue requirements, conduct tests, and send representatives to the design bureaus and production plants. The technical administrations work closely with the appropriate staffs, which are responsible for operational planning and combat training. Each service has R & D establishments that help it decide on its operational requirements, monitor foreign developments, and test and employ new equipment. These establishments may engage in some weapons development, but most of this is done in the design bureaus of the defence industry ministries. The military academies also play an important role in military R & D: the Zhukovskii Air Force Engineering Academy and the Malinovskii Academy of Armoured Forces, for example, have done considerable work on operational analysis and weapons design. No class of civilian defence analysts has grown up in the Soviet Union: analysis is done in military institutions.

The basic document regulating weapons development is the Tactical-Technical Instruction, which is prepared by the service and agreed with the design bureau. This sets out the purpose of the development; the operational and cost specifications; the composition and the stages of preparation of the technical documentation.[20] The instruction is used by the technical administration as the basis for monitoring development work. When a prototype or model is prepared it will undergo factory trials and then go for state trials, which determine how the system will perform under operational conditions; these latter trials are conducted by the services.

If the design is approved for series production, a document called the Technical Conditions is drawn up which sets out the purpose of the product, the basic tactical-technical data, the parameters that govern its suitability for delivery to the customer, the methods of quality control and so on.[21] This is in effect a contract between the technical administration and the production enterprise, and forms the basis for the quality control exercised by the military representatives at the plant. The representatives at large plants will consist of military engineers, technicians, and office personnel, and will be headed by a 'field grade officer equal in experience and status to the plant manager'.[22] They exercise quality control throughout the production process and conduct tests to ensure that equipment delivered to the Armed Forces meet the standards laid down in the Technical Conditions. They also have the right to supervise the calculation of production costs, and apparently try to exclude all indirect costs from such calculations.

It is generally true of the Soviet economy that vertical links (such as those between enterprise and ministry) prevail over horizontal ties (such as those between enterprises). This is true of military R & D too. The technical administration will be closely directed by the General Staff and the Deputy Minister of Armament, while the design bureaus are subordinate to their own ministries. Every large development or production decision will have to go to the Ministry of Defence Collegium and the Defence Council or the Politburo for approval, and large programs in which more than one ministry is involved will be coordinated by the Military-Industrial Commission.

The role of the Ministry of Defence in weapons acquisition seems to reinforce the tendency towards conservative and evolutionary technological change: the complex committee structure for approving new development programs is likely to inhibit innovation, while the different services might be expected to press for follow-on systems – pressure that may be welcome to the design bureaus, since it will keep them occupied with designs that are not too challenging.

There is one major element in the acquisition process that does not fall into the defence industry or the Armed Forces: the Academies of Sciences (the most important being the USSR Academy and its Siberian Division, and the Ukrainian Academy). The USSR Academy played a crucial role in military R & D in the 1940s and 1950s. In the early 1960s the Academy was reformed to concentrate on basic research, and many institutes (including the Kurchatov Institute of Atomic Energy and the Institute of Radio Engineering and Electronics) were transferred to the industrial ministries. The Academy still does applied research in very advanced technologies, some of which (for example, control systems, lasers and charged-particle beams) have military relevance. When Academy institutes become involved in military R & D programs it is probable that they, or the relevant parts, pass under the control of the Military-Industrial Commission.

## The Performance of Military R & D

The processes of technological innovation are more effective in the defence sector than in civilian industry. This is largely because the high priority given to defence by the Party leadership has helped to overcome the obstacles to innovation that are found elsewhere in the economy. Military R & D has received preferential treatment in the supply of scarce resources. The design bureaus and the Ministry of Defence have provided coordination and thus helped to overcome the customary departmental barriers to innovation. The Party leadership has exercised its political authority to make the system work well.

Three conclusions can be drawn about the innovativeness of the defence sector. First, the military R & D arrangements are well suited to the development of follow-on systems – for example, tanks – where no great shift in mission or technology is required. In such cases the R & D system ensures that user requirements are well understood in the development process, which is thus responsive to military needs.

Second, the Soviet Union has been able to organize large-scale projects to develop new weapons when the Soviet leaders have deemed it necessary. The Soviet system is well suited to the concentration of resources on specific goals, although past history indicates that the selection of such goals may be a complex and hazardous process. This suggests that if the United States enjoys a lead in a major new weapons technology – multiple warheads or cruise missiles, for example – the Soviet Union will try to close the gap by concentrating its effort on that area. Defence Minister Ustinov apparently holds this view, for in 1977 he commented that

> those who count on attaining military superiority over the Soviet Union with the help of such weapons [new types of weapons of mass destruction] should remember that the economy, science and technology in our country are now at such a high level that we are in a position to create in the shortest time any type of weapons on which the enemies of peace might wish to count.[23]

Third, the Soviet R & D system is not well adapted to the lateral or horizontal transfer of technology across departmental boundaries, unless this is organized as a matter of priority from the top. Low-level cross-fertilization between different branches of technology appears not to be encouraged by the Soviet R & D system. The reasons for this lie in the compartmentalization of Soviet industry, and especially of the defence sector where this rigidity is reinforced by secrecy. It is difficult to say how far this defect is overcome through central coordination. But Western studies indicate that ease of communication and movement of people and ideas are important factors in innovation, and these are lacking in Soviet military R & D. Engineer-Admiral Berg, who was Deputy Minister of Defence for Radar and Radioengineering from 1953 to 1957, said that 'we are stuck fast in secrecy like a fly in treacle'.[24] The prevailing secrecy is one of the main reasons why Soviet R & D is less innovative than its Western counterpart.

In spite of the relatively successful performance of Soviet military R & D, Soviet writers have pointed to problems in the weapons acquisition process. First, they have expressed anxiety about the costs of the R & D effort, and this has shown itself since the early 1960s in more open discussion of the need for cost-effectiveness and of the problem of rising intergenerational costs. Second, Khrushchev's fall was followed by expressions of concern about the way in which R & D decisions were being made. The military press underlined the need for 'scientific' policy-making in which the professionally competent – that is, the military – would have a greater say. This argument reflects real concern about the complexity of weapons decisions, and an extensive literature has grown up about operational analysis and weapons selection. Finally, concern has been expressed about the flexibility of the R & D system; in effect, this is anxiety about innovation, for the argument here is that new technological opportunities are not exploited quickly enough and that new ideas are translated too slowly into production.[25]

These arguments have accompanied a growing military R & D effort, a greater military voice in policy-making, and some attempts to improve the workings of the military R & D system. But there is no evidence that these concerns will lead to a major overhaul of the system. It is true that it is not as innovative as the American system, but it has been effective in helping to make the Soviet Union a military superpower. The present trend of reform in Soviet R & D is to transfer certain features of the military arrangements to the civilian sector, and this suggests that, whatever its shortcomings, military R & D is regarded as successful and worthy of emulation.

## Patterns of Military R & D

International competition with more advanced rivals has been the major driving force in Soviet military R & D. The Soviet leaders have created a large military R & D effort to meet what they have seen as the needs of this competition. Military doctrine has provided a general orientation for policy, and military science has studied how wars are to be fought.

Military doctrine and military science exercise an important but not a determining influence on Soviet weapons development. Military technology is not the product of military requirements alone. The Armed Forces have to formulate their requirements in the light of technological possibilities and production capacity, and hence negotiate them with the design bureaus and the defence industry. According to a Soviet study of weapons development, the starting-point for a new system is the recognition by the user that he faces new missions or that the missions he faces have changed in scope and character. Economic and technological analyses show what new systems are practicable. Doctrine (in the sense of operational doctrine)

> serves here as an organizing principle. Success in creating new systems and the appearance of types of systems which are new in principle influence, in their turn, the content of doctrine in a determining way. Thus in the process of creating systems there is an interaction between theory and practice: new missions – doctrine – conception of the system – the new system – doctrine.[26]

Here the interaction of doctrine and technology is stressed, with technology seen as a determining influence on doctrine, and doctrine ascribed a key role as the 'organizing principle' in formulating requirements. Another Soviet writer makes a similar point when he says that the customer cannot give the designer 'figures at will'.[27]

The way in which designers try to meet the customer's wishes is strongly influenced by the institutional arrangements for military R & D, which tend to discourage (as we have seen) any striving after major technological breakthroughs. Soviet designers have shown a marked preference for simple designs; for the common use of subsystems and components in different weapons systems; and for incremental or evolutionary technological change.[28] These preferences are the product of experience, and in some areas have been formulated as a self-conscious design philosophy. One of those who worked in the Tank Industry Commissariat during the war wrote later that the experience of the war shows that the design process ensures rapid introduction into series production only when it is based on assemblies which have been mastered earlier. Consequently, the continuous improvement of the basic assemblies is essential. To design a new tank, while at the same time creating new assemblies, means, as a rule, passing on for series production an uncompleted tank.[29]

Similar arguments have been advanced by others involved in the tank industry or in writing about the combat role of armoured forces.

These design preferences cannot, however, be applied in the same way in all areas of military technology. A leading Soviet aerodynamicist has written that 'the fact is that a new military aircraft is not set within the framework of well-established technical capabilities, but always represents a major step forward and is developed with means which have been recently tested or have not been checked at all.'[30] In high-technology areas, in other words, the use of existing tried-and-tested subsystems might be desirable, but may just not be possible. In such areas a large R & D effort in subsystem technologies (aeroengines, armament, avionics etc.) can provide the basis for major technological change between one generation and the next.

Even within the same general area of weapons development, different designers have espoused different philosophies. In aircraft development, for example, Tupolev argued that new systems should be created on the basis of available technology, and that operational doctrine should be adapted to what could be produced. Myasishchev, on the other hand, was known for his ambitious and innovative approach.[31] He, however, had his design bureau taken away from him in the 1940s and again in the late 1950s, and this shows the dangers of trying to be too innovative – though his fate had much to do with changing attitudes and long-range bombers. Myasishchev's case shows that different philosophies have existed in Soviet aircraft design. But it also suggests that Tupolev's approach works better in the Soviet system.

Soviet military R & D in the post-war period can be seen as the effort of a basically non-innovative system to cope with revolutionary technological change, which has been generated primarily by the Soviet Union's potential enemies. New paths of weapons development have been stimulated by foreign technological innovations – whether in emulation (atomic bomb development) or as a counter to enemy systems (air defence and ABM systems). In some cases the requirements formulated in response to foreign technology have pushed Soviet designers to develop systems that have been technologically overambitious. Two examples here are the SS-6 ICBM which, although it passed its state trials in August 1957, was unsatisfactory as a military missile, and the Galosh ABM system, which although deployed around Moscow is thought to be quite ineffective. Similar examples of systems that were overambitious were the Mya-4 *Bison* bomber and the first M(I)RVs, which were not successful enough to be deployed in any numbers. A civilian example is the Tu-144 supersonic transport plane.

The point here is not to disparage Soviet technological performance, but rather to stress that none of these systems conforms to a pattern in which Soviet designers create weapons that are within the state of the art. These examples suggest that the pressures of international competition – as these are defined by the Soviet leaders – have provided a major impetus to technological innovation.

Soviet military technological policy aims not only to create weapons in response to a foreign threat, but also to provide new technologies that can be exploited for military purposes. One of the leading Soviet commentators on the relationship between science and defence has argued that R & D used to play a quite subordinate role, responding to specific requests from the military authorities. Now, he writes, R & D plays an active role, throwing up ideas and possibilities for new types of weapons (nuclear and laser weapons are the examples he quotes).[32] Marshal Grechko wrote in 1975 that it was particularly important to direct fundamental research to the 'discovery of as yet unknown qualities of matter, phenomena and laws of nature, the working out of new methods for studying and using them for strengthening the defence capability of the state'.[33] Seen from an offensive point of view, a large R & D effort creates the possibility that fundamentally new types of weapons will emerge from research. Viewed defensively, it provides a hedge against the possibility of being overtaken by technological surprise.

Major innovation decisions cannot easily be handled within the standard operating procedure of the military R & D system, and require intervention from the top to authorize new funding and new institutional arrangements. The memoirs of the Stalin and Khrushchev years show how the Party leaders often acted to set up new programs or to change the direction of existing ones. The same kind of evidence does not exist for the Brezhnev period, but there is little doubt that a similar flexibility exists, even if the style of decision-making is different. Brezhnev was Central Committee Secretary with responsibility for heavy industry, including the defence industry, in the late 1950s, and Ustinov has been a leading manager of weapons development and production since before the war with Germany. The Soviet political leadership is probably more expert in matters of weapons development and production than any other leadership in the world.

The two main driving forces of Soviet military R & D are international military competition, which exerts both general and specific pressures, and a large research effort, which provides the basis for the development of new and improved weapons. Both of these forces act in a complex way on weapons acquisition. If the military R & D effort is rooted historically in international rivalry and strongly influenced by that rivalry, it is also true that the large military effort has created institutions that occupy a powerful position in the Soviet system and provide a dynamic and pattern of their own to weapons development and production. But the guiding force has been the exercise of political authority by the Party leaders to devote resources to the creation of military power and to initiate and expedite major weapons programs.

## ICBM Development

Some of the most important features of Soviet military R & D can be illustrated by sketching the history of ICBM development. The earliest experimental rocket work was done under the Red Army's auspices. In the early 1930s Tukhachevskii saw that rockets might play an important role in the operation in depth by inflicting deep strikes on enemy forces. In 1932 he wrote to the Chief of the Military-Engineering Academy that

> special promise is held out by the GDL's [Gas Dynamics Laboratory, which at the time came under Tukhachevskii's Technical Staff] experiments with a liquid-propellant rocket motor that has recently been designed in the laboratory. In artillery and chemical troops this motor will open up unlimited possibilities for firing projectiles of any power and any range.[34]

Tukhachevskii was instrumental in setting up the RNII (the Reaction Research Institute), which played the major role in Soviet rocket development after 1945.

Soviet rocket work suffered from the purge, but was revived towards the end of the war with Germany when it became clear that the Germans had made considerable progress in this field. By the middle of 1946 a network of institutes, design bureaus and factories had been set up to carry out rocket development. The first rocket units were formed in the

Army in 1946 on the basis of the Guards Mortar Units, which had the *Katyusha* rocket artillery.[35] Marshal of Artillery M.I. Nedelin oversaw the development of the rocket forces from 1946 until his death in an accident at a test launching in 1960.

In the 1940s and 1950s Soviet rocket development progressed rapidly because, in the words of Pilyugin, the Chief Designer of Control Systems, 'one rocket is being tested, the next modification is on the drawing-board, while the third is being conceived'.[36] Korolev's design bureau developed the earliest Soviet ballistic missiles on the basis of the German V-2, and then created the SS-3 MRBM and the SS-6 ICBMs. In 1954 M.K. Yangel', who had been one of Korolev's deputies since 1950, was given a design bureau of his own. Korolev and Yangel' did not get on well together.[37] They now competed in developing the SS-7 and SS-8 ICBMs, which have similar performance characteristics and entered service in the early 1960s; they also competed in designing the SS-9 and SS-10. In each case the Yangel' bureau won, with the SS-8 deployed only in small numbers and the SS-10 not deployed at all. After Korolev's death in 1966 his bureau seems to have stopped working on military missiles. Yangel's bureau designed the SS-4 MRBM and the heavy ICBMs: the SS-7, SS-9 and SS-18. Yangel' died in 1971, and it is not known who replaced him.[38]

In the late 1950s or early 1960s the design base for missiles was expanded when Myasishchev's aircraft bureau was taken over by V.N. Chelomei, who was already engaged in designing naval missiles. Chelomei is reported to have been responsible for the design of the SS-11, SS-17 and SS-19 ICBMs.[39] Another new bureau was set up, under V.N. Nadiradze, to develop solid-propellant missiles: the SS-13 and SS-16 ICBMs and the SS-20 IRBM. Most Soviet ICBMs have been powered by liquid-propellant motors developed by V.P. Glushko's design bureau.[41]

Competition has continued between these bureaus. The SS-11 and SS-13 have similar performance characteristics, although the former has a liquid-propellant, and the latter a solid-propellant, motor (the SS-13 may have been an unsuccessful attempt to develop a mobile ICBM). Over one thousand SS-11s were deployed, but only sixty SS-13s. The SS-17 and SS-19 may also have been competitive developments, with the latter deployed in greater numbers. The backbone of the ICBM force has been provided by the SS-7, SS-9, SS-11, SS-17, SS-18 and SS-19. The other ICBMs that have been flight tested have been deployed either in small numbers (SS-6, SS-8, SS-13) or not at all (SS-10, SS-16).

The design bureaus have maintained a steady and continuing effort along the lines indicated by Pilyugin. As a result, there has been a clear continuity in the Soviet program, with the heavy SS-18 following the SS-9 and SS-7, the solid-propellant SS-16 succeeding the SS-13, and the SS-17 and SS-19 replacing the SS-11. Yet it would be misleading to characterize Soviet ICBM development as evolutionary. Some systems have been modified and deployed in different models, but there have been major differences in the performance characteristics of the succeeding generations. The fourth generation (the SS-16 to the SS-20), which began to enter service in the mid-1970s, was marked by major improvements in warhead design, guidance systems and launch technology; the performance of these missiles is far superior to that of their predecessors.[42]

Institutes like the RNII and design bureaus such as Glushko's conduct applied research and develop subsystem technologies. Designers can draw on this continuing work in creating new systems and modifying existing ones, and this will encourage commonality and standardized design procedures. Soviet designers have had to work from a lower technological base than in the United States; they have faced specific deficiencies in electronics and in solid propellants. In spite of this, they have succeeded in creating very effective ICBMs. By stressing their advantages they have overcome their weaknesses: higher yield warheads, for example, compensated for poorer accuracy on the earlier missiles; the lack of on-board computers on earlier ICBMs was made less serious by the fact that the thrust of liquid-propellant motors can be regulated more easily than that of solid-propellant ones.[43]

Some consequences of technological backwardness turned out to be advantageous in the long run. The early Soviet ICBMs were very large, presumably because they had to carry heavy warheads and guidance systems. As warheads and guidance systems improved and became smaller, however, the heavy throw-weight was seen to be useful in accommodating high-yield warheads and MIRVs. The fact that the SS-18 heavy ICBM uses the 'cold launch' technique, which is designed to increase the missile's effective throw-weight, indicates that the size of this missile is not merely an accidental byproduct of early design decisions; it suggests that the designers wanted a missile with a heavy throw-weight. Since 1978 Soviet missile accuracy has improved significantly, thus making the SS-18 and SS-19 powerful countersilo weapons. It has been suggested that this improvement in accuracy was achieved with the help of grinding machines imported from the United States and Japan, but it is impossible to be sure that this was so.[44]

A new generation of ICBMs is reported to be under development, and past experience suggests that this will include a solid-propellant mobile ICBM and a heavy ICBM capable of carrying a large number of warheads. The main system in this generation will be a successor to the SS-19. How many of these systems will be flight tested and deployed is impossible to say, for it depends on the future of Soviet–American strategic arms control (under SALT II the Soviet Union can test only one new ICBM before 1985).

Contacts between the designers and the military customer have been close. Nedelin, for example, played an important role in managing early missile development. When the main problem was that of producing and testing missiles he held the post of Deputy Minister of Defence for Armament (January 1952–April 1953, March 1955–December 1959). When his main task was to introduce the new weapons into service he was made Commander of Artillery (March 1950–January 1952, April 1953–March 1955). Finally, in December 1959 he was appointed Commander-in-Chief of the newly formed Strategic Rocket Forces.[45] Although Nedelin worked closely with the designers and managers, he had his own interests to defend. According to Korolev, when it came to questions of quality control and delivery dates Nedelin was a demanding and 'principled' customer.[46]

Nedelin was an artillery officer, and the Strategic Rocket Forces have been dominated by artillery men. They have tended to see their missiles as extensions of artillery, not as pilotless bombers. It should not be surprising that this view has influenced ballistic missile development and nuclear strategy in the Soviet Union. When Nedelin was Deputy Minister for Armament he set up a special staff to work out 'the organizational-strategic bases of employing rocket units',[47] and this no doubt drew on the experience of Soviet artillery. One of the chief Soviet delegates to SALT, Academician Shchukin, once spoke of 'people who thought of nuclear weapons in terms of a needed number of wheels of artillery per kilometer of front'.[48]

The influence of this view has been pervasive. The concept of the 'operation in depth' may have encouraged Soviet designers to concentrate on extending the range of their rockets step by step, thus increasing gradually the Soviet capacity to launch deep strikes against the enemy. Similarly, the Soviet interest in reloading missile silos and reusing them in later salvos reflects a view of the silo as something akin to an artillery tube. The 'cold launch' technique may have been applied to ICBMs in order to make the silos easier to reuse. Finally, the idea of preemption, which is so important in Soviet nuclear strategy, seems to come directly from the artillery *kontrpodgotovka* (counterpreparation): 'a preplanned, brief, powerful, surprise burst of fire delivered by a defender against enemy groupings which are preparing for an offensive'.[49] Soviet missiles are intended to be able to break up an enemy attack before it can get under way, and this determines the kinds of targets that it is most urgent for them to strike.

ICBM development has been closely directed and monitored by the Party leadership. Stalin's role in the 1940s was noted earlier. Khrushchev too took a close interest in missile development. It is clear from his memoirs that he had frequent contact with Kurchatov, Korolev and M.V. Keldysh (who became director of RNII in 1946 and was later President of the Academy of Sciences); these men were known as the 'big three'.[50] Nedelin's biographer, Army General V.F. Tolubko, the present Commander-in-Chief of the Strategic Rocket Forces, makes it clear that he too had access to the top leaders in the 1950s: 'when it came to disputed or what seemed to be insoluble questions at the ministerial level, Nedelin with the knowledge of the Minister of Defence turned for help directly to the leaders of the Party and the government'.[51] According to Tolubko, when Brezhnev was responsible for heavy industry in the late 1950s his office was a 'kind of staff where the most important problems of rocket-building were solved, and meetings held with the participation of the most notable scientists, designers, and specialists from different fields of science, technology and production'.[52] The same kind of information is not available for the post-Khrushchev period, but there is no reason to doubt that the ICBM program is closely directed by the Party leaders, since ICBM development remains central to Soviet policy. The history of the ICBM program shows how the Party leadership has brought together designers, industrial managers and soldiers to create an effective strategic force.

## Conclusion

Soviet military thought has had to adjust to major technological changes in the postwar period, and Soviet military policy has devoted considerable resources to developing new weapons. But the Soviet view of war is not a purely technological one. Soviet theorists do not equate the level of technology with military effectiveness, for that is seen to depend on many other factors: the quantity of weapons, the way in which they are organized into forces, the skill and training of the troops. Moreover, as technological change grows more rapid, so the responsibilities of military thought are seen to increase, because attention has now to be directed to future technological possibilities. In the words of two Soviet theorists, scientific-technical progress

> is a guarantee that in future we can expect the appearance of new means of combat. Military strategy now has the task of developing in good time the methods of conducting military operations with the employment of these means, so that with the beginning of war we will not be forced as Engels expressed it, gropingly to 'adapt' strategic concepts to the new weapons.[53]

The Soviet leaders try to direct technological innovation to meet their military requirements. At the same time they recognize that they have to adapt their thinking to existing technological realities. Soviet statements about nuclear weapons, for example, stress both the need for systems that can carry out specific missions, and the technological character of the current strategic relationship with the United States, in which each side is vulnerable to devastating strikes by the other. Like the United States, the Soviet Union is working to develop anti-ballistic-missile systems. If one side or the other succeeds in making itself invulnerable to a nuclear strike by the other, the strategic relationship of the two countries will be transformed. There is, however, little prospect that either side will be able to escape from the relationship of mutual vulnerability in the foreseeable future.[54] The Soviet leaders apparently accept that they must live with this relationship for the time being. Nevertheless, technological development has the potential to transform the Soviet–American relationship, and the dynamism of technological innovation constantly threatens to tilt the balance in one direction or another. The fear that the balance may be upset by advances made by the other side is in turn used to justify the R & D efforts of each of the two superpowers; and these efforts provide the basis for the technological advances that are so much feared.

# CHAPTER EIGHT

# The Politics of Military Power

In an essay on 'Military Organization and State Organization', written at the beginning of this century, Otto Hintze argued that

> in the foreseeable future, matters will remain as they have been throughout history: the form and spirit of the state's organization will not be determined solely by economic and social relations and clashes of interest, but primarily by the necessities of defense and offense, that is, by the organization of the army and warfare.[1]

Hintze's argument was directed against those who sought to understand the state only in relation to the structure of social classes and ignored the effect that relations between states had on their internal organization. The Soviet Union provides a good illustration of Hintze's thesis, for its history is intimately bound up with war and the preparation for war. This is true both in the classical sense that armed force has established and maintained the territorial limits of the state, and in the sense that war and military preparation have had a profound effect on all aspects of Soviet life.

## A Military-Industrial Complex?

Military power has been of central importance for the Soviet state and its survival, but this has not given the Armed Forces or the defence industry a political position of commensurate significance. The early Bolsheviks, who saw strong parallels between the French Revolution and their own, were suspicious of any sign of 'Bonapartism' and took steps to ensure that the Red Army remained subordinate to the Party. Stalin, although he built up the Red Army during the 1930s, destroyed the Army's command in the military purge of 1937. After the war with Germany, he appropriated to himself the glory of victory. In July 1946 he removed Marshal Zhukov from his position as Commander-in-Chief of the Ground Forces and gave him the much less important post of Commander of the Odessa Military District. This (along with harsher treatment meted out to lesser figures) warned the High Command against making any attempt to convert the popularity they had gained during the war into an independent base of political power.[2]

Since 1953, the High Command has emerged as a more active force in politics. In each case of leadership change – Beria's arrest and execution in 1953, Malenkov's defeat by Khrushchev in 1955, Khrushchev's victory over the 'anti-Party group' in 1957, and Khrushchev's fall in October 1964 – members of the High Command have played some role. But their influence was one factor among many, and probably not the decisive one. Such intervention was made possible only by divisions in the Party leadership, and on no occasion has a situation arisen in which Party leaders were ranged on one side, and the High Command on the other. The Party and military leaderships are too closely intertwined for that.[3]

In October 1957, only months after helping Khrushchev to defeat the 'anti-Party group' of Molotov, Malenkov *et al.* in the Central Committee, Zhukov was removed from the Politburo and from his post as Minister of Defence. This shows that engaging in leadership politics can be a risky business for soldiers. He was accused of undermining the position of the Main Political Administration and of cutting back political education in the Armed Forces. He was also charged with wanting to pursue an adventurous foreign policy; even the spectre of Bonapartism was raised. Khrushchev exploited divisions within the High Command, calling on Zhukov's old rivals, notably Marshal Konev, to disparage him and his achievements. Whatever the justice of the charges against Zhukov (and his rehabilitation after 1964 suggests that while he may have posed a political threat to Khrushchev, he did not plot to overthrow Party rule), Khrushchev's action did underline the Party's determination to retain its supremacy over the Armed Forces.[4]

Although Party–military relations have not been completely harmonious, the principle of Party supremacy has never seriously been threatened. The Party maintains its control through a variety of institutions. It controls appointments through the *nomenklatura* system. It has its own structure of Party and Komsomol (Young Communist League) organizations in the Armed Forces, thus supplementing military discipline with Party discipline. The Main Political Administration and its political officers try to instil a positive commitment to the

Party and to sustain the morale of the troops. Finally, the KGB is active in rooting out any political opposition.

It is not so much the formal mechanisms of Party and secret police control that explain the political quiescence of the Armed Forces, however, as the way in which military interests have been given priority in Party policy. This is not to ignore Stalin's brutal treatment of the Red Army or to deny that Khrushchev pursued policies that the High Command opposed. But the Party, by stressing the importance of conflict between states and the need for cohesion and solidarity at home, has provided an ideology that gives clear purpose to the Armed Forces' existence. Party policy has given the officer corps a good standard of living and high status, and has furthered their professional interests by allocating generous resources to defence. Finally, the Party has provided capable and cautious leadership (with some glaring exceptions) in foreign policy, avoiding risky adventures that might provoke war.[5]

Since 1953 power has been diffused at the centre of the Soviet state; no individual has dominated policy-making in the way that Stalin did. The resulting political system has been called 'institutional pluralism', on the grounds that policy is now formed in the competition of different institutions and interests inside the Party-State apparatus.[6] This is a useful description as long as it is clear that this is not the pluralism of groups in civil society. Moreover, like any pluralism, this one is imperfect in the sense that some groups and institutions have more power than others. The Armed Forces have been well placed to take advantage of this diffusion of power. The Ministry of Defence and the General Staff are institutions of undisputed competence, and their monopoly of professional military expertise makes it difficult for others to challenge them. They seem to have benefited from the Brezhnev Politburo's emphasis on taking account of expert and technically competent advice. Besides, key elements of military policy are shrouded in secrecy, and this limits criticism of the resources devoted to defence and of the way in which those resources are used.

The defence industry too has occupied a privileged position, as a result of the high priority the Soviet leaders have given to building up military power. The managers of the defence industry form a cohesive group with interlocking careers. Many have held their positions for a long time. Ustinov, for example, became People's Commissar of Armament in 1941. Ye.P. Slavskii, the present Minister of Medium Machine Building (in charge of nuclear weapons development and production) has held that position since 1957 and first started to work in the nuclear weapons program in 1946. Yet in spite of the fact that these men form a clearly identifiable group, there is no evidence that they have an independent power base, or that they constitute a clearly defined lobby.[7]

The one occasion on which the defence industry ministers seem to have acted together was in the period from 1957 to 1963, when they took part, with some success, in the resistance to Khrushchev's decentralization of the economic system. In April 1963, after some recentralization had taken place, Khrushchev complained about the inefficiency of the defence sector. It is not clear, however, exactly what was in dispute. Specific weapons programs – in particular the ICBM program – may have been at issue. Or the defence industry ministers may have felt – along with other economic managers and some members of the Party leadership – that Khrushchev's reforms were weakening the economy and hampering their own operations.

Can one speak then of a Soviet 'military-industrial complex'? The Soviet Union certainly possesses a large defence industry and powerful Armed Forces, and the ties between them are close and numerous. But the mere existence of such institutions does not mean that they can dictate a government's policy. It cannot plausibly be argued, for example, that Stalin was forced to pursue the policies he did by pressure from the Red Army or the defence industry. They were his instruments, and he helped to create them in order to make the Soviet Union a powerful state. He controlled these institutions. He was not their prisoner – as his imprisonment of so many soldiers, designers and managers shows.

The question arises, however, whether the diffusion of power since Stalin's death has changed that relationship. The answer is that it has, but not to the extent of removing the power of final decision from the Party leaders. Military influence has grown in the making of defence policy, but it is still the Politburo that has to make the major decisions about resource allocation, and to reconcile the competing claims of defence, consumption and investment. No doubt the defence industry and the military do propose new weapons and ask for a greater defence effort, but it is the Politburo that disposes of the resources. Close ties exist between the military and the defence industry, but it is still the vertical relationships, culminating in the Party leadership, that predominate: it is far more important for the military to have allies in the Party leadership than in the defence sector. The Armed Forces and the defence industry do embody an historic commitment to military power, and would doubtless resist a major change in priorities. Such resistance might have considerable political significance if the Party leaders were divided on the issue. But priorities have been changed since Stalin's death (for example, in the greater investment in agriculture), and this suggests that while the old structures may make it difficult to adopt new priorities, they do not make it impossible. In other words, whatever momentum Soviet military policy may have acquired over the years, the build-up of military power since the late 1950s must be seen as the product of conscious political choices, and not only as the result of pressure from a military-industrial complex.

## Military-Patriotic Education

The Armed Forces have always served important social and political functions, above and beyond the defence of the Soviet Union. The Red Army was perhaps the most effective instrument of political education in the early years of Soviet rule; military service put uneducated recruits at the disposal of the Party during their term of duty. Under Brezhnev the Party has made growing use of military service and military-patriotic education to instil patriotism and social discipline. Brezhnev told the 25th Party Congress in 1976 that 'young men arrive in the family of soldiers with no experience in the school of life. But when they return from the Army they are already people who have gone through the school of tenacity and discipline, who have acquired technical and professional knowledge and political training.'[8] Three years later, on the anniversary of the Revolution, Ustinov declared that 'service in the Soviet Armed Forces is a wonderful school of labour and martial training, of moral purity and courage, of patriotism and comradeship'.[9] The Soviet leaders evidently believe that military service will strengthen the commitment of young men (65 to 70 per cent of whom are conscripted)[10] to the existing political order, and help to increase the social cohesion and solidarity of their multinational state.

It is not only conscripts who are exposed to the values of military life. In 1967 a new Law on Military Service, which reduced the length of service by one year, instituted pre-induction military training for children of fifteen and older. Military instructors – many of them retired officers – have been appointed to schools and factories to conduct the training programs. Pre-induction training is also provided by DOSAAF, the Voluntary Society for Cooperation with the Army, Aviation and the Navy. DOSAAF is open to all over the age of fourteen, and claims to have about 80 million members. Its main activities are: military-patriotic education; training for military service; training in technical skills, dissemination of military-technical knowledge;

organizing sports. It has clubs and facilities at factories, farms and educational institutions.[11]

These activities form part of the more general program of military-patriotic education. According to the *Soviet Military Encyclopedia*,

> military-patriotic education is called upon to instil a readiness to perform military duty, responsibility for strengthening the defence capability of the country, respect for the Soviet Armed Forces, pride in the Motherland and the ambition to preserve and increase the heroic traditions of the Soviet people. Military-patriotic education is carried out in the teaching process in secondary and higher educational establishments, in the system of political education, by means of propaganda in the press, on radio and television, and with the help of various forms of mass-political work and of artistic and literary works. Of great significance for military-patriotic education is the mastery of basic military and military-technical skills which young people acquire in secondary schools, technical schools, higher educational establishments, in studies at the houses of defence and technical creativity, aero-, auto- and radio clubs, at the young technicians' stations, in military-patriotic schools, defence circles, at points of pre-induction training, in civil defence formations. Physical training with an applied military bent presupposes the development of qualities of will, courage, hardiness, strength, speed of reaction, and helps to raise psychological stability, trains the sight, hearing etc.[12]

The emphasis on pre-induction military training and on military-patriotic education was strengthened in the late 1960s. But these activities are by no means new. The forerunners of DOSAAF were established in the 1920s, and military and patriotic themes have long been a feature of Soviet political education.[13] The program for pre-induction training in schools and factories marks a bigger change, and is designed to counteract the effects of the shorter terms of service introduced in 1967.

Military-patriotic education is intended to serve the wider political purpose of fostering loyalty to, and support for, the Party and the state. It represents an attempt to fuse nationalist, communist and military appeals. The Great Patriotic War occupies a central place in the program of military-patriotic education, as the source of examples and illustrations. The war with Germany was perhaps the time when Party and people were most closely united in a common cause. Military-patriotic education tries to recapture that bond, by identifying the

Soviet state with Russian nationalism and the prestige of the Armed Forces. Some of its extreme manifestations have been linked to neo-Stalinist sentiment, with its concern about the 'moral vacuum' in Soviet society, the lack of discipline, and the influence of foreign ideas. It does not signify growing military control over social and political life, but, rather, an attempt by the Party to use patriotic sentiment and military values for its own purposes.

It would be a mistake, however, to confuse the intention of military-patriotic education with its effect. The programs of training and propaganda have been widely criticized in the Soviet press for their ineffectiveness.[14] In an article in the Party's leading theoretical journal Marshal Ogarkov indicated that much remained to be done:

> the strengthening of ideological work in educating people in the spirit of Soviet patriotism and readiness to defend the socialist Fatherland is now acquiring enormous significance ... In 36 peaceful years there have actually grown up two new generations of Soviet people who do not know by their own experience what war is. In their view peace is the normal state of society. At the same time the ranks of those who took part in the Great Patriotic War and are ready to pass on to the young generation their combat and life experience are thinning out. Questions of the struggle for peace are sometimes understood not from class positions, but in a rather simplified way: any peace is good, any war is bad. And this can lead to unconcern, equanimity and complacency, to an underestimation of the threat of a possible war, which in contemporary conditions can be fraught with serious consequences.[15]

Yet, whatever its shortcomings, military-patriotic education is likely to foster an acceptance of the Party's military policy and a belief that peace is maintained by preparing for war. It will thus help to sustain the Soviet military effort and the special position of the defence sector and of the Armed Forces in Soviet society.

Military-patriotic education may help to explain why there appears to be so little opposition in the Soviet Union to Soviet military policy. Even in the dissident *samizdat* literature, where sharp criticism has been made of so many aspects of Soviet life, few voices have been raised against Soviet military power. The warnings that Sakharov has given the West about Soviet power are an important exception, but Sakharov's background in nuclear weapons development makes him in this context a very special case. By and large Soviet military policy appears to be regarded inside the Soviet Union as legitimate, and as pursuing legitimate goals.[16]

The Soviet leaders present their policy as essentially defensive and peaceful in purpose. The major justification they offer for Soviet military power is that it prevents war. In January 1980 Brezhnev claimed that the Soviet Union had succeeded in breaking the 'tragic cycle: world war – short peaceful breathing-space – world war again'.[17] This is undoubtedly a powerful argument, for the period of international peace that the Soviet Union has enjoyed since 1945 contrasts sharply with the wars of the first half of the century. Since 1945 Soviet forces have seen less combat than those of the leading Western powers: the war in Afghanistan is by far the largest action in which Soviet combat troops have been engaged on any scale. The assertion that Soviet military power secures peace does not, therefore, fly directly in the face of experience. The claim that Soviet military power contributes to peace goes hand in hand with military-patriotic education, which helps to sustain that power.

## The Politics of Doctrine

Soviet military writings often convey the impression that policy springs fully-armed from Marxist-Leninist theory, like Athena from the head of Zeus. They play down disagreements in order to emphasize the monolithic unity of the Communist Party and the Soviet state. Where alternative or dissenting views are alluded to, they are labelled 'mistaken' or 'incorrect'; the implication is that there are 'correct' policies that can be determined by applying theory to the issues in question. A similar picture of Soviet policy-making can be found in some Western studies, which portray Soviet policy as the implementation of a plan derived from military doctrine and Marxist-Leninist theory.

This is a misleading picture. Policy cannot be derived directly from military doctrine because doctrine is too general to do more than provide broad guidelines. Policy must be understood as the product of a political process, in which both low politics (bureaucratic infighting and struggles for power) and high politics (disagreement over the direction of policy or over its implementation) play their part. This politics of Soviet defence policy is difficult to study because key aspects are shrouded in secrecy, but an important role has been played by debates about doctrine itself.

Soviet military doctrine allows for substantial ambiguities, cross-currents and differences of emphasis, especially if one takes both its military-political and military-technical sides into account. Stress can be laid on the preparation for war, or on political measures to prevent it; on the possibility of victory in nuclear war, or on the destructiveness of nuclear weapons. Within the framework of military doctrine esoteric and stylized debate has taken place about nuclear war and its utility as an instrument of policy. In 1954 Malenkov argued that a nuclear war would lead to the destruction of world civilization, and was criticized for holding this view. At the 20th Congress Khrushchev said that world war was not 'fatalistically inevitable', but he did not endorse Malenkov's view of the consequences of nuclear war. In the late 1950s and early 1960s, the goal of victory coexisted with the recognition that nuclear war would bring immense and unprecedented destruction. Nuclear war was not seen as inevitable, or as necessary for the triumph of socialism, or as an expedient instrument of policy. But it was to be prepared for.[18]

In the early 1960s Clausewitz's thesis that war is a continuation of politics by other means was challenged in the Soviet press, mainly by civilian commentators, one of whom wrote that now 'war can be a continuation only of madness'.[19] This challenge to Clausewitz was made in the context of the polemics with China, but it proved to be contentious in the Soviet Union, for it seemed to imply that nuclear war was indeed unthinkable, and that consequently there was little point in preparing to fight it. This may have been Khrushchev's own view.[20] In any event, not long after his removal from office, a vigorous debate on Clausewitz's thesis was conducted in the Soviet press. In May 1965 Major General Talenskii, a leading military theorist who had retired from active service in 1958, wrote that 'in our days there is no more dangerous illusion than the idea that thermonuclear war can still serve as an instrument of politics, that it is possible to achieve political aims by using nuclear weapons and still survive'.[21] Later in the year Talenskii was attacked in the journal of the Main Political Administration by Lt. Col. Ye. Rybkin, who wrote that

> to assert that victory is not at all possible in a nuclear war would not only be untrue on theoretical grounds, but dangerous as well from the political point of view . . . Any *a priori* rejection of the possibility of victory is harmful because it leads to moral disarmament, to a disbelief in victory and to fatalism and passivity. It is necessary to wage a struggle against such attitudes.[22]

Other theorists, chiefly from the Lenin Military-Political Academy (the academy of the Main Political Administration), weighed in to support Rybkin's view that victory was possible in a nuclear war, and that it was both wrong and harmful to argue the contrary.[23]

The real issues at stake in this debate were made clearer in an article by Major General K. Bochkarev, Deputy Chief of the General Staff Academy, in the General Staff journal *Military Thought* in 1968. Bochkarev took exception to the view that in a world nuclear war civilization would be destroyed and there would be neither victor nor vanquished. Three things, in particular, seem to have worried him about this view. The first was that it provides no answer to the question: if there is a nuclear war, what should be done? Military strategy, which concerns itself with how wars are fought and won, would lose its significance. Second, if this happened, the whole rationale behind Soviet military policy would collapse:

> the armed forces of the socialist states at the present time, in principle, will not be able to set for themselves the goal of defeating imperialism . . . and our military science should not even work out a strategy for the conduct of war since the latter has lost its meaning and its significance . . . In this case the very call to raise the combat readiness of our armed forces and improve their capability to defeat any aggressor is senseless.[24]

Third, the idea that there could be no victory in a nuclear war would, in Bochkarev's opinion, undermine the morale of Soviet troops, who are instilled with 'unflagging confidence in the indestructibility and final triumph of socialism'.[25]

The argument about Clausewitz's formula touched on vital questions about nuclear war, and behind the published discussion there may have been even more intense disagreement. In 1967 Andrei Sakharov gave an interview (which was not published in the Soviet Union) in which he too addressed the Clausewitzian thesis and, incidentally, gave the best answer to the argument that a nuclear war could be won. (This was before he came out as a dissident.)

> *Sakharov:* Don't you think there are crazy politicians and generals who would seize on the creation of such a 'shield' [an ABM system] to argue that thermonuclear war could serve as a modern 'continuation of politics by other means' – to use the formula of Clausewitz?
> *Henry:* I have been writing for years about such irrational politicians and generals in the capitalist world. Of course you are right.
> *Sakharov:* But if Clausewitz's formula were applied across the board in our day and age, we would be dealing not with the 'continuation of politics by other means' but with the total self-destruction of civilization, despite the existence of a 'shield'. The destruction of

hundreds of millions of people, the genetic deformation of future generations, the destruction of cities and industry, transport, communication, agriculture, and the educational system, the outbreak of famine and epidemics, the rise of a savage and uncontrollable hatred of scientists and 'intellectuals' on the part of civilization's surviving victims, rampant superstition, ferocious nationalism, and the destruction of the material and informational basis of civilization – all of this would throw humanity centuries back, to the age of barbarism, and bring it to the brink of self-destruction. This is a gloomy prognosis, but you can't just brush the facts aside.[26]

The debate of the 1960s did not lead to the abandonment of the Clausewitzian view of war; but most Soviet writers have been careful to distinguish between the essence of nuclear war and its practical utility as an instrument of policy.[27]

The issue of victory in a nuclear war reemerged in 1973 and 1974. Once again the argument was conducted mainly by civilian writers on one side, and by military theorists from the Lenin Academy on the other. G.A. Arbatov, director of the Academy of Sciences' Institute of the USA and Canada, wrote that 'with the emergence of nuclear missiles any correspondence between the political ends and the means was lost, since no policy can have the objective of destroying the enemy at the cost of complete self-annihilation'.[28] In another article, V.N. Dolgin, an *apparatchik* in the Central Committee Secretariat, wrote that 'one, several or many nuclear devices will wipe from the face of the earth cities and even entire states, and turn our planet into a chaos of chain reactions, global disasters and undermine the conditions of the existence of mankind'.[29] A leading newspaper commentator, Alexander Bovin, argued that nuclear war would be suicidal for both sides and that it could not serve as an instrument of policy.[30]

This view of nuclear war and its consequences was attacked by Major-General A. Milovidov of the Lenin Military-Political Academy, who wrote that some Soviet writers had made mistakes in their analysis of the 'essence and consequences of missile-nuclear war'. This was because they 'absolutized the quantitative analysis and arithmetical calculations of the destructive power of nuclear weapons', and failed to take account of the qualitative factors that would determine the outcome of war.[31] Rybkin entered the fray once again to argue that 'class and defence vigilance' would be weakened by denying that war could serve as an instrument of policy.[32] Early in 1974 Rear Admiral Shelyag, also a political officer, attacked 'arguments about the death of civilization and about there being no victors in nuclear war' as the product of a 'one-sided approach' and 'over-simplified mathematical calculations'. Any war fought by the Soviet Union, even with nuclear weapons, would serve as a 'means of defending civilization'.[33]

It is difficult to tell whether debates like these reflect policy differences in the Politburo. In this case there is no evidence that they did. Nor is it clear whether they were linked to specific weapons decisions. If they were, it was probably, as the Sakharov interview suggests, with ABM systems. In the mid-1960s the Soviet Union was deploying such a system around Moscow and, while some, like Sakharov, thought it would be both ineffective and dangerous, others evidently hoped that it would extricate the Soviet Union from its vulnerability to American attack. The debate in 1973 and 1974 took place after the ABM Treaty had been signed and each side was clearly vulnerable to retaliatory attack by the other.

These esoteric debates are difficult to interpret. They appear to reflect differences in thinking about nuclear war. They also reflect different political currents inside the Soviet Union, for the Main Political Administration has been one of the centres of neo-Stalinist sentiment. Arbatov and the other civilian commentators have been more involved in detente and may feel more strongly the need for cooperative, and not merely autarkic, solutions to the problems of security.

The debate of 1973–74 may also have been a prelude to the reformulation or clarification of doctrine that has taken place since the mid-1970s. The destructiveness of nuclear war has been strongly emphasized in the Soviet press, and the suicidal nature of any decision to start such a war has been underlined by Brezhnev. At the same time, however, it is asserted that such a war has to be prepared for: strategy, in other words, has not been made redundant. Parity has been affirmed by Brezhnev as the goal of Soviet policy, and the pursuit of superiority has been disavowed. Parity is a key concept here, for it approximates to the idea of mutual deterrence in that it recognizes that for the time being the basic nature of the Soviet–American strategic relationship is one of mutual vulnerability to devastating retaliatory strikes. But parity does not carry two of the most important connotations of mutual deterrence: it does not suggest that the nuclear balance is a foolproof mechanism for preventing war, and it does not imply that war should not be prepared for.[34]

From this it should be clear that military thought is not merely a matter of intellectual activity. It is also a matter of domestic politics, of currents of political thought and institutional interests. This is not to say that military doctrine merely legitimates domestic interests; but the shape of doctrine and its evolution cannot be understood without reference to them.

## Economic Choices

In 1961 the Communist Party adopted a Program which proclaimed that the Soviet Union would surpass the United States in production per head of population before 1970, and build the material-technical basis of a communist society by 1980.[35] These economic hopes have not been fulfilled. The rate of economic growth has declined steadily since the 1950s, whether measured in Soviet national income statistics, or in Western estimates of Soviet GNP. From 1956 to 1960 Soviet national income (produced) grew at 9·1 per cent a year; from 1975 to 1979 it grew at an annual rate of 4·5 per cent.[36] According to CIA estimates, Soviet GNP grew at an annual rate of 5·8 per cent from 1956 to 1960; from 1976 to 1980 the rate was 2·8 per cent a year.[37] The decline in the growth rate has been secular, and neither the 11th Five Year Plan for 1981−5 nor the projections of Western observers point to a major reversal of the trend. The 26th Party Congress in 1981 called for a new Program to be drawn up, and this is likely to make fewer specific promises than Khrushchev's Program did.

In the late 1950s Khrushchev believed that growing Soviet strategic power would enable him to make important gains in foreign policy, and in 1960 he claimed that the Soviet Union would maintain its lead over the United States in ICBMs. But his foreign policy led to the debacle of the Cuban missile crisis; and by 1965 the United States had a very substantial numerical and technological lead in strategic forces. Since then, however, the Soviet Union has built up its military power, though at considerable cost. During the Brezhnev years, Soviet military expenditure has risen at an annual rate of 4−5 per cent, according to the CIA estimate.[38] The proportion of GNP devoted to defence remained at about 11−13 per cent for most of this time, but rose to 12−14 per cent, in the CIA estimate, as the military effort continued to increase alongside the slowdown in economic growth. Some Western analyses argue that the rate of growth of military expenditure was even higher; and that it absorbs a greater share of the GNP. Others claim that the CIA overstates the growth rate of military outlays and the proportion of GNP devoted to defence. But there seems, in any event, to be little disagreement that Soviet military expenditure has grown steadily for twenty years or more.

For most of the post-Stalin period the Soviet leaders have been able to combine the growth in military expenditure with steady improvements in the standard of living and a continuing high rate of investment. By the late 1970s, however, they were no longer able to sustain this pattern. The rate of growth of capital investment was cut in the 10th Five Year Plan (1976–1980) and is to fall further in the 11th Plan.[39] In the 1970s, especially towards the end of the decade, the rate of growth of per capita consumption fell off considerably, compared with the 1960s.[40] Of the three major categories of resource use, only defence has so far been protected against the effects of the economic slowdown.

The choices facing the Soviet leaders are not likely to become easier. A leading economist and member of the Party Central Committee wrote after the 26th Congress that

> in the '80s we will have to solve simultaneously such large-scale tasks as further raising the standard of living of the people, continuously increasing the economic and scientific-technical might of the country, reliably ensuring its security. And these tasks have to be solved, as was emphasized at the Congress, in conditions that are far from easy, since several factors which complicate economic development will be operative. Among them are the reduction in growth of labour resources, the increasing cost of exploiting the East and the North, expenditure on preserving the environment and on the infrastructure, above all transport and communications, and the necessity for more rapid renewal of productive funds.[41]

Energy will be more expensive to produce, because mineral fuels are becoming harder to extract. The growth rate of the labour force will diminish. Increases will come primarily in Central Asia and the Transcaucasian Republics, whose people seem reluctant to emigrate, and not in the European part of the Soviet Union, where labour is most needed. The government may have to direct industrial investment to the south.[42]

The Soviet leaders face declining rates of growth in both labour and capital, but they nonetheless intend the 11th Five Year Plan to halt the economic slowdown and improve the lot of the consumer. They hope, no doubt, for better weather and better harvests than in the last Five Year Plan period; their hopes on this score were disappointed in 1981, however. They are continuing to try to improve the workings of the system of economic planning and management, and they have stressed the need for more effective technological innovation. There are no signs, however, that the current effort to improve planning and innovation will yield far-reaching results, and that is why even the modest goals of the 11th Five Year Plan may prove difficult to achieve.

The CIA's estimate of the economic burden of military expenditure can be read in two ways. It can be taken, first, as indicating that the Soviet leaders are seriously committed to increasing their military power and therefore likely to ignore the economic costs. It is clear (and from better evidence than Soviet military outlays) that the Soviet leaders have been committed to making their country a great military power. They have also been committed to making it a great economic and technological power. They have been more successful in pursuing the former goal than the latter, but there is no evidence that they have abandoned the pursuit of economic growth and technological progress. Since the 1920s Soviet policy has been based on the assumption that military power must rest on a strong economic and technological foundation. It seems improbable, therefore, that the Soviet leaders would put the economic basis of their military power in jeopardy in order to maintain the rate of growth of military expenditure (though it is not clear at what point they might decide that that was the effect of their policy). Furthermore, both Khrushchev and Brezhnev have made the improvement of living standards a central element in their political strategy, in order to secure popular support for their rule. The targets in the 11th Plan suggest that this remains an important priority. To say that the Soviet leaders are firmly committed to military power does not tell us what choices they will make, for they are committed to other objectives too.

The economic burden of defence can be interpreted, secondly, as showing that the cost of the military effort is high and might have to be cut if other objectives are to be met. It is not clear, however, what impact a cut in military expenditure – or in its rate of increase – would have on the rest of the economy. How great the benefit would be depends on what resources – skilled labour, scarce materials, or scientists and engineers – were released, and how quickly they could be absorbed into the civilian economy. Besides, it would also depend on how efficiently the resources would be used in comparison to the way in which they are being used now. These factors make it difficult to estimate the effects a change in expenditure might have. A cut in the rate of growth might have an immediate effect by loosening supply constraints and thus alleviating bottlenecks in the civilian economy. For any perceptible effect on investment or consumption, however, five years might be needed. In the longer term, the effects would be greater: a decision taken in 1982 to reduce the rate of growth in military expenditure would show up in economic performance at the end of the decade.[43] An actual cut in outlays would presumably have a more profound impact, more quickly.

The level of military expenditure has been, presumably, a factor in the Soviet economic slowdown. But it is by no means the only one; many other obstacles to growth have been identified by Soviet and foreign economists alike. In the 1930s the 'war economy' enabled the Soviet Union to build up its industry and its military power by concentrating high levels of investment and a rapidly growing industrial labour force in key sectors. Now, however, the planning system, which is unchanged in its basic features, has become a brake on economic growth, and in particular on technological progress. This is a serious problem because innovation has become a more important factor in economic growth as the opportunities for increasing the labour force and capital investment have diminished. In the 1930s the planning system served both industrial and military policy equally well. But now a contradiction has emerged between the two, for while the system hinders progress in civilian industry, it allows the state to protect the defence sector and ensure that it is more successful in pursuing technological progress.

In the 1960s many economists, both Soviet and foreign, assumed that the Soviet Union would have to undertake a major reform in order to improve its economic performance. The cause of reform was set back, however, by the crisis in Czechoslovakia in 1968, because political developments in that country were widely interpreted as resulting from the economic reform of 1966. Full-scale reform now looked politically risky. After 1968 Brezhnev adopted several partial measures to try to improve economic performance: one was to use the defence industry as a technological dynamo for the economy as a whole (another was to place more stress on buying foreign technology). In 1971 he told the 24th Party Congress that 'taking into account the high scientific-technical level of the defence industry, the transmission of its experience, inventions and discoveries to all spheres of our economy acquires the highest importance'.[44] In the piecemeal reforms of the 1970s some of the defence industry's organizational features and management techniques – especially in the area of R & D – have been transferred to civilian industry. At the October 1980 Plenary Session of the Central Committee Brezhnev returned to the same theme when he called for the mobilization of the country's 'strongest scientific collectives', which he defined as the Academy of Sciences and scientists and designers in the defence sector, to improve civilian machine-building.[45]

This approach to reform has not had a dramatic effect on economic growth. This is partly because not all the conditions that explain the better technological performance of the defence sector can be reproduced in civilian industry: the powerful role of the military customer, for example, cannot be transferred to civilian production.[46] Further, a very clear redefinition of priorities is needed if the inertia of day-to-day management is to be overcome.

The 9th Five Year Plan (1971–5) called – for the first time since plans were instituted – for a faster rate of growth for Group B industries (those producing consumer goods) than for Group A industries (those producing the means of production). But the traditional priorities were not in fact reversed. One of the reasons why was suggested by an article in *Literaturnaya Gazeta* in 1972, which pointed out that in numerous ways – in prestige, in the priority given by other ministries (for example, in construction projects), in wages, in cultural and housing facilities, in labour turnover – Group B industries fared worse than those in Group A.[47] One of the letters provoked by the article claimed that

> the best conditions are given to the so-called 'leading' branches. Then we have the remaining enterprises in Group A. Last in line are the Group B enterprises. Naturally, the most highly skilled cadres – workers, engineers, or technicians – find jobs or try to find them where the pay is highest, so they are concentrated in the 'leading' branches of industry. What is more, these branches receive the best materials, the most advanced technology, the latest equipment, etc. etc. . . . ).[48]

There is little doubt that within Group A the defence industry occupies the position of highest prestige and therefore shows these features to the highest degree. The 11th Plan once again reverses the traditional priorities between Group A and Group B; it remains to be seen whether the new priority will be realized in practice.

A shift of resources from defence would require, to be effective, a clear redefinition of priorities. The question of priorities could raise once again the issue of economic reform, since the present planning system seems to favour the defence sector over civilian industry. If that happened, a change of priorities might become more difficult because it would be more far-reaching in its consequences. It is possible, therefore, that military expenditures will become the focus of a broad and bitter argument about the future of Soviet policy – an argument that could be as significant as the industrialization debate of the 1920s.

## *The Politics of Change*

In the 1980s the present generation of Party leaders will be succeeded by another, and this will provide the opportunity for new policies and new priorities to emerge. The departure of the present generation of leaders is, as Seweryn Bialer has written, 'an important turning-point in Soviet *political* history. This circumstance, coinciding as it does with another turning-point in Soviet *economic* history, marks a time of unusual opportunities and openings for change.'[49] Foreign and defence policy are also at a turning-point: Soviet–American detente has collapsed; a new round of the arms race is under way; a new encirclement has been forming; economic and political difficulties in Eastern Europe pose sharp problems for Soviet policy. The existence of different crosscurrents and tendencies in Soviet military thinking, and of different conceptions of the Soviet position in the world, suggests that foreign and defence policy will be an issue during the political succession. Past experience indicates that, if a major turning-point takes place in domestic politics, it will be accompanied by a shift in external policy.

The Soviet leaders face important choices in the 1980s. It is difficult to be specific about the courses of action they might take, for there are many combinations of external and internal policies that they could pursue. It is very unlikely, however, that any Soviet leadership would be willing to sacrifice the Soviet position in the world in order to attend to domestic reforms. Consolidation and the search for a breathing-space are possible objectives; retreat is not. Brezhnev has made it clear, for example, that the Soviet Union will respond to the Reagan strategic arms program, which the Soviet press has portrayed as an attempt to achieve military superiority over the Soviet Union.

The Reagan program does present a formidable challenge to the Soviet Union because it will give the United States weapons that can destroy (in theory) the ICBMs on which about three-quarters of Soviet strategic nuclear warheads are deployed (as compared with about one-quarter of American strategic warheads). The Soviet Union, however, can take measures to counteract the American program. It can diversify its strategic forces by putting more warheads on SLBMs and by deploying a mobile ICBM. By the end of the decade the structure of the Soviet strategic forces will be different from what it is today. The Soviet leaders may also adopt a launch-on-warning policy, or drop hints that they have done so; then the U.S. President could not be sure that Soviet ICBMs would still be in their silos if the United States launched a nuclear strike. The Soviet Union could also strengthen its air defences against cruise missile attacks, in particular around command and control installations and missile silos. There is evidence that all of these steps are being undertaken.

At the same time the Soviet Union could deploy a new bomber to strike NATO's nuclear forces in Europe. It could improve the accuracy of its own strategic missiles in order to increase their ability to strike hardened targets. It will no doubt continue to do research and development work in ABM systems technologies and anti-submarine warfare techniques. It might also try to increase its capacity to strike the United States with little warning by deploying missiles closer to the North American continent, either at sea or perhaps even in Cuba. The Soviet Union has a variety of defensive and offensive measures to choose from in countering the Reagan program. These will ensure that, whatever shifts might take place in the strategic balance, the Soviet Union will continue to possess a powerful retaliatory force. Moreover, although expensive, these measures could be accommodated within the present level of defence expenditure: strategic arms production, for example, would not have to reach the levels of the 1960s and 1970s.

The Soviet leaders' response to the Reagan program may well depend on how far they see it as an attempt to apply pressure by forcing the Soviet Union to spend money on new and difficult technologies. If they do see it in this light, they may decide that the appropriate response is a moderate arms program, allied with diplomatic efforts to improve relations with Western Europe, China and Japan. In this way the potential encirclement would be forestalled. Such an emphasis in foreign and defence policy could well be coupled with a determined effort to carry through economic reform at home.

If the Soviet Union can meet the Reagan program by adopting countervailing measures, there is little force in the argument that the Soviet leaders will pursue a highly aggressive policy in the early 1980s because it will lose its powerful position vis-à-vis the West by the 1990s. The combination of present strength and future weakness, it is sometimes claimed, might lead the Soviet Union to exploit its temporary advantage to make some lasting foreign policy gains – for example, by destroying China's nuclear forces, or by seizing control of the Persian Gulf.

This thesis overstates both the present strength and the future weakness of the Soviet Union. Besides, there is no evidence that the present Soviet leaders see the choices facing them in such stark terms. Brezhnev's speech to the 26th Party Congress conveyed neither an impression of overweening arrogance, nor a sense of desperation at the problems to come. It may be, of course, that the present leaders are too sanguine, and that the problems they face will turn out to be less tractable than they think. But they would have to see their choices in this stark way if they were to act as this argument suggests.

Another thesis about the relationship between internal and external politics argues that the Soviet Union must pursue an aggressive and expansionist policy because otherwise the state will lose its legitimacy. There is some force in this argument. The creation of military power is the area in which the Soviet Union has most clearly attained the goal of 'catching up and overtaking' the advanced capitalist states. The Soviet Union's international influence demonstrates the power and prestige of the state, and a serious foreign policy setback might diminish its legitimacy by showing it to be weak or incompetent. But the Soviet Union has had such setbacks, most notably in its relations with China, and it survives.

Moreover, legitimacy might also be lost if the rate of growth continues to decline, for rapid growth has been claimed as a mark of the system's success. If economic decline results in falling living standards this too might affect support for the state. It has been a central objective of Soviet policy since 1953 to raise living standards, and events in Poland have shown that it can be dangerous to neglect this goal. Consequently the thesis about legitimation through expansion is not a sound basis on which to predict future policy, for, although it points to an important aspect of Soviet politics, it neglects other sources of legitimation. (Perhaps it also exaggerates the need for legitimacy in a state with a powerful repressive apparatus.)

It is conceivable that the Soviet leaders might pursue adventures abroad in order to divert attention from problems at home. But there is no evidence that they have done so. That was not the reason why they intervened in Afghanistan; nor have they used the war there to stir up nationalist sentiment in the Soviet Union. On the other hand, they can point to the worsening international situation, and to bellicose statements from the Reagan Administration, to justify the continuing high level of military effort, and can explain economic difficulties by saying that the defence of the country has to be secured in the face of new threats. The appeal to patriotism is likely to be effective because there appears to be widespread acceptance of the need for strong armed forces to maintain peace and security.

It might be argued, as an alternative hypothesis, that the Soviet Union does not really have choices to make. In 1929 and again in

1945–6 Stalin embarked on economic and military policies that gave lowest priority to popular standards of living. Stalin was willing to tolerate famine in the country and not import grain. On the basis of this precedent it might be claimed that, no matter what happens, defence expenditure will continue to grow at its present rate, because defence has absolute priority. But Soviet priorities, and the political system through which they are enforced, have changed since Stalin's death. Defence still has the highest priority, but other policy areas, such as agriculture, for example, have become more important: the Soviet Union does import grain now, not to prevent people from starving, but to maintain livestock production. Since 1953 the Soviet leaders have been able to pursue their more complex priorities without having to make major choices between them. The decline in economic growth has been forcing them to make choices. So far defence has been protected, but its position may be questioned during the political succession.

There is a great deal to suggest that the 1980s will be a major turning-point in Soviet politics: the change of leadership, economic difficulties and foreign policy problems all point towards this. Important questions are likely to be raised about the system of economic planning and management and its suitability for the present stage of economic development, and about the ability of the system as a whole to adapt to new conditions and new challenges. At the same time, however, the forces of inertia are strong, especially in the area of defence policy. This is where the Soviet Union has been most successful. The priority of defence has been built into the economic system. The High Command can be expected to make a forceful case for maintaining a large military effort – indeed Marshal Ogarkov has been doing this already, with his outspoken warnings about the threatening international situation. A succession crisis might give the High Command a more important political role as champions of a strong defence. They might also emerge as advocates of economic reform on the grounds that poor economic performance threatens the country's future defence potential. Unless there is a complete collapse of Party rule, however, General Jaruzelski's action will not provide a model for the Soviet military. Such a collapse is extremely unlikely, and the Polish crisis will have served as a warning to the Soviet Party leaders not to let it happen.

There are strong pressures for change in the Soviet Union, but the forces of inertia are also powerful. It is difficult to be certain, therefore, that the opportunities for change will be taken. The 1980s may be an important turning-point in Soviet history; or they may prove to be (to paraphrase Namier's comment on the European revolutions of 1848) a 'turning-point that fails to turn'.

## Conclusion

Hintze was right. The military factor has been, and will continue to be, a crucial element in Soviet politics. Soviet military power is not something separate from the Soviet state, but forms part and parcel of it. Soviet military power must be understood not only in terms of the international environment, but also in the context of domestic politics, for its domestic roots – ideological, political, social and economic – are very strong. This does not necessarily mean that internal politics has primacy over foreign policy considerations, but rather that issues of military policy are crucial in domestic politics. The major turning-points in Soviet military policy have been the same as those in domestic politics: the launching of Stalin's industrialization drive, the purges of the late 1930s, the war with Germany, the decisions on post-war reconstruction, Khrushchev's attempts at reform, and the consolidation and stability of the Brezhnev years. If the 1980s are a major turning-point in Soviet domestic politics, then military policy too will be affected. But if the Soviet leaders determine, for whatever reason, that they will not or cannot alter their military policy, then that will have a major influence on domestic politics. The Soviet leaders may decide that economic reform would jeopardize their military policy; or they may conclude that major reforms are needed to strengthen the economic and technological basis of the state and its military power.

# Conclusion

I have attempted in this book to explore the historical experience, the policy objectives and the institutions that sustain the Soviet military effort. I have tried to show that Soviet policy has been the product of specific decisions taken in a distinctive institutional setting, under the influence of a particular historical experience. I have not undertaken a comprehensive account of Soviet policy, but have chosen, instead, to explore some specific aspects of Soviet military power. Nor have I sought to provide a history of Soviet military policy: much more research needs to be done – and the Soviet Union needs to be more open about its past decisions – before that becomes possible. Nevertheless I have tried to set my discussion of Soviet military power in its historical context.

One reason why a historical perspective is important is that Soviet policy is not easily explained by the theoretical models of the arms race to be found in the social science literature. There are, it is true, elements of the action-reaction phenomenon (in which each side reacts to actions, or potential actions, by the other side) in the history of Soviet – American nuclear weapons competition, with the Soviet Union less innovative, and therefore more reactive, than the United States. At a broader level too it is possible to identify important points at which American policy seems to have been crucial for Soviet decisions: the atomic bomb decision of 1945; decisions about the development of thermonuclear weapons in the late 1940s and early 1950s; decisions in the early 1960s about strategic forces; decisions about ABM systems and strategic missiles in the years before the SALT I Agreements; and perhaps at the present time too. It is more difficult to trace the interaction for the later decisions than for the earlier ones, but the evidence is strong that interaction exists. It is not helpful, therefore, to view Soviet policy as autistic, unresponsive to external stimuli.

At the same time, however, Soviet decisions cannot be understood only as reactions to Western actions. The Soviet leaders have had their own purposes to pursue, their own conception of what military forces they need in order to pursue those purposes, and their own way of doing things. All these influences have imparted a special quality to Soviet policy and policy-making. Even in the history of the early nuclear program, when the Soviet Union was clearly reacting to developments abroad, the important point to understand is not how Stalin reacted, but why he reacted: what political feelings, what fears and ambitions, lay behind the decision to enter the nuclear arms race? The answer to this question cannot be provided by the action-reaction model of the arms race, but has to be sought in Soviet history.

The Soviet Union has approached the problem of nuclear war in the way that states have traditionally approached the question of war. It has sought to ensure its own security by increasing its military strength. The Soviet leaders have presented their country as powerful, even to the point of hiding its weakness by deception and bluff, as in the bomber gap episode of the mid-1950s and the missile gap episode of 1959−61. They have not wanted to advertise their vulnerability, and their concern not to do so has contributed to their reluctance to accept mutual deterrence, with its stress on mutual vulnerability, as a sound basis for Soviet−American relations.

The Soviet leaders have treated nuclear weapons like conventional weapons in regarding them as instruments of military power and political influence, and at the same time have recognized their qualitatively new character and the devastation they could bring. The Soviet Union has built up powerful nuclear forces not only in preparation for a possible nuclear war, but also to deprive the United States of any political advantage that superiority might bring. In 1946 Stalin said that it would take at least fifteen years to be ready for all contingencies. But in the nuclear age complete readiness is not possible. The Soviet leaders have been forced to recognize that their relationship with the United States is in reality one of mutual vulnerability to devastating nuclear strikes, and that there is no immediate prospect of escaping from this relationship. Within the constraints of this mutual vulnerability they have tried to prepare for nuclear war, and they would try to win such a war if it came to that. But there is little evidence to suggest that they think victory in a global nuclear war would be anything other than catastrophic.

The Soviet Union has tried to manage the strategic relationship with the United States through arms control negotiations. 'Manage' is an ambiguous term here, and appropriately so, for the Soviet commitment to parity is by no means so strong as to rule out the search for unilateral advantage. It is hard to see, however, that arms control, as it has been pursued up to now, will lead to anything better than a regulated arms race, for reasons given in Chapter Four. There is no evidence that the Soviet leaders recognize that this is the best that arms control, as practised in the 1960s and 1970s, can achieve. Nonetheless, arms control has become an important element in the Soviet relationship with the West, and a major arena for pursuing both common goals and conflicting objectives.

The Soviet leaders have valued nuclear weapons not only for their potential military utility, but also for their political effect. When they lacked nuclear weapons they felt themselves to be the targets of 'nuclear diplomacy'. In the late 1950s and early 1960s Khrushchev tried to extract political gains from the ability the Soviet Union was now acquiring to strike the United States with nuclear-armed missiles. When that failed the Soviet Union pressed ahead with building up its strategic nuclear forces and in the 1970s claimed strategic parity with the United States. Strategic nuclear power is the clearest symbol of Soviet superpower status, and the claim to strategic parity shades into the assertion that the Soviet Union is the United States's political equal. But it is not clear what the Soviet Union means by equality in practical terms, or what it implies for Soviet–American relations: an equal right to intervene in third countries, a Soviet–American condominium, a new world order designed with Soviet participation? If the Soviet claim to equality is to provide the basis for better Soviet–American relations it will have to be explained more fully.

The Soviet leaders have been successful in making their country a military superpower. The defence economy has been able to sustain a high level of military effort, and military R & D has been more effective than its civilian counterpart in generating technological innovation. But the military effort has placed a heavy burden on the economy, absorbing resources that could contribute to economic growth and the welfare of the people. The current economic slowdown will force the Soviet leaders to make difficult choices, not only about the allocation of resources, but also about the system of economic planning and management. The 1980s may see fundamental questions raised about the economic system, and about the ability of the political institutions to cope with change. These questions may become the focus of political conflict during the succession, and, if they do, military policy is likely to be a central issue in the argument. The problems that confront the Soviet leaders are indeed serious, but they are not the portents of imminent collapse; whatever choices the Soviet leaders make, the Soviet Union will remain a great military power and a major force in world politics.

My main purpose in this book has been to throw light on Soviet military power, not to make recommendations for Western policy. The problem of understanding Soviet policy should, I think, be kept analytically distinct from prescriptions for Western policy. Too often Soviet policy is presented in such a way as to justify whatever Western policy is being recommended; Western fears about nuclear war or (much less frequently) hopes about disarmament are projected onto the Soviet Union, with little attention to the substance of Soviet policy. Moreover, in devising Western policy, considerations other than Soviet power have to be taken into account, and criteria other than military effectiveness (economic, political and moral criteria, for example) have to be applied. With these reservations in mind, however, it seems appropriate to point to some broad implications that might be drawn from the analysis given in this book.

The conclusion that the Soviet Union faces major choices about the direction of its policy is relevant for Western policy. The United States now seems to be intent only on preparing for confrontation, and on applying pressure on the Soviet economy in order to force a reduction in the military effort. The Reagan Administration appears to be unwilling to concede equal status of any kind to the Soviet Union. The difficulty with this approach is that it exaggerates the external strength of the Soviet Union (great though that is) and overemphasizes the Soviet Union's internal problems (considerable though those are). Moreover, if the Soviet Union is at a turning-point in its history, the West should prepare also for cooperation. This is not an argument for acceding to all Soviet demands, but rather for thinking out more clearly the basis on which better East–West relations might be conducted and preparing for the pursuit of such relations.

It is probably a mistake to suppose that Western governments can have much effect on Soviet domestic politics. But a policy of confrontation that appears to preclude the possibility of cooperation might well affect the outcome of internal Soviet arguments, and thus of the political succession. If the Soviet leaders see themselves challenged to another round in the arms race, they may well respond, as they did in 1945–6 and in the early 1960s, by concentrating their efforts on continuing to increase their military power. If, on the other hand, they see the possibility of accommodation, they may decide that that is the course to pursue. In the immediate aftermath of Stalin's death, important shifts took place in Soviet foreign and defence policy, as the Soviet leaders moved to resolve some of their major differences with the West (the Korean War and the German Problem, for example) and to revise their defence policy. No one can say for certain whether the political succession will lead to similar moves this time or to a major shift in the direction of policy, but it seems, at the very least, extremely ill-advised for the United States to pursue a policy that makes any Soviet move towards accommodation and cooperation less likely.

Perhaps the most important conclusion is that the Soviet Union does not have satisfactory answers to the problems posed by nuclear war and nuclear weapons. The answers the Soviet leaders have arrived at are not very different from those given by Western governments: nuclear weapons are both instruments of power and influence, and the potential agents of catastrophic devastation. Nor are Soviet answers much better than Western answers. The Soviet Union has not been able to escape from the threat of nuclear annihilation. Its leaders and its people share our predicament. We have a common interest in preventing nuclear war.

It follows from this, I think, that negotiations to halt the nuclear arms race should be pursued as vigorously as possible. This conclusion is reinforced by the Soviet economic slowdown and the shifts in Soviet military doctrine which suggest that the Soviet Union may be particularly interested in arms reductions. It is sometimes argued that the Soviet rejection of the American proposal of March 1977, which called for lower ceilings for strategic arms than had been agreed at Vladivostok in November 1974, shows that the Soviet Union will not accept cuts in existing force levels. Such a conclusion is unwarranted, for that proposal was ineptly presented (it was made public in Washington before being delivered to Moscow), and came at a time when a SALT II Agreement seemed close at hand. Moreover, the Soviet Union regarded the proposal as one-sided and was clearly unwilling to rethink its negotiating position at such a late stage in the talks.[1] It is wrong, therefore, to conclude from this episode that the Soviet Union will not accept radical cuts under any circumstances. Indeed, the subsequent fate of the SALT II Treaty may have indicated to the Soviet leaders that it was a mistake to reject the American proposal out of hand.

It is also objected sometimes that Soviet secrecy makes effective verifiable arms control agreements difficult, or even impossible, to achieve. It is true that Soviet secrecy is an obstacle, and that it complicates negotiations. Recently, however, the Soviet Union has given some indication that it recognizes this, for in the Comprehensive Test Ban negotiations it accepted that seismic recorders and on-site inspections on Soviet territory would be necessary for a verifiable agreement.[2] At a more general level the Soviet Union, though still extremely secretive, has been more forthcoming about the size of its own forces, and about its view of the military balance, where these are relevant for arms control negotiations. This was especially so in the prelude to the Geneva talks on Intermediate Range Nuclear Forces. Even the battle of the books, in which the Soviet Ministry of Defence responded to the Pentagon's *Soviet Military Power* by issuing a similar pamphlet of its own, *Whence the Threat to Peace?*, showed an increased willingness on the part of the Soviet Union to discuss the details of its military relationship with the Western powers.[3]

It may seem curious to recommend arms control talks when the argument has been made in Chapter Four that such talks can speed up the arms race. That will indeed be the result of such talks unless negotiations are accompanied by unilateral steps to slow down the competition in nuclear weapons. Western governments have to take account of Soviet power, of course, but they should not allow their policies to be determined by it. Too often Western governments try to justify their policies merely by reference to what the Soviet Union is doing, as though that were a good reason in itself. (Such an argument conveys the historically incorrect impression that Western governments have merely reacted to Soviet actions.) Similarly it is too often argued that Soviet power makes it impossible to take unilateral steps to slow down the nuclear arms race. But that is not so. There is considerable scope, for example, for Western governments to reduce unilaterally their heavy reliance on nuclear weapons, especially in Europe.[4] Not every step of this kind need be, or should be, made conditional on Soviet reciprocity. Actions should be judged on their merits by asking whether they contribute not only to Western security, but also to the common human interest in reducing the risk of nuclear war. Only by applying this principle alongside arms control may it be possible to prevent negotiations from stimulating, rather than slowing down, the East–West arms competition.

This point is, I think, relevant for the peace movements in the West. The political arrangements in the Soviet Union and Eastern Europe make it extremely difficult, if not impossible, to bring public opinion to bear on the authorities in those countries. The emergence of a peace movement in East Germany and the recent formation of a small peace group in Moscow are signs that the Western movements have touched a chord in those countries. While this is encouraging (and to be encouraged), it would be a mistake to link the success of Western peace movements in influencing Western governments to the success of such groups in reviving civil society and influencing their governments. To make everything conditional on the growth of similar movements in the Soviet Union and Eastern Europe would be to make the Western peace movement hostage to the policies of the Soviet and Eastern European authorities.

On the other hand it is intellectually unsatisfying and politically dangerous to ignore Soviet military power and the threat that it can pose to Western countries. The Soviet Union is a powerful state and has shown itself willing to use military force. In pressing Western governments to move away from reliance on nuclear weapons the peace movement should consider alternative policies for defence against possible aggression. It is precisely in this area that the scope for unilateral action by Western governments seems to be greatest.[5] This is not the place to explore possible courses of action. But the point needs to be made that while Soviet military power cannot be ignored, we should not allow the fact of that power to deprive us of all freedom of choice in the courses of action we pursue.

# Notes

## Notes to Chapter One

1.   In his report to the 8th Party Congress; see V.I. Lenin, *Pol'noe Sobranie Sochinenii*, vol. 38, Moscow: Politizdat, 1963 pp. 139–40.

2.   Yu. I. Koroblev, *V.I. Lenin i zashchita zavoevanii velikogo Oktyabrya*, 2nd ed., Moscow: Nauka, 1979, chs. 2 and 4.

3.   John Erickson, 'The Origins of the Red Army', in Richard Pipes (ed.), *Revolutionary Russia*, Cambridge, Mass.: Harvard U.P., 1968, pp. 224–56.

4.   N. Bukharin and E. Preobrazhensky, *The ABC of Communism*, Ann Arbor: The University of Michigan Press, 1966, p. 218.

5.   John Erickson, 'Some Military and Political Aspects of the "Militia Army" Controversy, 1919–1920', in C. Abramsky (ed.), *Essays in Honour of E.H. Carr*, London: Macmillan, 1974, pp. 204–28.

6.   Speech of 15 March at the Tenth Party Congress, in V.I. Lenin, *Pol'noe sobranie sochinenii*, vol. 43, Moscow: Politizdat, 1963. Quoted in E.H. Carr, *The Bolshevik Revolution 1917–1923*, vol. 2, London: Macmillan, 1952, p. 277.

7.   This important topic has not received the analysis it merits. But see Manfred von Boetticher's recent study, *Industrialisierungspolitik und Verteidigungskonzeption der UdSSR 1926–1930*, Düsseldorf: Droste Verlag, 1979.

8.   Quoted in *50 let Vooruzhennykh Sil SSSR*, Moscow: Voenizdat, 1968, p. 198.

9.   Quoted in E.H. Carr, *Foundations of a Planned Economy 1926–1929*, vol. 2, London: Macmillan, 1971, p. 314.

10.   *Istoriya vtoroi mirovoi voiny* (hereafter *IVMV*), vol. 1, Voenizdat, 1969, pp. 264–6.

11.   *KPSS o Vooruzhennykh Silakh Sovetskogo Soyuza*, Moscow: Voenizdat, 1969, pp. 264–6.

12.   *IVMV*, vol. 1, Moscow: Voenizdat, 1973, pp. 257–8.

13.   Quoted by S. Kozlov, in 'The Formulation and Development of Soviet Military Doctrine', *Voennaya Mysl'*, 1966, no. 7. All references to this classified journal are to the CIA translations made available through the Library of Congress.

14.   J.V. Stalin, *Problems of Leninism*, Moscow: Foreign Languages Publishing House, 1947, p. 213.

15.   E.H. Carr, *Socialism in One Country 1924–1926*, vol. 2, London: Macmillan, 1959, p. 50.

16.   Julian Cooper, *Defence Production and the Soviet Economy 1929–1941*, CREES Discussion Paper, University of Birmingham, 1976, pp. 28–30.

17.   M.N. Tukhachevskii, 'O Novom Polevom Ustave RKKA', in *Izbrannye Proizvedeniya*, vol. 2, Moscow: Voenizdat, 1964, pp. 255–6.

18.   Oskar Lange, *Papers in Economics and Sociology*, Oxford and Warsaw: Pergamon Press and Panstwowe Wydawnictwo Naukowe, 1970, p. 102.

19.   Cooper, *op. cit.*, pp. 26–7.

20.   See Marshal Biryuzov's Introduction in Tukhachevskii, *op. cit.*, vol. 1, pp. 12–13.

21.   On this see Seweryn Bialer, *Stalin's Successors. Leadership, Stability and Change in the Soviet Union*, Cambridge: Cambridge U.P., 1980, p. 22.

22.   'On the Draft Constitution of the USSR', 25 November 1936, in I.V. Stalin, *Sochineniya*, vol. 1/xiv/ 1934–1940, ed. by Robert H. McNeal, Stanford, California: The Hoover Institution on War, Revolution and Peace, Stanford University, 1967, p. 148.

23.   'Report to the 18th Party Congress, 10 March, 1939', in Stalin, *op. cit.*, pp. 385–7.

24.   On the military purge see John Erickson, *The Soviet High Command*, London: Macmillan, 1962, chs. 14–15.

25.   M.V. Zakharov, in *Voprosy strategii i operativnogo iskusstva v Sovetskikh Voennykh Trudakh* (1917–1940gg), Moscow: Voenizdat, 1965, p. 22.

26.   G.S. Kravchenko, *Ekonomika SSSR v gody Velikoi otechestvennoi voiny*, Moscow: Ekonomika, 1970, pp. 123–4.

27.   Kozlov, *loc. cit.*, p. 60.

28.   John Erickson, *The Road to Stalingrad*, London: Weidenfeld and Nicolson, 1975, ch. 2.

29.   On the way in which Soviet historiography treated the events of 1941 before 1967 see P. Maslov, 'Literatura o voennykh deistviyakh letom 1941 goda', *Voenno-istoricheskii zhurnal*, 1966, no. 9, pp. 88–95.

30.   *Khrushchev Remembers*, New York: Bantam Books, 1971, pp. 640–7.

31.   A.M. Nekrich, *1941 22 iyunya*, Moscow: Nauka, 1965. An English translation of Nekrich's book, along with a commentary on the whole affair, a translation of the attack on Nekrich, and an account of an interesting Soviet discussion of his book is to be found in Vladimir Petrov, *'June 22, 1941'*, Columbia, S.C.: University of South Carolina Press, 1968. For another analysis of the whole affair, by the dissident Major-General P.G. Grigorenko, see 'Sokrytie istoricheskoi pravdy – prestuplenie pered narodom', in his *Mysli sumasshedshego*, Amsterdam: Fond imeni Gertsena, 1973, pp. 31–93.

32.   Note, for example, the different treatment given to Stalin in the works of the General Staff historian V.A. Anfilov, *Nachalo velikoi otechestvennoi voiny*, Moscow: Voenizdat, 1963, and *Bessmertnyi podvig*, Moscow: Nauka, 1971. See also the views expressed by Anfilov in the discussion of Nekrich's book, in Petrov, *op. cit.*, pp. 252–3.

33.   See the next chapter. See also Army General S.P. Ivanov (ed.), *Nachal'nyi period voiny*, Moscow: Voenizdat, 1974, a study of the opening campaigns and operations of the Second World War.

34.   Alexander Werth, *Russia at War*, London: Pan Books, 1965, pp. 162–9.

35.   Alexander Dallin, *German Rule in Russia 1941–1945*, London: Macmillan, 1957, p. 678.

36.   Quoted by Robert C. Tucker, in 'Swollen State, Spent Society: Stalin's Legacy to Brezhnev's Russia', *Foreign Affairs*, Winter 1981/2, p. 217; see also Alexander Gershenkron, 'Economic Backwardness in Historical Perspective', in his book of the same title, New York: Praeger, 1965, pp. 5–30.

37.   Quoted in V.A. Anfilov, *Bessmertnyi Podvig*, Moscow: Nauka, 1971, p. 509.

38.   'Speech at the Reception in the Kremlin in Honor of the Commanders for the Red Army Troops, May 24, 1945', in I.V. Stalin, *Sochineniya*, vol. 2/xv/ 1941–1945, ed. by

Robert H. McNeal, Stanford, California: The Hoover Institution on War, Revolution and Peace, Stanford University, 1967, p. 204.

39. Election speech, February 9, 1946, in I.V. Stalin, *Sochineniya*, vol. 3/xvi/ 1946–1953, ed. by Robert H. McNeal, Stanford, California: The Hoover Institution on War, Revolution and Peace, Stanford University, 1967, pp. 6–7.

40. *Ibid.*, p. 20.

## Notes to Chapter Two

1. On Bohr's activities see Margaret Gowing, *Britain and Atomic Energy*, London: Macmillan, 1964, pp. 347–66 and Martin Sherwin, *A World Destroyed*, New York: Vintage Books, 1977, pp. 91–8.

2. Harry S. Truman, *1945: Year of Decisions*, New York: Doubleday, 1965, p. 458.

3. Quoted by Herbert York, in *The Advisors: Oppenheimer, Teller and the Bomb*, San Francisco, Calif.: W.H. Freeman & Co., 1976, p. 29. Unless otherwise noted, the material in this section is taken from David Holloway, 'Entering the Nuclear Arms Race: The Soviet Decision to Build the Atomic Bomb, 1939–45', *Social Studies of Science*, vol. 11, 1981, pp. 159–97.

4. A.I. Ioirysh, I.D. Morokhov, S.K. Ivanov, *A-Bomba*, Moscow: Nauka, 1980, p. 377.

5. Yu. V. Sivintsev, *I.V. Kurchatov i yadernaya energetika*, Moscow: Atomizdat, 1980, p. 11.

6. A.I. Ioriysh *et al.*, *op. cit.*, p. 390.

7. Alexander Werth, *Russia at War 1941–1945*, London: Pan Books Ltd., 1965, p. 925.

8. *Foreign Relations of the United States, 1945*, vol. II, Washington D.C.: Department of State, 1967, p. 83.

9. *Foreign Relations of the United States, 1945*, vol. V, Washington D.C.: Department of State, 1967, p. 923.

10. Quoted by A. Lavrent'yeva in 'Stroiteli novogo mira', *V mire knig*, 1970, no. 9, p. 4.

11. Margaret Gowing, *Science and Politics*, The Eighth J.D. Bernal Lecture, Birkbeck College, London, 1977, p. 11.

12. V.P. Glushko, *Rocket Engines GDL-OKB*, Moscow: Novosti Press Agency Publishing House, 1975, pp. 7, 8, 11; Ye. K. Moshkin, *Razvitie otechestvennogo raketnogo dvigatelestroeniya*, Moscow: Mashinostroenie 1973, pp. 170–180; N.A. Pilyugin, interview in *Pravda*, 17 May 1978. See also David Holloway, 'Innovation in the Defence Sector: Two Case Studies', in R. Amann and J. Cooper (eds.), *Industrial Innovation in the Soviet Union*, New Haven and London: Yale University Press, 1982, pp. 386–92.

13. A.G. Zverev, *Zapiski ministra*, Moscow: Politizdat, 1973, p. 227.

14. See Holloway in Amann and Cooper, *op. cit.*, pp. 390–1; the figure for the proportion of research done in prison institutes is taken from Roy A. Medvedev and Zhores A. Medvedev, *Khrushchev. The Years in Power*, New York: Columbia U.P., 1976, p. 38.

15. Ioirysh, Morokhov, Ivanov, *op. cit.*, p. 395.

16. A.P. Romanov, *Raketam pokoryaetsya prostranstvo*, Moscow: Politizdat 1976, p. 51; G.A. Tokaev, *Comrade X*, London: Harvill Press, 1956, pp. 310–30. Romanov confirms Tokaev's report that meetings were held then, though he does not discuss, as Tokaev does, what was decided.

17.  Antony C. Sutton, *Western Technology and Soviet Economic Development 1945 to 1965*, Stanford, California: Hoover Institution Press, 1973, chs. 2, 20, 21.

18.  See Frederick I. Ordway III and Mitchell R. Sharpe, *The Rocket Team*, New York: Thomas Y. Crowell, 1979, chs. 13, 14 and 17.

19.  Pilyugin, *loc. cit.*; P.A. Agadzhanov, in *S.P. Korolev. Sbornik statei*, Moscow: Znanie, 1977, p. 20.

20.  David Holloway, 'Military Technology', in R. Amann, J. Cooper and R.W. Davies (eds.), *The Technological Level of Soviet Industry*, New Haven and London: Yale University Press, 1977, p. 458.

21.  See Table 2.1.

22.  Robert J. Donovan, *The Devastating Time: Truman, The Hydrogen Bomb, China and Korea*, Washington D.C.: ISSP, Wilson Center, Working Paper No. 6, 1979, p. 20.

23.  Quoted in York, *op. cit.*, p. 156.

24.  See, for example, A.I. Ioirysh, I.D. Morokhov, *Khirosima*, Moscow: Atomizdat, 1979, p. 279.

25.  See York, *op. cit.*, esp. pp. 75–110; see also David Holloway, 'Soviet Thermonuclear Research', *International Security*, Winter 1979/80, vol. 4, no. 3, pp. 192–7.

26.  Holloway, 'Soviet Thermonuclear Research', *loc. cit.*, pp. 192–6.

27.  I.N. Golovin, *I.V. Kurchatov*, Moscow: Atomizdat, 3rd ed., 1978, p. 94.

28.  V.M. Molotov, *28aya godovshchina Velikoi Oktyabr'skoi Sotsialisticheskoi revolyutsii*, Moscow: Gospolitizdat, 1945, pp. 28–9.

29.  *Sovetskie Vooruzhennye Sily. Istoriya stroitel'stva*, Moscow: Voenizdat, 1978, pp. 384–7, 391–6. Matthew Evangelista, 'Stalin's Army Reappraised', unpublished manuscript, Peace Studies Program, Cornell University, 1982.

30.  *Pravda*, 25 September 1946.

31.  Maj-Gen. S. Kozlov, 'The Development of Soviet Military Science After World War Two', *Voennaya Mysl'*, 1964, no. 2, p. 35.

32.  *Ibid.*, p. 33.

## Notes to Chapter Three

1.  M.V. Frunze, 'Yedinaya voennaya doktrina i Krasnaya Armiya', in *Izbrannye proizvedeniya*, Moscow: Voenizdat, 1977, pp. 29–46. This was first published in June 1921.

2.  Leon Trotsky, 'Military Doctrine or Pseudo-Military Doctrinairism', in *Military Writings*, New York: Merit Publishers, 1969, pp. 31–69. This dates from December 1921.

3.  *Sovetskaya Voennaya Entsiklopediya* (hereafter *SVE*), vol. 3, Moscow: Voenizdat, 197, p. 225.

4.  *SVE*, vol. 2, Moscow: Voenizdat, 1976, p. 184.

5.  *Ibid.*, p. 221.

6.  See, for example, Col. Gen. N.A. Lomov, 'O Sovetskoi voennoi doktrine', and Maj. Gen. S.N. Kozlov, 'Voennaya doktrina i voennaya nauka', in *Problemy revolyutsii v voennom dele*, Moscow: Voenizdat, 1965, pp. 40–56, 57–69.

7.  Besides the references in note 6 see *Spravochnik ofitsera*, Moscow: Voenizdat, 1971, pp. 73–9. Subjectivism is a term often used to refer to Khrushchev's mistaken policies, and voluntarism to Stalin's.

8.  Col. Gen. A. Radzieyevskii, 'Thirty Years of the Military Academy of the General Staff', *Voennaya Mysl'*, 1966, no. 10, p. 8.

9. I.V. Stalin, 'Ekonomicheskie problemy sotsializma v SSSR', in *Sochineniya*, vol. 3/xvi/ 1946–1953, ed. by Robert H. McNeal, Stanford, California: The Hoover Institution on War, Revolution and Peace, Stanford University, 1967, p. 230.

10. Raymond L. Garthoff, 'The Death of Stalin and the Birth of Mutual Deterrence', *Survey*, 1980, no. 2, pp. 10–16.

11. H.S. Dinerstein, *War and the Soviet Union*, New York: Frederick A. Praeger, 1962, pp. 28–63, 70–7.

12. F. Burlatskii and A. Galkin, *Sotsiologiya. Politika. Mezhdunarodnye otnosheniya*, Moscow: Izd. 'Mezhdunarodnye otnosheniya', 1974, p. 287.

13. N.S. Khrushchev, *Report of the Central Committee to the 20th Congress of the CPSU*, London: Soviet News Booklet, 1956, p. 28.

14. D.F. Ustinov, *Izbrannye rechi i stat'i*, Moscow: Politizdat, 1979, p. 329. This is taken from an article originally published in *Kommunist*, 1977, no. 3.

15. Henry Trofimenko, *Changing Attitudes Toward Deterrence*, ACIS Working Paper No. 25, Center for International and Strategic Affairs, University of California, Los Angeles, July 1980, pp. 53–4.

16. Burlatskii and Galkin, *op. cit.*, pp. 286–8. This part of the study was written by Burlatskii and has been published in English, in Fyodor Burlatskii, *The Modern State and Politics*, Moscow: Progress Publishers, 1978.

17. Maj. Gen. S. Kozlov, 'The Formulation and Development of Soviet Military Doctrine', *Voennaya Mysl'*, 1966, no. 7, p. 48; Army General S. Ivanov, 'Soviet Military Doctrine and Strategy', *Voennaya Mysl'*, 1969, no. 5, pp. 40–51.

18. The manpower figures were given by Khrushchev. *Pravda*, 15 January 1960. On naval programs see Michael MccGwire, 'The Turning Points in Soviet Naval Policy', in MccGwire (ed.) *Soviet Naval Developments, Capability and Context*, New York: Praeger Publishers, 1973, p. 202.

19. Col. Gen. M. Povaliy, 'The Development of Soviet Military Strategy', *Voennaya Mysl'*, 1967, no. 2, p. 64.

20. On American policy see, for example, George H. Quester, *Nuclear Diplomacy. The First Twenty-Five Years*, New York: Dunellan, 1970, pp. 89–144. On nuclear weapons deployment and stockpiles see Milton Leitenberg, 'Background Materials in Tactical Nuclear Weapons (primarily in the European context)', in SIPRI, *Tactical Nuclear Weapons: European Perspectives*, London: Taylor and Francis Ltd., 1978, pp. 12, 75.

21. Army General V.G. Kulikov (ed.), *Akademiya General'nogo Shtaba*, Moscow: Voenizdat, 1976, p. 129; *Atomnaya Energiya. Sbornik Statei*, Moscow: Voenizdat, 1954; *50 let Vooruzhennykh Sil SSSR*, Moscow: Voenizdat, 1967, p. 502; Harriet Fast Scott and William F. Scott, *The Armed Forces of the USSR*, Boulder, Colorado: Westview Press, 1979, p. 40.

22. Matthew P. Gallagher, *The Soviet History of World War II. Myths, Memories and Realities*, New York: Frederick A. Praeger, 1963, ch. 2; Dinerstein, *op. cit.*, pp. 167–74.

23. Dinerstein, *op. cit.*, p. 186.

24. *Ibid.*, p. 187.

25. Marshal of Tank Forces P. Rotmistrov, *Krasnaya Zvezda*, 24 March 1955. Quoted in Raymond L. Garthoff, *Soviet Strategy in the Nuclear Age*, London: Stevens and Sons Ltd., 1958, p. 84.

26. *50 let . . .*, *op. cit.*, p. 521; Scott and Scott, *op. cit.*, pp. 41, 74–5; Kulikov, *op. cit.*, pp. 157, 164; *SVE*, vol. 7 Moscow: Voenizdat, 1979, p. 52; Khrushchev's speech is in *Pravda*, 15 January 1960.

27. *Pravda*, 15 January 1960.

28. On the debates of the period see Thomas W. Wolfe, *Soviet Strategy at the Cross-roads*, Cambridge, Mass: Harvard U.P., 1964.

29. Marshal of the Soviet Union V.D. Sokolovskii (ed.), *Voennaya Strategiya*, Moscow: Voenizdat, 1962, p. 16.

30. *Ibid.*, p. 237.

31. *Ibid.*, p. 239.

32. *Ibid.*, p. 238—9.

33. Wolfe *op. cit.*, pp. 149—50; 50 let . . . , *op. cit.*, p. 510.

34. John Erickson, 'Soviet Theater-Warfare Capability: Doctrines, Deployments, and Capabilities', in Lawrence L. Whetten, *The Future of Soviet Military Power*, New York: Crane, Russak and Co. Ltd., 1976, p. 125.

35. Sokolovskii, *op. cit.*, 3rd ed., p. 228; in a book review in *Voennaya Mysl'*, 1965, no. 10, p. 64, Lt. Col. Ye. Rybkin calls for more attention 'to the problems of conducting local wars'.

36. Sokolovskii, *op. cit.*, pp. 222—4.

37. Soviet Government Statement – Reply to Statement Made by the Chinese Government, September 21, 1963, in William E. Griffith, *The Sino—Soviet Rift*, London: George Allen and Unwin Ltd., 1964, p. 444.

38. Open Letter from the CPSU Central Committee to Party Organizations and All Communists of the Soviet Union, 14 July 1963, *ibid.*, p. 300.

39. Robert L. Arnett, 'Soviet Attitudes towards Nuclear War: Do They Really Think They Can Win?' *Journal of Strategic Studies*, September 1979, pp. 173—5.

40. Maj. Gen. N. Talenskii, 'Anti-Missile Systems and Disarmament', *International Affairs*, 1964, no. 10, p. 18.

41. Quoted by John Newhouse, *Cold Dawn. The Story of SALT*, New York: Holt, Rinehart and Winston, 1973, p. 90.

42. Raymond L. Garthoff, 'SALT and the Soviet Military', *Problems of Communism*, January—February 1975, pp. 21—4.

43. Maj. Gen. V.M. Zemskov, 'Wars of the Modern Era', *Voennaya Mysl'*, 1969, no. 5, p. 60. On this period in Soviet military thought see Raymond L. Garthoff, 'Mutual Deterrence and Strategic Arms Limitation in Soviet Policy', *International Security*, Summer 1978, pp. 114—33.

44. Gerard Smith, *Doubletalk. The Story of SALT I*, New York: Doubleday, 1980, p. 83.

45. *Ibid.*, p. 85.

46. *Ibid.*, p. 147.

47. *Pravda*, 30 September 1972.

48. See, for example, G.A. Trofimenko, *S.Sh.A. Politika, Voina, Ideologiya*, Moscow: Mysl', 1976, pp. 285—332; A. Arbatov, *Bezopasnost' v yadernyi vek i politika Vashingtona*, Moscow: Politizdat, 1980, pp. 104—48.

49. Smith, *op. cit.*, pp. 280—98.

50. *Ibid.*, p. 139—44.

51. See the discussion in Garthoff, 'Mutual Deterrence . . . ', *loc. cit.*, pp. 133ff.

52. *Pravda*, 19 January 1977.

53. *Pravda*, 2 August 1979.

54. *Pravda*, 24 February 1981.

55. *Ibid.*

56. *New York Times*, 2 October 1981, p. A26.

57. *Pravda*, 20 October 1981.

58.  Smith, *op. cit.*, p. 460.

59.  Paul H. Nitze, 'Assuring Strategic Stability in an Era of Detente', *Foreign Affairs*, vol. 54, no. 2 (January 1976), pp. 207–32. See also Congressional Budget Office, U.S. Congress, *Counterforce Issues for the U.S. Strategic Nuclear Forces*, Washington D.C.: USGPO, 1978.

60.  *Pravda*, 2 August 1979.

61.  Alexander and Andrew Cockburn, 'The Myth of Missile Accuracy', *New York Review of Books*, 20 November 1980, pp. 40–4; J. Edward Anderson, 'First Strike: Myth or Reality', *Bulletin of Atomic Scientists*, November 1981, pp. 6–11.

62.  V. Zhurkin, in *Literaturnaya Gazeta*, 19 September 1980.

63.  See, for example, N. Ogarkov, 'Na strazhe mirnogo truda', *Kommunist*, 1981, no. 10, pp. 81–3.

64.  David R. Jones, 'Civil Defense' in David R. Jones (ed.) *Soviet Armed Forces Review Annual*, vol. 2, Gulf Breeze: Academic International Press, 1978, pp. 289–350; Leon Goure, *War Survival in Soviet Strategy. USSR Civil Defense*, University of Miami: Center for Advanced International Studies, 1976.

65.  Committee on Banking, Housing, and Urban Affairs, U.S. Senate, *Civil Defense*, Hearings, January 8, 1979, Washington, D.C.: USGPO, 1979, pp. 263–76; James Fallows, *National Defense*, New York: Random House, 1981, pp. 159–62.

66.  For some of the uncertainties see Fred M. Kaplan, 'The Soviet Civil Defense Myth', in *Bulletin of the Atomic Scientists*, March 1978, pp. 15–20, and April 1978, pp. 41–51; U.S. Arms Control and Disarmament Agency, 'An Analysis of Civil Defense in Nuclear War', December 1978, in Committee on Banking . . . , *op. cit.*, p. 93.

67.  Ogarkov, *loc. cit.*, *Kommunist*, 1981, no. 10, p. 85.

68.  *Komsomol'skaya Pravda*, 10 April 1981.

69.  *SVE*, vol. 7, Moscow: Voenizdat, 1979, p. 564.

70.  The entry on 'military-technical superiority' in *SVE*, vol. 2, Moscow: Voenizdat 1976, p. 253, states that 'Soviet military doctrine . . . gives a program of actions for ensuring military-technical superiority over the armed forces of probable enemies'.

71.  See the article on strategy referred to in note 69.

72.  For example, M.A. Mil'shtein, 'Nekotorye kharakternye cherty sovremennoi voennoi doktriny S.SH.A.', in *SShA*, 1980, no. 5, pp. 9–18.

73.  See Garthoff, 'Mutual Deterrence . . . ', *loc cit.*, pp. 129–31.

## Notes to Chapter Four

1.  G.A. Tokaty, 'Soviet Rocket Technology', in E.M. Emme (ed.), *The History of Rocket Technology*, Detroit: Wayne State U.P., 1964, p. 281.

2.  *Pravda*, 27 August 1957.

3.  Thomas W. Wolfe, *Soviet Power and Europe 1945–1970*, Baltimore and London: The Johns Hopkins Press, 1970, p. 179.

4.  Robert Berman and John C. Baker, *Soviet Strategic Forces*, Washington D.C.: The Brookings Institution, forthcoming.

5.  Jean Alexander, *Russian Aircraft Since 1940*, London: Putnam, 1975, pp. 289–93, 384–7; A.N. Ponomaryov, *Sovetskie aviatsionnye konstruktory*, Moscow: Voenizdat 1977, pp. 198–200; N.S. Khrushchev, *Khrushchev Remembers. The Last Testament*, London: Andre Deutsch, 1974, pp. 39–40.

6.  David Holloway, 'Military Technology', in R. Amann, J. Cooper, R.W. Davies

(eds.), *The Technological Level of Soviet Industry*, New Haven and London: Yale U.P., 1977, pp. 458–9.

7.　Berman and Baker, *op. cit.*

8.　Maj. Gen. M. Cherednichenko, 'Ob osobennostyakh razvitiya voennogo iskusstva v poslevoennyi period', *Voennoistoricheskii zhurnal*, 1970, no. 6, p. 25; see also Raymond L. Garthoff, *Soviet Strategy in the Nuclear Age*, London: Stevens and Sons, 1958, pp. 221–2.

9.　Quoted in Arnold L. Horelick and Myron Rush, *Strategic Power and Soviet Foreign Policy*, Chicago and London: The University of Chicago Press, 1966, p. 94.

10.　Committee on Foreign Affairs, U.S. House of Representatives, Special Studies on Foreign Affairs Issues, vol. 1, *Soviet Diplomacy and Negotiating Behavior: Emerging New Context for U.S. Diplomacy*, by Joseph G. Whelan, Washington D.C.: USGPO, 1979, p. 283.

11.　*Pravda*, 15 November 1958.

12.　*Pravda*, 28 May 1959.

13.　*Pravda*, 15 January 1960.

14.　Berman and Baker, *op. cit.*

15.　Edward I. Warner III, *The Military in Contemporary Soviet Politics. An Institutional Analysis*, New York: Praeger Special Studies, 1977, p. 195; Gregory Treverton, *Nuclear Weapons in Europe*, Adelphi Papers No. 168, London: International Institute for Strategic Studies, 1981, p. 6.

16.　Warner, *op. cit.*, p. 195.

17.　Warner, *op. cit.*, p. 194; Treverton, *op. cit.*, p. 6.

18.　Berman and Baker, *op. cit.*

19.　Simon Lunn, 'Cruise Missiles and the Prospects for Arms Control', *ADIU Report*, September/October 1981, pp. 1–5.

20.　Lawrence Freedman, *Britain and Nuclear Weapons*, London: Macmillan, 1980, p. 109.

21.　N.V. Ogarkov, 'V interesakh povysheniya boevoi gotovnosti', *Kommunist Vooruzhennykh Sil*, 1980, no. 14, p. 26.

22.　Raymond L. Garthoff, 'The TNF Tangle', *Foreign Policy*, No. 41, Winter 1980–81, pp. 92–3; Raymond L. Garthoff, 'Soviet Perspectives', in Richard K. Betts (ed.), *Cruise Missiles. Technology, Strategy, Politics*, Washington D.C.: The Brookings Institution, 1981, p. 345.

23.　See, for example, M.A. Mil'shtein and L.S. Semeiko, 'Problema nedopustimosti yadernogo konflikta (o novykh podkhodakh v SShA)', *SShA*, 1974, no. 11, pp. 2–13.

24.　Desmond Ball, *Can Nuclear War Be Controlled?*, Adelphi Papers No. 169, London: International Institute for Strategic Studies, 1981, pp. 30–5.

25.　*Pravda*, 24 February 1981.

26.　Thomas W. Wolfe, *The SALT Experience*, Cambridge, Mass: Ballinger, 1979, pp. 103–6; Strobe Talbott, *Endgame. The Inside Story of SALT II*, New York: Harper Colophon Books, 1980, pp. 72, 189, 304–5, 322–3.

27.　*Pravda*, 7 October 1979.

28.　*Strategic Survey 1980–81*, London: The International Institute for Strategic Studies, 1981, pp. 81–3, 109–10.

29.　*Der Spiegel*, 2 November 1981, pp. 144–7.

30.　*New York Times*, 19 November 1981, p. A17.

31.　Treverton, *op. cit.*, p. 32.

32.　Flora Lewis, 'A Start on the Nukes', *New York Times*, 28 December 1981.

33.  *Der Spiegel*, 2 November 1981, pp. 44–7; *New York Times*, 19 November 1981, p. A17.
34.  V.S. Shaposhnikov, 'Dvizhenie obshchestvennykh sil za mir i razryadku mezhdunarodnoi napryazhennosti', in G.I. Morozov *et al.*, *Obshchestvennost' i Problemy Voiny i Mira*, Moscow: izd. 'Mezhdunarodnye Otnosheniya', 1976, p. 9.
35.  *The Times*, 6 May 1981.
36.  *Pravda*, 24 November 1981.
37.  *Pravda*, 17 March 1981.
38.  William G. Hyland, 'Soviet Theatre Forces and Arms Control Policy', *Survival*, 1981, no. 5, p. 197.
39.  Gerard Smith, *Doubletalk. The Story of the First Strategic Arms Limitations Talks*, New York: Doubleday, 1980, pp. 130–1.

## Notes to Chapter Five

1.  D.A. Volkogonov *et al.* (eds.), *Voina i Armiya*, Moscow: Voenizdat 1977, pp. 354–5.
2.  Michael J. Deane, 'Soviet Perceptions of the Military Factor in the "Correlation of World Forces" ', in Donald C. Daniel (ed.), *International Perceptions of the Superpower Military Balance*, New York: Praeger Publishers, 1978, pp. 72–94; Vernon V. Aspaturian, 'Soviet Global Power and the Correlation of Forces', *Problems of Communism*, May–June 1980, pp. 1–18; Seweryn Bialer, *Stalin's Successors. Leadership, Stability and Change in the Soviet Union*, Cambridge: Cambridge U.P., 1980, pp. 241–53.
3.  Army General I. Shavrov, 'Lokal'nye voiny i ikh mesto v global'noi strategii imperializma', *Voenno-istoricheskii Zhurnal*, March 1975, p. 60.
4.  Army General I. Shavrov, 'Lokal'nye voiny i ikh mesto v global'noi strategii imperializma', *Voenno-istoricheskii Zhurnal*, April 1975, p. 93.
5.  Shavrov, *loc. cit.*, March 1975, p. 64.
6.  Arnold Horelick and Myron Rush, *Strategic Power and Soviet Foreign Policy*, Chicago: the University of Chicago Press, 1966, p. 212.
7.  *Ibid.*, p. 120.
8.  1963 Chinese Government statement quoted in Stephen S. Kaplan, *Diplomacy of Power. Soviet Armed Forces as a Political Instrument*, Washington, D.C.: The Brookings Institution, 1981, p. 95.
9.  N.S. Khrushchev, *Khrushchev Remembers*, New York: Bantam Books, 1970, p. 480.
10.  Herbert S. Dinerstein, *The Making of a Missile Crisis: October 1962*, Baltimore and London: The Johns Hopkins University Press, 1976, pp. 127–35.
11.  Lawrence Freedman, *US Intelligence and the Soviet Strategic Threat*, London: Macmillan, 1977, p. 73.
12.  William E. Griffith, *The Sino–Soviet Rift*, London: George Allen and Unwin Ltd., 1964, p. 90.
13.  Kaplan, *op. cit.*, pp. 139–40.
14.  Thomas W. Robinson, 'The Sino–Soviet Border Conflict', in Kaplan, *op. cit.*, pp. 265–313.
15.  William G. Hyland, *Soviet–American Relations: A New Cold War?* R–2763–FF/rc, Santa Monica: RAND Corporation, 1981, pp. 21–2.

194 *Notes to pages 88–100*

16. Philip Hanson, *Trade and Technology in Soviet Western Relations*, New York: Columbia U.P., 1981, pp. 96–7.
17. Basic Principles of Relations Between the USA and the USSR, *Department of State Bulletin*, June 26, 1972, pp. 898–9.
18. *Pravda*, October 28, 1962, quoted by Horelick and Rush, *op. cit.*, p. 178.
19. Hyland, *op. cit.*, p. 27.
20. *Ibid.*
21. *Ibid.*, pp. 26–8.
22. Quoted in Alexander Dallin, 'The Road to Kabul: Soviet Perceptions of World Affairs and the Afghan Crisis', in *The Soviet Invasion of Afghanistan*, ACIS Working Paper No. 27, Center for International and Strategic Affairs, UCLA, September 1980, p. 57.
23. Marshal A.A. Grechko, 'Rukovodyashchaya rol' KPSS v stroitel'stve armii razvitogo sotsialisticheskogo obshchestva', *Voprosy istorii KPSS*, May 1974, p. 39.
24. Shavrov, *loc. cit*, April 1975, p. 96.
25. *Pravda*, 25 February 1976.
26. Colin Legum, 'Angola and the Horn of Africa', in Kaplan (ed.), *op. cit.*, pp. 605–37.
27. *New York Times*, 18 January 1981.
28. *Pravda*, 13 August 1978.
29. *Pravda*, 26 June 1978.
30. *Strategic Survey 1979*, London: International Institute for Strategic Studies, 1980, pp. 67–72; *Strategic Survey 1980–1981*, London: International Institute for Strategic Studies, 1981, pp. 103–4.
31. Marshal N.V. Ogarkov, 'V interesakh povysheniya boevoi gotovnosti', *Kommunist Vooruzhennykh Sil*, 1980, no. 14, July, p. 26.
32. *Ibid.*, p. 25.
33. For speculation about possible Soviet military intervention see Louis Dupree, 'Afghanistan under the Khalq', *Problems of Communism*, July–August 1979, pp. 49–50; David Chaffetz, 'Afghanistan in Turmoil', *International Affairs*, January 1980, p. 35.
34. On the intervention see Fred Halliday, 'War and Revolution in Afghanistan', *New Left Review* 119, January–February 1980; Zalmay Khalilzad, 'Soviet-Occupied Afghanistan', *Problems of Communism*, November–December 1980; Dev Murarka, 'The Russian Intervention: A Moscow Analysis', *The Round Table*, April 1981; *The Soviet Invasion of Afghanistan*, ACIS Working Paper No. 27, *op. cit.*; Jiri Valenta, 'From Prague to Kabul: The Soviet Style of Invasion', *International Security*, Fall 1980.
35. *New York Times*, 17 December 1981, p. A15.
36. *Pravda*, 5 August 1981.
37. Fred Halliday, *Soviet Policy in the Arc of Crisis*, Washington, D.C.: The Institute for Policy Studies, 1981, p. 89.
38. *Pravda*, 24 February 1981.
39. State of the Union Address, 23 January 1980.
40. *Pravda*, 19 November 1978.
41. *Pravda*, 26 September 1968.
42. Christopher D. Jones, *Soviet Influence in Eastern Europe*, New York: Praeger, 1981, p. 1.
43. Michel Tatu, 'Intervention in Eastern Europe', in Kaplan (ed.), *op. cit.*, pp. 262–3.
44. Letter sent by the Central Committee of the CPSU to the Central Committee of

the Polish United Workers Party on 5 June 1981. Text in *Soviet News*, 16 June 1981.
45.   *Ibid.*
46.   As in his speech announcing the imposition of martial law on 13 December 1981; the text may be found in the *New York Times*, 14 December, p. 16.
47.   James M. McConnell, 'Doctrine and Capabilities', in Bradford Dismukes and James M. McConnell (eds.), *Soviet Naval Diplomacy*, New York: Pergamon Press, 1979, pp. 1–36.
48.   Zdenek Mlynar, *Nightfrost in Prague*, New York: Karz Publishers, 1980, pp. 239–40.
49.   Quoted in Aspaturian, *loc. cit.*, p. 1.
50.   V.M. Molotov, *Problems of Foreign Policy*, Moscow: Foreign Languages Publishing House, 1949, p. 28.
51.   Walter C. Clemens Jr., *The USSR and Global Interdependence: Alternative Futures*, Washington, D.C.: American Enterprise Institute for Public Policy Research, 1978; Franklyn Griffiths, 'Ideological Development and Foreign Policy', in Seweryn Bialer (ed.), *The Domestic Context of Soviet Foreign Policy*, Boulder, Colorado: Westview Press, 1981, pp. 41–5.
52.   N. Inozemtsev, 'XXVI s''yezd KPSS i nashi zadachi', *Mirovaya Ekonomika i Mezhdunarodnye Otnosheniya*, 1981, no. 3, pp. 12–13.
53.   Ogarkov, for example, argues that 'the situation demands that we keep our powder dry'; *loc. cit.*, p. 27.
54.   See M. Maksimova, 'Global'nye problemy mirovogo razvitiya', *Mirovaya Ekonomika i Mezhdurarodnye Otnosheniya*, 1981, no. 1; and I. Ivanov, 'Perestroika mezhdunarodnykh otnoshenii i global'nye problemy', *ibid.*, 1981, no. 2; also Elizabeth Kridl Valkenier, 'The USSR, the Third World, and the Global Economy', *Problems of Communism*, July–August 1979.

## Notes to Chapter Six

1.   Gerard C. Smith, *Doubletalk. The Story of SALT I*, New York: Doubleday, 1980, pp. 408, 415, 424, 430.
2.   *Sovetskaya Voennaya Entsiklopediya*, vol. 1, Moscow: Voenizdat, 1976, p. 588.
3.   Harriet Fast Scott and William F. Scott, *The Armed Forces of the USSR*, Boulder, Colorado: Westview Press, 1979, pp. 99–102
4.   Maj. Gen. N. Komkov and Col. P. Shemanskiy, 'Certain Historic Trends in the Development of Troop Control', *Voennaya Mysl'*, 1974, no. 10, p. 13.
5.   Scott and Scott, *op. cit.*, pp. 102–13.
6.   Raymond L. Garthoff, 'SALT and the Soviet Military', *Problems of Communism*, January–February 1975, p. 29.
7.   David Holloway, 'Innovation in the Defence Sector', in R. Amann and J. Cooper (eds.), *Industrial Innovation in the Soviet Union*, New Haven and London: Yale U.P., 1981, pp. 296–303.
8.   P.V. Sokolov (ed.) *Voenno-ekonomickeskie voprosy v kurse politiekonomii*, Moscow: Voenizdat, 1968, pp. 286–7.
9.   N.S. Khrushchev, *Khrushchev Remembers*, vol. 2., *The Last Testament*, Harmondsworth: Penguin Books, 1977, pp. 55ff, 70–2.
10.   Henry A. Kissinger, *White House Years*, Boston: Little, Brown, 1979, pp. 1220–2, 1229, 1234.

11. Col. Gen. G. Sredin, 'Istochnik sily i mogushchestva', *Voennyi Vestnik*, 1977, no. 10, p. 10.

12. See, for example, Khrushchev's speech in *Pravda*, 15 January 1960; the Statement of Data on the Numbers of Strategic Offensive Arms as of the Date of Signature of the SALT II Treaty, in Strobe Talbott, *Endgame. The Inside Story of SALT II*, New York: Harper Colophon Books, 1980, p. 324; the Brezhnev interview in *Der Spiegel*, 3 November 1981.

13. *Statement on the Defence Estimates 1981*, Cmnd. 8212, London: HMSO, April 1981, p. 4.

14. On the problems of using Soviet data see Franklyn D. Holzman, *Financial Checks on Soviet Defense Expenditure*, Lexington, Mass: Lexington Books, 1975.

15. This approach is adopted by William T. Lee, *The Estimation of Soviet Defense Expenditures, 1955–1975. An Unconventional Approach*, New York: Praeger Publishers, 1977; for sceptical discussions see Abraham S. Becker, 'The Meaning and Measure of Soviet Military Expenditure', in Joint Economic Committee, U.S. Congress, *Soviet Economy in a Time of Change*, Washington, D.C.: USGPO, 1979, vol. 1, pp. 352–66, and Philip Hanson, 'Estimating Soviet Defence Expenditure', *Soviet Studies*, July 1978, pp. 403–10.

16. A. Marshall, in Joint Economic Committee, U.S. Congress, *Allocation of Resources in the Soviet Union and China – 1975*, Hearings before the Subcommittee on Priorities and Economy in Government, Part I, Washington, D.C.: USGPO, 1975, p. 156.

17. CIA: *A Dollar Comparison of Soviet and U.S. Defense Activities 1965–1975*, SR 76–10053, February 1976; CIA: *Estimated Soviet Defense Spending in Rubles, 1970–1975*, SR 76–10121U, May 1976.

18. Steven S. Rosefielde, in Permanent Select Committee on Intelligence, U.S. House of Representatives, *CIA Estimates of Soviet Defense Spending*, Hearings before the Committee on Oversight, Washington, D.C.: USGPO, 1980, p. 14.

19. CIA: *Estimated Soviet Defense Spending in Rubles, 1970–75*, SR 76–10121U, May 1976, p. 6.

20. Marshall, *loc. cit.*, p. 163.

21. See the testimony of Steven S. Rosefielde and William T. Lee in Permanent Select Committee, *op. cit.*, pp. 10–28.

22. The testimony of Franklyn D. Holzman in Permanent Select Committee, *op. cit.*, pp. 43–7; see also his 'Are the Russians Really Outspending the U.S. on Defense?', *International Security*, Spring 1980, pp. 86–104, and 'Soviet Military Spending: Assessing the Numbers Game', *International Security*, Spring 1982, pp. 78–101.

23. Joint Economic Committee, U.S. Congress, *Statement of Maj. Gen. Richard X. Larkin, Deputy Director and Edward M. Collins, Vice Director for Foreign Intelligence, Defense Intelligence Agency*, before the Subcommittee on International Trade, Finance and Security Economics, 8 July 1981, p. 83.

24. *Ibid.*

25. *Materialy XXIV s"yezda KPSS*, Moscow: Politizdat, 1971, p. 46.

26. CIA, National Foreign Assessment Center, *Estimated Soviet Defense Spending: Trends and Prospects*, SR 78–10121, June 1978, p. 2.

27. David Holloway, 'Innovation in the Defence Sector', in Amann and Cooper (eds.), *op. cit.*, pp. 303–14.

28. Julian Cooper, *Defence Production and the Soviet Economy 1929–1942*, CREES Discussion Paper, University of Birmingham, 1976, p. 24: L.M. Ol'shchevits, N.A. Orlov (eds.), *Organizatsiya, planirovanie i ekonomika aviatsionnogo proizvodstva,*

Moscow, 1963, p. 70; P.M. Stukolov (ed.), *Ekonomika elektronnoi promyshlennosti*, Moscow, 1976, pp. 14–15.

29.   Joint Economic Committee, U.S. Congress, *Allocation of Resources in the Soviet Union and China – 1977*, Hearings before the Subcommittee on Economy and Priorities in Government, Part 3, Washington, D.C.: USGPO, 1977, p. 40.

30.   Secretary of Defense, *Annual Report to Congress FY 1982*, p. I–20.

31.   *Ibid.*; Joint Economic Committee, U.S. Congress, *Statement of Maj. Gen. Richard X. Larkin. . . . op. cit.*, p. 63.

32.   On the Ground Forces see A.Kh. Babadzhanyan, *Tanki i Tankovye Voiska*, Moscow: Voenizdat, 1970, ch. 5; on bombers, A.V. Glichev, *Ekonomicheskaya effektivnost' tekhicheskikh sistem*, Moscow: Ekonomia, 1971, pp. 64–5; James McConnell, 'Doctrine and Capabilities' in Bradford Dismukes and James M. McConnell (eds.), *Soviet Naval Diplomacy*, New York: Pergamon Press, 1979, pp. 10–21.

33.   Joint Economic Committee, U.S. Congress, *Allocation of Resources in the Soviet Union and China – 1978*, Hearings before the Subcommittee on Priorities and Economy in Government, Part 4, Washington, D.C.: USGPO, 1978, p. 224.

34.   P.V. Sokolov, *Political Economy*, Moscow: Voenizdat, 1974; quoted in Joint Economic Committee, U.S. Congress, *Statement of Maj. Gen. Richard X. Larkin. . . . op. cit.*, p. 40.

35.   U.S. Arms Control and Disarmament Agency, *World Military Expenditures and Arms Transfers, 1969–78*, Washington, D.C.: ACDA, 1980, pp. 159–62; in addition, the Soviet Union exported $525 million worth of arms to Yugoslavia, and $50 million to Finland.

36.   CIA: National Foreign Assessment Center, *Communist Aid Activities in Non-Communist Less Developed Countries, 1979 and 1954–1979*, ER–10318U, October 1980, p. 5. Kampuchea, Laos and Vietnam are included for the years before 1975. The figures refer to estimated Soviet export prices; see CIA: National Foreign Assessment Center, *Arms Flows to LDCs: US–Soviet Comparisons, 1974–77*, ER 78–10494U, November 1978, pp. 3–4.

37.   CIA: National Foreign Assessment Center, *Communist Aid. . . . op. cit.*, p. 4.

38.   U.S. ACDA, *op. cit.*, p. 150.

39.   For the calculation see David Holloway, 'The Soviet Defense Industry', in N. Ball and M. Leitenberg (eds.) *Defense Industries*, forthcoming.

40.   *Ibid.*

41.   CIA: National Foreign Assessment Center, *Communist Aid . . . op. cit.*, p. 1; Roger F. Pajak, 'Soviet Arms Transfers as an Instrument of Influence', *Survival*, July–August 1981, p. 168.

42.   CIA: National Foreign Assessment Center, *Communist Aid . . . op. cit.*, p. 5.

43.   *Ibid.*

44.   Wharton Econometric Forecasting Associates, *Centrally Planned Economies. Current Analysis*, Washington, D.C.: 22 January 1982, p. 2.

45.   The U.S. Defense Intelligence Agency has reported increases in the capacity for submarine, aircraft and tank production over the last ten years; see Joint Economic Committee, *Statement of Maj. Gen. Richard X. Larkin . . . op. cit.*, p. 84. Plant expansion might also be designed to accommodate a greater output of civilian goods.

46.   On the work of the prison institutes and design bureaus see G.A. Ozerov, *Tupolevskaya Sharaga*, Frankfurt-am-Main: Possev, 1973.

47.   M. Agursky, *The Research Institute of Machine-Building Technology*, The

Hebrew University of Jerusalem, The Soviet and East European Research Center, Soviet Institutions Series Paper no. 8, September 1976, pp. 13–15.
48. See chapter 1, note 23.
49. H.H. Gerth and C. Wright Mills (eds.), *From Max Weber*, London, 1970, p. 233.
50. Marshal M.V. Zakharov made this point in his damning assessment of Khrushchev's leadership in *Red Star*, 4 February 1965.
51. *Pravda*, 26 April 1963.
52. *Ibid.*
53. Permanent Select Committee . . . , *op. cit.*, p. 83.
54. See, for example, Admiral of the Fleet S.G. Gorshkov, *Morskaya Moshch' Gosudarstva*, 2nd ed., Moscow: Voenizdat, 1979, pp. 373–407.
55. Secretary of Defense, *Annual Report FY 1983*, p. I–20.

## Notes to Chapter Seven

1. F. Engels, *Anti-Dühring*, Moscow: Foreign Languages Publishing House, 1962, p. 230.
2. *Ibid.*
3. *Ibid.*, p. 236.
4. Marx to Engels, 25 September 1857, and 7 July 1866, in Marx and Engels, *Selected Correspondence*, Moscow: Foreign Languages Publishing House, n.d., pp. 118, 218.
5. Quoted in A.I. Babin, *F. Engels – vydayushchiisya voennyi teoretik rabochego klassa*, Moscow: Voenizdat, 1970, p. 180.
6. G.A. Ozerov, *Tupolevsakaya Sharaga*, 2nd ed., Frankfurt-am-Main: Possev, 1973, p. 57.
7. *Ibid.*
7. A.C. Sutton, *Western Technology and Soviet Economic Development 1930–45*, Stanford: Hoover Institution Press, 1971, pp. 207–48, 363–72; and his *Western Technology and Soviet Economic Development 1945–65*, Stanford: Hoover Institution Press, 1973, pp. 255–79.
9. David Holloway, 'Innovation in the Defence Sector', in R. Amann and J. Cooper (eds.) *Industrial Innovation in the Soviet Union*, New Haven and London: Yale U.P., 1982, pp. 356–66.
10. CIA: National Foreign Assessment Center, *Estimated Soviet Defense Spending: Trends and Prospects*, SR 78–10121, June 1978, p. 3.
11. Louvan E. Nolting and Murray Feshback, 'R & D Employment in the USSR – Definitions, Statistics and Comparisons', in Joint Economic Committee, U.S. Congress, *Soviet Economy in a Time of Change*, vol. 1, Washington, D.C.: USGPO, 1979, p. 746. According to the US Department of Defense Program for Research, Development and Acquisition for FY 1981, 'over half' of Soviet 'scientific workers' (estimated at over 1,000,000) were engaged in military R & D. Committee on Armed Services, US House of Representatives, *Hearings on Military Posture, Research and Development, Title II*, Washington, D.C.: USGPO, 1980, p. 79.
12. *Sovetskaya Voennaya Entsiklopedia*, vol. 2, Moscow: Voenizdat, 1976, p. 253. Note that this was published before Brezhnev's speech of January 1977 in Tula (see chapter 3).

13.  R. Amann, J. Cooper, R.W. Davies (eds.), *The Technological Level of Soviet Industry*, New Haven and London: Yale U.P., 1977, p. 66.

14.  David Holloway, 'Military Technology', in Amann, Cooper and Davies (eds.), *op. cit.*, pp. 407–89.

15.  Joint Economic Committee, U.S. Congress, *Allocation of Resources in the Soviet Union and China – 1977*, Hearings before the Subcommittee on Economy and Priority in Government, Part 3, Washington, D.C.: USGPO, 1977, p. 40.

16.  Joint Economic Committee, U.S. Congress, *Allocations of Resources in the Soviet Union and China – 1977*, Hearings before the Subcommittee on Economy and Priority in Government, Part 3, Washington, D.C.: USGPO, 1977, p. 40.

17.  *Ibid.*, p. 87.

18.  Unless otherwise noted this section is taken from David Holloway, 'The Soviet Style of Military R & D', in F.A. Long and Judith Reppy (eds.), *The Genesis of New Weapons. Decisionmaking for Military R & D*, New York: Pergamon Press, 1980, pp. 139–58.

19.  On Nedelin see Army General V.F. Tolubko, *Nedelin*, Moscow: Molodaya Gvardiya, 1979; on Berg see Irina Radunskaya, *Aksel' Berg. Chelovek XXogo veka*, Moscow: Molodaya Gvardiya, 1971; on Alekseev see the comments in Gerard Smith, *Doubletalk, the Story of SALT I*, New York: Doubleday, 1980, pp. 48–9.

20.  *Sovetskaya Voennaya Entsiklopedia*, Vol. 3, Moscow: Voenizdat, 1977, pp. 616–17.

21.  *Ibid.*

22.  Andrew Sheren, in Joint Economic Committee, U.S. Congress, *Economic Performance and the Military Burden in the Soviet Union*, Washington, D.C.: USGPO, 1970, p. 126.

23.  D.F. Ustinov, 'Strazh mirnogo truda; oplot vseobshchego mira', *Kommunist*, 1977, no. 3, p. 18.

24.  Mark Popovsky, *Science in Chains: The Crisis of Science and Scientists in The Soviet Union Today*, London: Collins and Harvill Press, 1980, p. 72.

25.  Holloway, 'Innovation . . .', *loc. cit.*

26.  S.A. Sarkisian and E.S. Minaev, *Ekonomicheskaya otsenka letatel'nykh apparatov*, Moscow: Mashinostroenie, 1972, pp. 27–9.

27.  Lt. Gen. of Engineering-Technical Service V. Pyshnov, 'Certain Problems in the Development of Military Aircraft', *Voennaya Mysl'*, 1963, no. 10, p. 6.

28.  Arthur Alexander, 'Research in Soviet Defence Production', *NATO's Fifteen Nations*, October–November 1981, pp. 52–60, 74.

29.  I.V. Yurasov, in P.N. Pospelov (ed.), *Sovetskii Tyl v Velikoi Otechestvennoi voine. Kniga II. Trudovoi Podvig Naroda*, Moscow: Mysl', 1974, p. 113.

30.  Pyshnov, *loc. cit.*, p. 6.

31.  Ozerov, *op. cit.*, pp. 48–60.

32.  Lt. Col. V.M. Bondarenko, 'Nauchno-tekhnicheskii progress i ukreplenie oboronsposobnosti', *Kommunist Vooruzhennykh Sil*, 1971, no. 24, p. 15.

33.  Marshal A.A. Grechko, *Vooruzhennye Sily Sovetskogo Gosudarstva*, 2nd ed., Moscow: Voenizdat, 1975, p. 193.

34.  V.P. Glushko, *Rocket-Engines GDL-OKB*, Moscow: Novosti Press · Agency Publishing House, 1975, p. 11.

35.  Holloway, 'Military Technology', *loc. cit.*, pp. 457–8.

36.  N.A. Pilyugin, interview in *Pravda*, 17 May 1978.

37.  V. Gubarev, *Konstruktor. Neskol'ko stranits iz zhizni Mikhaila Kuzmicha Yangela*, Moscow: Politzdat 1977.

38.  Holloway, 'Innovation in the Defence Sector: Two Case Studies', in Amann and Cooper, eds.), *op. cit.*, pp. 391–2.

39.  Robert Berman and John Baker, *Soviet Strategic Forces*, Washington, D.C.: The Brookings Institution, forthcoming.

40.  *Ibid.*

41.  V.P. Glushko, *Development of Rocketry and Space Technology in the USSR*, Moscow: Novosti Press Agency Publishing House, 1973, p. 20.

42.  For a discussion see Holloway, 'Military Technology', *loc. cit.*, p. 468.

43.  Holloway, 'Military Technology', *loc. cit.*, pp. 468–82; Joint Economic Committee, U.S. Congress, *Allocation of Resources in the Soviet Union and China – 1977*, Hearings Before the Subcommittee on Economy and Priority in Government, Part 3, Washington, D.C.: USGPO, 1977, pp. 90–1.

44.  Philip Hanson, *Trade and Technology in Soviet–Western Relations*, New York: Columbia U.P., 1981, p. 225; Holloway, 'Military Technology', *loc. cit.*, p. 477.

45.  Tolubko, *op. cit.*, pp. 181, 215, 216.

46.  *Ibid.*, p. 176.

47.  *Ibid.*, p. 182.

48.  Smith, *op. cit.*, p. 47.

49.  *Slovar' osnovnykh voennykh terminov*, Moscow: Voenizdat, 1965, p. 111.

50.  N.S. Khrushchev, *Khrushchev Remembers. Vol. 2. The Last Testament*, London: Andre Deutsch, 1974, pp. 46, 61; A. Romanov, *Spacecraft Designer*, Moscow: Novosti Press Agency Publishing House, 1976, photographs between pp. 64–5.

51.  Tolubko, *op. cit.*, p. 185.

52.  *Ibid.*, p. 183.

53.  Lt. Gen. G. Semenov and Maj. Gen. V. Prokhorov, 'Scientific-Technical Progress and Some Question of Strategy', *Voennaya Mysl'*, 1969, no. 2, p. 23. It is not always easy to form arms, men and doctrine into an effective fighting force, as is shown by the history of Soviet armour in the 1930s. See Benjamin Miller, 'The Origin of the Soviet Armored Forces and the Concept of the Operation in Depth', Unpublished Manuscript, Peace Studies Program, Cornell University.

54.  See the discussion in Spurgeon M. Keeny Jr. and Wolfgang K.H. Panofsky, 'The Mutual Hostage Relationship of the Superpowers', in *Foreign Affairs*, Winter 1981/82, pp. 287–304.

## Notes to Chapter Eight

1.  Felix Gilbert (ed.), *The Historical Essays of Otto Hintze*, New York: Oxford University Press, 1965, p. 215.

2.  Malcolm Mackintosh, *Juggernaut. A History of the Soviet Armed Forces*, New York: Macmillan, 1967 p. 276.

3.  Timothy J. Colton, *Commissars, Commanders and Civilian Authority*, Cambridge, Mass.: Harvard U.P., 1979, pp. 221–49.

4.  See Colton, *ibid.*, pp. 175–95.

5.  *Ibid.*, pp. 250–78.

6.  Jerry Hough, 'The Soviet System: Petrification or Pluralism', in his *The Soviet Union and Social Science Theory*, Cambridge, Mass.: Harvard U.P., 1977, pp. 19–48.

7.  John McDonnell, 'The Soviet Defense Industry as a Pressure Group', in Michael

McGwire, Ken Booth, John McDonnell (eds.) *Soviet Naval Policy. Objectives and Constraints*, New York: Praeger Publishers, 1975, pp. 87–122.

8. *Pravda*, 8 November 1979.

10. CIA: National Foreign Assessment Center, *Estimated Soviet Defense Spending: Trends and Prospects*, SR 78-10121, June 1978, p. i.

11. See William E. Odom, 'The "militarization" of Soviet Society', *Problems of Communism*, 1976, no. 5, pp. 34–51; David Holloway, 'War, Militarism and the Soviet State', in E.P. Thompson and Dan Smith (eds.), *Protest and Survive*, Harmondsworth: Penguin Books, 1980, pp. 129–69; Timothy J. Colton, 'The Impact of the Military on Soviet Society', in Seweryn Bialer (ed.), *The Domestic Context of Soviet Foreign Policy*, Boulder, Colorado: Westview Press, 1981, pp. 119–38.

12. *Sovetskaya Voennaya Entsiklopediya*, vol. 2, Moscow: Voenizdat, 1976, p. 245.

13. William E. Odom, *The Volunteers*, Princeton: Princeton U.P., 1974; and Herbert Goldhamer, *The Soviet Soldier*, New York: Crane Russak, 1975.

14. Colton, *loc. cit.*, pp. 127–8.

15. N. Ogarkov, 'Na strazhe mirnogo truda', *Kommunist*, 1981, no. 10, p. 90.

16. See, for example, Roy A. Medvedev and Zhores A. Medvedev, 'A Nuclear Samizdat on America's Arms Race', *The Nation*, 16 January 1982, p. 49.

17. *Pravda*, 13 January 1980.

18. Raymond L. Garthoff, 'Mutual Deterrence and Strategic Arms Limitation in Soviet Policy', *International Security*, Summer 1978, p. 115.

19. Boris Dmitriyev, in *Izvestiya*, 25 September 1963, quoted in Garthoff, *loc. cit.*; see also Thomas W. Wolfe, *Soviet Strategy at the Crossroads*, Cambridge, Mass.: Harvard U.P., 1965, pp. 70–8.

20. Garthoff, *loc. cit.*, p. 115.

21. N.A. Talenskii, in *Mezhdunarodnaya Zhizn'*, no. 5, May 1965, p. 23, quoted in Garthoff, *loc. cit.*, p. 115.

22. Lt. Col. Ye. Rybkin in *Kommunist Vooruzhennykh Sil*, 1965, no. 17, pp. 55–6, quoted in Edward L. Warner III, *The Military in Contemporary Soviet Politics*, New York: Praeger, 1977, p. 88.

23. See Warner, *op. cit.*, pp. 88–9.

24. Garthoff, *loc. cit.*, p. 120.

25. *Ibid.*

26. Andrei Sakharov and Ernst Henry, 'Scientists and Nuclear War', in Stephen F. Cohen (ed.) *An End to Silence. Uncensored Opinion in the Soviet Union*, New York: W.W. Norton and Co., 1982, p. 230.

27. Robert L. Arnett, 'Soviet Attitudes Towards Nuclear War: Do They Really Think They Can Win?', *Journal of Strategic Studies*, September 1979, pp. 173–5.

28. In *Problemy Mira i Sotsializma*, 1974, no. 2, p. 42; quoted in Warner, *op. cit.*, p. 253.

29. in *Voprosy filosofii*, 1974, no. 1, p. 64; quoted in *ibid*.

30. Warner, *op. cit.*, p. 252.

31. In *Krasnaya Zvezda*, 17 May 1973; quoted in Warner, *op. cit.*, p. 252.

32. Warner, *op. cit.*, p. 252.

33. *Krasnaya Zvezda*, 7 February 1974; quoted in Warner, *op. cit.*, p. 253.

34. See Chapter 3.

35. The 1961 Party Program, in Leonard Schapiro (ed.), *The USSR and the Future*, New York: Praeger, 1962, p. 284.

36. Philip Hanson, *Trade and Technology in Soviet–American Relations*, New York:

Columbia UP, 1981, p. 32, and Abram Bergson, 'Soviet Economic Slowdown and the 1981–85 Plan', in *Problems of Communism*, 1981, p. 26.
37. *ibid.*
38. CIA: National Foreign Assessment Center, *op. cit.*, p. i.
39. Bergson, *loc. cit.*, p. 26.
40. *Ibid.*
41. N. Inozemtsev, 'XXVI s''yezd KPSS i nashi zadachi', *Mirovaya Ekonomika i Mezhdunarodnye Otnosheniya*, 1981, no. 3, p. 7.
42. Bergson, *loc. cit.*, p. 29.
43. Abraham S. Becker, *The Burden of Soviet Defense. A Political-Economic Essay*, R–2752–AF, Santa Monica: Rand Corporation, 1981, pp. 68–72.
44. *Materialy XXIV s''yezda KPSS*, Moscow: Politizdat, 1971, p. 46.
45. *Pravda*, 22 October 1980.
46. See David Holloway, 'Innovation in the Defense Sector', in R. Amann and J. Cooper (eds.), *Industrial Innovation in the Soviet Union*, New Haven and London: Yale UP, 1981, p. 354.
47. A. Levikov, ' "A''i''B" ', *Literaturnaya Gazeta*, 15 November 1972, p. 11.
48. *Literaturnaya Gazeta*, 7 February 1973, p. 10.
49. Seweryn Bialer, *Stalin's Successors. Leadership, Stability and Change in the Soviet Union*, Cambridge: Cambridge U.P., 1980, p. 300.

## Notes to Conclusion

1. Strobe Talbott, *Endgame. The Inside Story of SALT II*, New York: Harper Colophon Books, 1980, pp. 38–87
2. Barry M. Blechman, 'The Comprehensive Test Ban Negotiations; Can They Be Revived?', *Arms Control Today*, June 1981, p. 3.
3. *Soviet Military Power*, Washington, D.C.: USGPO 1981; *Whence the Threat to Peace?*, Moscow: Ministry of Defence Publishing House, 1982.
4. McGeorge Bundy, George F. Kennan, Robert S. McNamara and Gerard Smith, 'Nuclear Weapons and the Atlantic Alliance', *Foreign Affairs*, Spring 1981, pp. 753–68.
5. Anders Boserup, 'Nuclear Disarmament: Non-Nuclear Defence', in Mary Kaldor and Dan Smith (eds.), *Disarming Europe*, London: The Merlin Press, 1982, pp. 185–92.

# INDEX